STREETWISE®

MAXIMIZE WEB SITE TRAFFIC

STREETWISE®

MAXIMIZE WEB SITE TRAFFIC

Build Web Site Traffic
Fast and Free by
Optimizing Search
Engine Placement

**by Robin Nobles &
Susan O'Neil**

Adams Media
Avon, Massachusetts

Published by Adams Media, an F+W Publications Company
57 Littlefield Street, Avon, MA 02322. U.S.A.
www.adamsmedia.com

ISBN: 1-58062-369-7

Printed in the United States of America.

J I H G F E D C B

Library of Congress Cataloging-in-Publication data
available upon request from publisher.

This publication is designed to provide accurate and authoritative information with regard to the subject matter covered. It is sold with the understanding that the publisher is not engaged in rendering legal, accounting, or other professional advice. If legal advice or other expert assistance is required, the services of a competent professional person should be sought.
— From a *Declaration of Principles* jointly adopted by a Committee of the
American Bar Association and a Committee of Publishers and Associations

Many of the designations used by manufacturers and sellers to distinguish their products are claimed as trademarks. Where those designations appear in this book and Adams Media was aware of a trademark claim, the designations have been printed in initial capital letters.

Cover illustration by Eric Mueller.

This book is available at quantity discounts for bulk purchases.
For information, call 1-800-872-5627.

Contents

SECTION IV: DOORWAY PAGES: IMPORTANT ADDITIONAL WAYS TO "GET FOUND" ON THE WEB

SECTION V: SEARCH ENGINE STRATEGIES

SECTION VI: LEARN FROM SUCCESSFUL WEB SITES

SECTION VII: PREVENTING PROBLEMS WITH THE ENGINES

SECTION VIII: OTHER FACTORS THAT CAN AFFECT WEB POSITIONING

Contents

Acknowledgments

This book is built from our experiences, of course, but also on the experience of many others. Thanks to our colleagues and former students who have been generous with their ideas and encouragement. To those who allowed us to use their work as examples, thank you, and we applaud your success!

Thanks to those in the field who answered our questions and helped with our research. We are particularly appreciative of the contributions from the search engines and directories themselves.

Thanks to our literary agent, Richard Curtis, who sold the book in record time, and to Adams Media Corporation for their foresight in publishing a book that, to some, seemed ahead of its time.

Special thanks to our families for their understanding and support.

T his is an Internet book in more ways than one. When the authors began writing this book, they'd never met nor even spoken on the phone. They had been e-chatting for over a year—at first at a distance-learning course as teacher (Robin in Mississippi) and student (Susan in New Hampshire), but later, as colleagues in a new and exploding industry.

The book was conceived and developed via e-mail. It wasn't until the end of the project that the authors finally met, coming together in a Vermont ski chalet for a final, week-long editing blitz. But the conviction that drove them from the start remained solid to the end—that "There had to be an easier way!"

Since search engine positioning is a new field, aspiring practitioners—the authors included—have had to painstakingly identify fairly new and/or emerging sources of information in order to learn their craft. They have had to find their way to various resource Web sites, somehow gauge the reliability and freshness of the information found there, and integrate it across differences in terminology, approach, and assumptions. Then, they've had to roll it all together to form the framework of experiments in positioning, the results of which became *knowledge*.

In working with new staff members and class members, the authors came to appreciate how helpful a manual for search engine positioners would be. This is that manual.

The Importance of Web Site Positioning

Overview of Section I

In this section, you'll learn what search engine positioning is and why it's so important to the success of your online business. Who are the major players in the search engine industry? How large are the engines, and which ones are the most popular? How can you put the search engines to work marketing your site?

Chapter 1

How Web Positioning Fits into a Comprehensive Web Site Promotion Plan

You've spent weeks in creating your Web site, and you're finally ready to introduce it to the world. You've read everything you can get your hands on about designing a Web site, and you have full confidence in the effectiveness of yours.

You've carefully taken into consideration your unique customers, the purpose of your site, simple navigational strategies, and all the other crucial aspects of Web design. Your page loads fast, doesn't contain annoying frames, and your shopping cart setup is simple enough for even a child to use.

Using the tactics of an online marketing book, you've advertised your Web site in all the "right" places. You've announced it to all of your friends, and you've even told your local customers that they can begin to order online.

Now, you're ready to kick back and rake in the business. With your calculations, you should be able to retire in a few years with what you'll be making on your Web site.

A great scenario, but one with a fatal flaw: you've failed to take into account the search engines.

Between 85 and 90 percent of all Web site traffic comes from the major search engines. Okay, no problem. You'll use one of those handy-dandy submission services that will submit your site to 980 search engines for a mere $19.95. That will take care of it, won't it?

Hardly.

Just because your Web site is listed in the engines doesn't mean your customers can find it.

Visit any search engine and type in a few words, like "software programs." You will be immediately told that there are 223,023 results, and you'll be presented with the top 10 on the first page. How many of those 223,023 results are you going to glance through? The first 100, which would be 10 pages? Probably not. The first 30, or 3 pages, is more like it, and some Web surfers won't even go past the first page of 10 results.

What does this tell us?

That if our own Web sites don't rank in the top 30 listings for our important keywords, we won't be found. Simple as that.

So how on earth do we get our Web sites ranked high in the engines?

> If our own Web sites don't rank in the top 30 listings for our important keywords, we won't be found. Simple as that.

By using "Web positioning" strategies that are designed to give the engines what they want and need in order to find your site among those other 223,023 pages. We call this making "spider food" for your Web site.

When you submit your site to one of the engines, the engine immediately sends its "spider" to visit your site. A spider is a sophisticated software program operated by the search engine that will record, or index, the words on your Web site. The engine then uses this information to rank your site in its index.

So, your ultimate goal in Web positioning is to create search engine–friendly Web pages that will boost your site to the top of the rankings and significantly increase your Web site traffic for your important keywords.

You'll find a direct correlation between a top ranking and an increase in traffic to your site. An increase in traffic, coupled with effective Web site design aimed toward selling your goods and services, is what it takes to create a successful online business.

That all sounds pretty easy, doesn't it?

Web positioning is challenging at best. It's not a simple matter of adding a few tags that contain your important keywords. Web positioning is an art—and a science—since it is applying creative techniques to an in-depth study of the search engines.

Each engine has a different ranking algorithm, which means that they each have different likes and dislikes that affect the ranking of your site. So, it's crucial to study those guidelines and craft your site around them to get the maximum benefit for your online business.

Not all of the search facilities are "engines." Some are directories. And many of the top search facilities offer both options.

A search engine uses a spider to crawl the Web to gather information, then builds its index based on that information. However, a directory uses information that you submit directly to it to build its index.

Another important distinction between engines and directories is that with engines, each **page** of your Web site is handled on its own so that with some search engines you can submit separate pages and get them ranked for various keyword phrases. The engine looks at individual pages rather than your Web site as a whole.

> Create search engine–friendly Web pages that will boost your site to the top of the rankings and significantly increase your Web site traffic for your important keywords.

Directories, however, look at whole Web sites, not individual pages. With directories, you submit the main page of your site only. You'll complete an online form, listing information about your site, and the directory uses that information, as well as the appraisal of human editors who may visit your site, to determine your ranking, as opposed to information gathered from a spider's search.

In the following table, you'll see which of the major search facilities are engines and which are directories. Keep in mind that most of the engines also have a directory component to go along with the search options they offer. The details for submitting to them will be described in chapters on the individual engines.

> Directories, however, look at whole Web sites, not individual pages.

NAME	SEARCH ENGINE?	DIRECTORY?
AltaVista	Yes	
Excite	Yes	
Google	Yes	
HotBot	Yes	
GO/InfoSeek	Yes	
Lycos	Yes	
Northern Light	Yes	
WebCrawler	Yes	
Yahoo!		Yes
Open Directory Project		Yes
Snap		Yes

Now that you understand the basic goals of Web positioning, let's take it one step further.

Note: For your convenience, a listing of the URLs mentioned throughout this book will also be available as "live links" from the authors' Web site: *www.searchengineadvice.com*.

For more information on this topic, visit our Web site at www.businesstown.com

Search Technology & Marketing

As the Internet has exploded into an infinite cataloging of the human experience, search technology has become the requisite tool for finding and using *any* of it. Today, the major search engines are hard-pressed to keep up with the phenomenal growth of the Internet, which hosts approximately 800 million indexable Web pages currently (*Accessibility and Distribution of Information on the Web* by Steve Lawrence and Lee Giles, *www.wwwmetrics.com*), with many thousands more being added every day.

Sorting through this ever-growing sea of data challenges our very human knowledge base. The search engines continually experiment and evolve as they try to give their visitors search results that are the closest matches to queries. Where once the algorithms of a search engine may have been quite simple, perhaps as simple as counting the instances of the search word's appearance within any indexed Web page and returning the Web page with the highest incidence of search word repetition to the top of the rankings, today's engines have developed complex algorithms.

These algorithms may reflect the influences, variously, of the type of design elements within a Web page; the number of links pointing to that Web page from other, independent sites; the content of the META data, the words used in headings and subheadings; and much more. Some engines, like GoTo, have skirted the entire problem of determining which Web sites should be returned at the top of the rankings by subscribing to the "You Get What You Pay For" theory and letting Web sites *pay* for their rankings' success.

In addition to managing all this data, the search services are also always working to increase the speed at which information may be found by its users. According to the GVU's WWW User Survey, their efforts are paying off. In 1998, the survey determined that average search times to achieve desired results at the engines had decreased by 5 percent (*www.gvu.gatech.edu/user_surveys/survey-1998-04/#exec*).

The Beginnings of Search Technology

The Internet began as a research project, and the search engines began as attempts to quantify and qualify the data that was collected, so that other researchers could access it and add to it. Of course, sooner or later, a few people came along who thought: "Hey, how can we make some money off this thing?" The result is today's sometimes stormy marriage between information and money, as the search engines become publicly traded portals reaping profits because they are critical to the commercial success of the Internet. All the while, marketers are learning more and more ways to use the search engines to sell their wares.

Who Are the Major Search Services, and Why Do We Care?

Why, as Web marketers, do we care so much about the search engines? Purely because they have more marketing muscle than anything ever seen on planet Earth. ActivMedia Research reports that search engine positioning has become Webmasters' preferred method of Web site promotion, and here's why. According to the GVU's Tenth Annual WWW User Survey, 84.8 percent of visitors to a Web site are ushered there via the major search engines (*www.cc.gatech.edu/gvu/user_surveys/survey-1998-10/graphs/use/q52.htm*).

Obviously, if you can't get people to your Web site, you can't sell to them. With e-commerce revenues pegged at $37.5 billion in 1999 (*Business 2.0* magazine), it's easy to see why attracting traffic to Web sites has become big business, creating an entirely new industry—search engine positioning. In this era of declining banner ad click-throughs and difficulties in tracking the effectiveness online of other, traditional media, positioning has become the critical first step for creating e-commerce viability—through e-commerce *visibility*!

> Search engines have more marketing muscle than anything ever seen on planet Earth.

If people had told us ten years ago—or even two years ago—that a one-person company with no track record and no financing, but with one good idea could establish an international presence for free, we would have told them they were crazy. But we are seeing time and time again what a powerhouse like Yahoo! can do for an indexed Web site. Getting a Web site accepted into the right Yahoo! category, and with the right title and description, can drive thousands of qualified leads to a Web site every month—without the Web site owner ever paying Yahoo! one penny.

Talk about leveling the playing field! It's the American way—hard work and perseverance can get you ahead. Interestingly enough, in the worldwide scope of the Internet, it is the Americans who have been the pioneers in search technology.

Many of those American pioneers in search technology still exist today; in fact, some remain among the leaders. Yahoo! was the first major directory, making its debut in late 1994, and WebCrawler was the first major search engine, opening its virtual doors in April 1994. Among the other early birds are AltaVista, Infoseek (now GO), and Excite in 1995. But you wouldn't recognize these important players now from their earlier selves.

> Free e-mail services, instant stock quotes, weather, horoscopes, the daily soaps—you name it, you can get it from the home pages of many of the major engines and directories.

Free e-mail services, instant stock quotes, weather, horoscopes, the daily soaps—you name it, you can get it from the home pages of many of the major engines and directories. Although most of these search services do not charge Web sites to be listed, they depend on high traffic numbers to sell ads on their site. So, in addition to trying to give visitors user-friendly yet robust search features, most of the major engines also offer everything else they can think of that will attract traffic.

They also want to give visitors large databases of information through which to search. The increases in the size of searchable databases over the past five years and the advances in search technology are mind-boggling. Following are two charts presenting today's leaders in the field of search engines. These engine and directory listings are organized, first, according to the size of their indexes. Second, they are ranked according to their popularity. Think of this as the number of potential customers they could send to your site.

Size of Index

If you rank them by the size of their indexes, here are some of the players, according to SearchEngineWatch.com* (*searchenginewatch.com/reports/sizes.html*).

AltaVista	250	million Web pages indexed
Northern Light	211	
Fast	300	
Excite	214	
Google	138	
Inktomi	110	
GO	50	
Lycos	50	

*as of February 3, 2000

Popularity

Listed here is the percentage of search engine referrals that can be attributed to the following search engines and directories on December 19, 1999, according to StatMarket.com (*statmarket.com/SM?c=WeekStat*).

Yahoo!	56%
AltaVista	11.18%
Excite	9.66%
GO	8%
Lycos	5%
GoTo	2.76%
WebCrawler	2.15%
Snap	1.58%
MSN	1.25%
Ask Jeeves	0.82%

Think of this as the number of potential customers they could send to your site.

According to MediaMetrix.com (*mediametrix.com*), February 2000, the popularity of the major engines and directories according to unique visitors who visited the site during the month is as follows.

Yahoo.com	44,698,000
Lycos.com	23,121,000
GO.com	19,487,000
Excite.com	15,552,000
AltaVista Search Svcs.	11,969,000
Snap.com Search & Serv.	10,923,000
LookSmart.com	8,812,000
Ask Jeeves.com	7,631,000
GoTo.com	7,208,000
Iwon.com	6,480,000

Understanding Algorithms

A search engine uses its proprietary software to travel through the Internet, following seemingly impenetrable networks of links to grab and index Web pages. Then it uses additional software to move the data about within one or more databases. Layered onto that is more software—we hope software with a friendly GUI (graphic user interface) to enable visitors to easily retrieve information through the searchable database.

Each of these software tasks is guided by distinctly different **algorithms**, or different criteria used by a particular engine when determining keyword relevancy, link popularity, or other ranking issues for its search returns. Each engine's ranking algorithm is different from each other engine's and depends on the automated "sorting" that is programmed for each engine's database. This means that one engine may consider a particular factor to be important, whereas another engine may consider that same factor of no importance whatsoever.

Of course, this creates myriad challenges for Web designers and Web marketers. In the section of the book called "Meet the Search Engines," you'll find chapters detailing with each of the major engines and directories. You'll learn design and submission techniques for each search service and discover how to put search engine algorithms to work for the success of your Web site.

Algorithms are different criteria used by a particular engine when determining keyword relevancy, link popularity, or other ranking issues for its search returns.

Where to Begin?

Web positioning is a process, where each concept and strategy builds on the concept introduced before. For this reason, it is important not to try implementing a strategy from Chapter 19 without having the firm foundation in Web positioning strategies that you'll gain in Chapters 1–18.

It's so tempting to want to jump ahead and try to get top rankings immediately! But don't do it. The result would be disappointing and could get you into big trouble.

Instead, the goal of this book is to explain the Web positioning process in a step-by-step fashion, to bring you to a thorough understanding of the basic concepts. In this manner, you'll be able to use the more advanced concepts presented in later chapters without confusion or difficulty.

So, start at the beginning of the book and work forward. The results will be worth it!

Basic Steps to Creating Top-Ranking Pages

To give you an idea of where we're headed and how the whole process will work, here is the strategy we'll use to guide us through the complete Web positioning process.

1. Consider your overall Web site. What is the goal of your site? What are you trying to accomplish? What pages are so important on their own that they should be able to be found separately from your home page?
2. Determine what your rankings are now at each of the major engines. You can do this by manually searching for important keywords associated with your site at each of the engines. Or you can purchase software or online services to accomplish this. More on this later. At the end of this chapter, you'll find a listing of the URLs for each of the major engines.
3. Consider what keywords are important to your site. Under what keywords do you want your Web site or individual Web pages to be found?
4. Determine where to place those keywords for optimum findability by the engines.

Extra Hints and Tips

You'll submit each of your important pages individually to some of the search engines, not just the home page of your site.

5. Develop doorway pages to increase your coverage in the engines.
6. Every time you make changes, submit your pages again!
7. Monitor your progress by checking your rankings frequently.
8. Consider other changes that could be made to help boost your rankings.
9. Correct problem areas.
10. Don't be afraid to try new things—as long as you stay far away from using spamming techniques.
11. Record your positioning work step by step. Buy a notebook and write down everything you do. By keeping good records, you'll learn what techniques work best for each particular engine at any point in time. This is crucial, because if you make changes that cause your rankings to go down, you'll be able to backtrack and take out those problematic changes. And when you find something that works, you'll know how to repeat the process for your other pages or sites!
12. Don't give up! Following this path will turn you into an effective Web positioner to the benefit of all the Web sites you touch.

Important Things to Remember

When studying this book, please keep these important points in mind.

General Optimization Strategies Will Be Introduced First

In the beginning of the book, we'll cover general Web positioning strategies that are effective with most of the major engines. However, each engine has its own unique ranking "algorithm" that it uses when determining the ranking of a Web page.

Beginning with Chapter 23, we'll cover specific strategies that work for each particular engine. But for the purpose of introducing the concepts in the beginning chapters of this book, we'll discuss what works best for most of the major engines.

> Web positioning is a process, where each concept and strategy builds on the concept introduced before.

Need More Info?

Keyword weight refers to the number of times a particular keyword is used on your Web page in relation to the total number of words appearing on that page. Keyword weight is also referred to as "keyword density."

Generally speaking, it's almost impossible to achieve a perfect keyword weight as determined by a particular engine for more than one or two keywords per page.

Create Pages Designed for Each Specific Engine

The best way to get to the top of the rankings in a particular engine is to give that engine's spider the right "food." In other words, what works for Excite might not work for AltaVista, so you'll want to craft your Web pages accordingly. Ideally, you should create engine-specific pages that incorporate each particular engine's unique likes and that avoid its dislikes. You can do this by optimizing interior Web pages for individual engines, or by creating doorway pages that are built with a particular engine in mind. We'll cover doorway pages in Chapters 10–12.

Optimize Each Page for One or Two Keywords Only

Although it certainly would be a time saver if you could optimize one page and have it achieve top rankings for every one of your keywords, it doesn't work that way. It's difficult, if not impossible, to achieve the right combination of keyword use both in the META tags and on the visible page for more than one or two keywords per Web page.

Your ranking in the engines is determined by how relevant the engine considers your Web page to be for a particular keyword or keyword phrase. In order to have a top ranking for a keyword, you have to use that keyword throughout your tags and body text and arrive at an appropriate "keyword weight."

The solution to this limitation? Optimize your subpages for those other important keyword phrases, or build doorways for them.

Stay on Top of Your Rankings!

Once you submit your pages to the engines, it's easy to want to move on to something else and to feel as though your job is done. But it isn't.

Your job is to get your pages indexed and ranked high in the engines and *to keep them there*. The only way to achieve this goal is to stay on top of your rankings. Check them frequently by visiting the major engines and searching for your important keywords, or by using a software program as mentioned earlier.

You can't make effective changes until you know exactly what your rankings are. Obviously, if your page is in the top ten, you have no reason to make changes. If your page is number 130, you do.

Resubmitting your pages has to be an important part of your ongoing search engine strategy. As a general rule, resubmit your pages once a week until they get indexed. And then resubmit any time you see a page slip in the rankings. Sometimes this is enough to get back into the engines' "good graces" without making any changes to the page. More on this later.

If a simple resubmission doesn't do the trick, analyze your Web page and reread our chapter on the engine in question to see what changes you can make to boost those rankings back into the top ten.

Rules, Rules, Rules!

In this book, we share proven techniques for achieving top rankings in the major search engines—the rules to follow for bringing in the traffic necessary for a successful Web site. However, you'll find exceptions to these "rules" frequently.

Don't concentrate on those exceptions. Instead, concentrate on what works best for you. Even if it looks as if someone else is getting away with something, be careful about emulating that person because the strategy could constitute spamming, and spamming an engine is dangerous.

However, there may be times when you can break the rules and have it work to your benefit. Experiment with *expendable* pages and domains, if you have them. Rejoice when an inventive technique works, but first concentrate on learning what works best *most* of the time.

The only rules that should *never* be broken are spamming guidelines because they can get your Web site banned from the engines. We'll cover the topic of spamming in Chapter 17.

Extra Hints and Tips

An exception to the resubmitting your pages once a week rule is with AltaVista, where you won't want to resubmit pages unless you've made several changes to them.

Extra Hints and Tips

An exception to the one or two keyword rule is with Excite, where you can sometimes optimize a page for five or six keywords and be effective.

Conflicting Information

You'll find many "experts" in the field of Web positioning, and some of their ideas about what works and what doesn't may conflict with other information you might come across.

So, Whom *Do* You Believe?

It can be confusing. You'll find Web sites that have gotten top-ten rankings, yet they seem to defy every rule in the Web positioning game. Further, what works for one page doesn't necessarily work for another. And this leads to conflicting information throughout the industry.

What we present in this book has been learned through trial and error. At the time of printing, the techniques included here have worked for *most* sites *most* of the time. There are other reputable sources out there, like Danny Sullivan's Search Engine Watch (*www.searchenginewatch.com*), but it is best to take tips from every source with "a grain of salt." Until you've implemented a strategy and have tracked its path to success, don't assume that what you read online or elsewhere is a proven technique. Pick your sources carefully and learn from your own successes (and mistakes!).

> Until you've implemented a strategy and have tracked its path to success, don't assume that what you read online or elsewhere is a proven technique.

Here's an Example

Here's an example of conflicting information. There's some controversy over the number of pages that can be indexed with Excite. Some authorities believe that a total of 25 pages can be indexed with the engine. If you submit more than 25 pages, you stand a chance at getting your Web site tossed out of the index.

Other authorities believe that you can submit only 25 pages in one day but that more than 25 pages per site can be listed.

Yet another expert believes that a 25-page per site listing limit at Excite has never existed. He believes that Excite has a 25-page per week submission limit, but submitting to Excite has little impact on the actual pages that get listed, so this limit really doesn't matter.

We'll put our own spin on this in Chapter 24, along with information *straight from the horse's mouth*!

Quickly Changing Guidelines

One of the many challenges of search engine positioning is that the engines change their ranking algorithms quite frequently. What works today may not work next week, which is why we sometimes resort to trial-and-error techniques to determine what works.

If your rankings slip, consider it an indication that your pages no longer meet the requirements for a top-ranking page in that particular engine. So, make changes to your pages based on what you believe that particular engine's ranking preferences have become.

How can you keep up with the changes in the search engines? In our appendix, you'll find several subscription services that provide the most up-to-date guidelines for each of the major areas. Read them regularly and test, test, test!

Begin with Your Home (or Main) Page

As we'll learn in Chapter 5, the engines assign more relevancy to your home page, also called your index or main page, than other pages of your site. Therefore, it's critical to use general Web positioning strategies for your main page and submit it to each of the major engines. What's more, because you have an automatic edge with a home page over your other pages, you may want to optimize that page for your most important keyword phrase, or even the most competitive.

Work your home page as hard as you can, and then consider what other pages of your site can be optimized for the other search engines to bring in more traffic.

The Engines Like Simplicity!

Sometimes we try too hard with our Web positioning strategies. We get in a hurry, and we want to implement all the possible changes recommended by a wide variety of sources to try to immediately get in the top-ten rankings.

There are a lot of reasons to go slowly. First of all, if you implement a few changes at a time, you'll be able to determine what really is working, which will help you with subsequent pages in that engine.

Need More Info?

Search Engine Watch is one of the best sources of information about the search engines. You can subscribe to a free monthly newsletter and access a mountain of information at the Web site. Or for a subscription fee, you'll be able to enter the password-protected area of the site, and you'll receive a newsletter twice a month. It's well worth the fee.

searchenginewatch.com

If you implement ten changes at the same time, you won't know why your rankings have gone up. Plus, one of those changes might actually be hurting your rankings somewhat, but because you changed so many things at once, you won't have any way of knowing that.

Further, many of the engines like simplicity. In Chapter 15, we'll study our competitors' Web sites to see if we can learn from their success. In some cases, you'll see that the "simplest" sites rank the highest.

Why? Because those sites aren't using techniques that confuse the engines or that cause the engine's spider to have to dig through a mountain of code to get to the real heart of the site—the keyword-containing areas.

So, start out slowly with a few changes at a time. Check your rankings, and make a few more changes. Write down everything. Try not to use techniques that present problems for the engines because it will put your Web site at an immediate disadvantage. We'll discuss those problem areas in Chapter 19.

Remember: more isn't always better in this business!

Don't Be Afraid to Try New Things!

Web positioning is not an exact science, and that's an enormous understatement. As long as you're not trying blatant spamming techniques, don't be afraid to try new things. You never know when you might discover something that can make a huge difference in your rankings.

But try to go slowly. Don't test a handful of new things at once. If you try one or two new things at a time, you'll be able to tell what's really working and what isn't.

Remember that if you test something that doesn't work and your rankings go down, backtrack and take out the changes. This proves the importance of keeping good notes. If you don't take good notes, you may not remember how to get back a previous better ranking.

> Web positioning is not an exact science, and that's an enormous understatement.

How to Determine Your Ranking

1. Visit each of the engine's Web sites (see the following chart
   for addresses) and type in the search window the keywords
   that are important to your site. If you're using keyword
   phrases rather than single keywords, which we'll discuss in
   Chapter 4, place those keyword phrases in quotation marks
   when searching, like this:
   "Washington red apples"
2. In the results, look for your Web site. Can it be found in the
   first 50 rankings (first 5 pages)? Write down your rankings
   for each of your keywords for each of the major engines.

Further, there are software programs available, such as TopDog,
that will search for your site and determine your rankings.

URLs for the Major Engines and Search Facilities

AltaVista	*www.altavista.com*
AOL Search	*search.aol.com*
Excite	*www.excite.com*
GO/InfoSeek	*infoseek.go.com*
Google	*www.google.com*
HotBot	*www.hotbot.com*
Lycos	*www.lycos.com*
Northern Light	*www.northernlight.com*
Open Directory Project	*dmoz.org*
WebCrawler	*www.Webcrawler.com*
Yahoo!	*www.yahoo.com*

Need More Info?

TopDog's Web site address is:

www.topdogg.com

For more information on this topic, visit our Web site at www.businesstown.com

It All Begins with a Simple Keyword

Overview of Section II

Since every search engine positioning strategy depends on successfully identifying your most important keywords, Section II helps you determine what those keywords are, then explains where you can place those keywords for maximum effectiveness.

Chapter 4

How to Choose Effective Keywords

The key to successful Web optimization begins with a simple keyword phrase. Everything depends on that keyword phrase.

When people visit a search engine looking for links to relevant sites, they'll put keywords in the search window that they feel will get them the information they need. As search engine positioners, it is our job to determine which keywords the visitors will most likely use when trying to find our Web pages.

Of course, for most sites, more than one or two keyword phrases can attract desirable visitors. This is why we optimize each page of a site separately and uniquely, which means we'll need to determine which keywords are important for each particular page.

So, carefully consider which keywords are important to your site. Under what keywords is it important for your site to be found?

Let's take a moment to study how people really search.

How Do People Search?

When considering which keywords to use on our pages, we need to understand how people really search. Do they use single words or groups of words? Do they search in all capital letters? Let's see.

Use Two- or Three-Word Phrases Instead of Single Words

As Web visitors get more and more Internet savvy, they're learning that they can fine-tune their search results considerably by searching for two- or three-word phrases instead of single words. When searching for single words, like "computers," for example, you'll get literally millions of Web pages in your search results, many of which aren't relevant to what you're looking for. But if you combine "computers" with another word or two, such as "large screen computers," you'll effectively eliminate most of those irrelevant results, saving yourself time and hassle.

Here's an example: as of this writing, at AltaVista you'll find approximately 12,863,812 pages when you search for "computers." But if you search for "large screen computers" (using quotation marks around the phrase), you'll find 38 pages. Quite a difference!

Searches Using Keyword Phrases in Quotation Marks

More and more Web searchers are using search strategies that will cut down on the number of results they get, while also making those results more relevant to what they're looking for. One such strategy is to put their search terms in quotation marks.

If you search for "large screen computers" without using quotation marks, you'll find 22,820,870 results. Add those little quotation marks, and you'll find 38 pages. This is because with most of the search engines, putting quotes around the term tells the engine that you're interested in that *exact term*, not in the *individual* words in that term. Without those quotation marks around the keyword phrase, you're telling the engine to search for "large," "screen," and "computers" separately as well as a group, so your list of results is larger and less relevant.

So what does this mean to you as a search engine positioner? Simply put, you need to make sure to fine-tune your keyword phrase. Of course, your goal is to get found both when searchers use quotation marks and when they don't. But because the amount of competition is generally much less when you use quotes, you'll have an easier time getting a top ranking when searchers use quotes.

Search in Lowercase Letters

Most Web viewers search using all lowercase letters. In other words, if they're looking for "New York City," they'll type in "new york city."

So what does this mean to you as a search engine positioner?

Simply, you'll need to use your keyword phrase with all lowercase letters at least once in your META tags, even if your keyword phrase is a proper noun. This is because some of the engines are case sensitive, which means that they will search for exactly what you have specified in the search query window. For example, if you type in "new york city," case-sensitive engines may not search for "New York City" or "NEW YORK CITY." Other engines are partially case sensitive, meaning that their search will include capitalized forms but not in all uppercase letters.

> The key to successful Web optimization begins with a simple keyword phrase.

To ensure that your approach to each particular engine is ideal, you can search for your keyword phrase in all variations: all lowercase letters, upper- and lowercase, and all uppercase letters. If you get different results for some or all, you'll need to include those variations in your tags for that engine.

Consider These Important Facts

Please keep these important facts in mind.

Fine-Tune Your Keywords and Narrow the Competition

How difficult do you think it would be to get a top-10 ranking, or even top 30, under the very generic keyword of "computers"? You would be competing against 12 million other Web pages. And even if you were to achieve that, how "qualified" would your traffic be? How many Web surfers would you irritate when they come to your site looking for *laptop* "computers" or *IBM* "computers," while your site sells only *large screen* "computers"?

Don't make the mistake of trying to go after very generic keywords. The possibility of your getting top rankings under those words is slim, your frustration level would be great, and we've already shown you how your target audiences will be refining their searches anyway by adding additional keywords to their search phrases.

By fine-tuning your keyword phrase, you're targeting traffic that is looking for your particular Web page. You'll stand a much greater chance at getting top rankings under that keyword phrase. Once you've achieved this, consider going after the more competitive keyword phrases to enhance the stream of qualified leads you are already generating.

Pair a General Keyword with a More Specific One

If your Web site deals with insurance, pairing a more specific keyword with a general keyword is another way of fine-tuning your

> Don't make the mistake of trying to go after very generic keywords.

keyword phrase. For example, combine keywords like "whole life insurance" or "high risk automobile insurance." Take your very general keyword and add words to it to make it more specific to your particular Web page.

Ask Your Customers for Advice!

We often think that we know which keywords our customers will use when trying to find our site. We often are wrong! Don't consider keyword phrases that *you* would use—use keyword phrases that *they* would use.

Ask a few customers how they would search for your site. Ask a family member, a close friend, or your next-door neighbor how he or she might try to find your site in the search engines. Get different opinions. In many cases, you'll find that you would search for your site in a different way from other people.

If you have a referrer log program, which we'll cover in Chapter 21, look in your log file and see how people are currently finding your site. What search terms are they using?

> **Ask Your Customers for Advice!** Don't consider keyword phrases that you would use—use keyword phrases that they would use.

Consider Combining Keywords That Are Distantly Related

Let's say that you're in real estate, which is a very competitive area on the Web. Besides choosing a keyword phrase like, "new orleans real estate," consider keyword phrases like "new orleans school districts" or even "new orleans shopping malls."

If someone is considering moving to that area, he or she may very well search the Web to find out about the area schools or shopping malls. Capitalize on that by using keyword phrases that will bring you that business.

Is Your Keyword Commonly Misspelled?

The Web is full of bad spellers, and they're certainly not going to crack open a dictionary before typing in a search term. So, if you're using a keyword phrase that is commonly misspelled, take advantage of that by including the misspelled version as one of your keywords.

For example, if your keyword phrase is "Los Angeles restaurants," consider variations like "Las Angeles restaurants" or "Los Angeles restarants." You don't have to use the misspelled versions on your visible page since using it in the tags will pull in many misspelled searches.

Are Your Services Region Specific?

In our preceding example, we would be concentrating on restaurants in one certain area: Los Angeles. If you're in a region-specific field like the real estate business, you will want to use keywords that pertain to your particular region, whether it's a county, a city, or an area of a city.

Use the Longest Variation of Your Keywords

If you're in the advertising business, you would want to use keywords such as "advertising" or "advertisements" rather than simply "ads" or "advertise." This is because many of the engines use *word stemming*, which means that they will search for the root word and include all variations of that word in the search results. By using the longest form as your keyword, you'll also receive traffic from the shorter forms.

Further, when you use the longer variations, you won't have to use every single one of the variations in your tags or on the page because the search engines that practice word stemming will return your page for searches on those word variations.

A simple but important way to gain traffic with one common longer variation is to include the plural of most keyword phrases by adding an "s" to them, such as "English bulldogs."

> A simple but important way to gain traffic with one common longer variation is to include the plural of most keyword phrases by adding an "s" to them, such as "English bulldogs."

Different Terminology for Different Regions

People in other areas of the world express themselves differently. You may call the carts that you use in a grocery store "shopping carts," whereas someone else might call them "buggies."

In your area, seventh graders may go to junior high, whereas in other areas, they're in middle school.

Try to determine what people in other regions might call your keyword phrase, and if enough potential traffic is involved, optimize a page for that keyword phrase.

Stop Using "Stop" Words!

"Stop" words are common words that are often totally ignored by the search engines as a way to save storage space and speed up searches. When your keyword phrase contains stop words, the engine won't "stop" to look for those words when it's searching its index.

Examples of stop words are:
and, the, a, an, am, for, of, that, this, it

In some of the engines, common Web-related words may be stop words, such as:
web, internet, net

The best way to tell if a word is a stop word is to search for it in each of the major engines. If you receive a statement such as, "No document matches your query," you'll know that the word is a stop word for that particular engine. Each engine has different stop words, so it's important to check each one.

If your site contains stop words in areas where the search engine spider looks for information to index (such as your title tag), it will ignore the stop words, possibly affecting how you're indexed. Or if the prominence of a keyword in your title is crucial for a particular engine's ranking scheme, having the first word in your title be "the" could damage your ranking.

If a stop word is an important part of your title, try to come up with another title that doesn't contain the stop word, or put the stop word in quotes, which will tell the engine that it is indeed important.

If your keyword phrase contains stop words and if you put the phrase in quotes, take time to search for your site to see what your description looks like in the search engine results.

> If your keyword phrase contains stop words and if you put the phrase in quotes, take time to search for your site to see what your description looks like in the search engine results.

Be Careful When Using Trademarked Terms

The illegitimate use of trademarked terms has gotten a lot of coverage in the news recently. Some ambitious Web marketers learned that if they optimize their pages for a very popular trademarked name, one that they had no legal right to themselves, they could get visitors who were searching for that popular trademark.

Now the courts are getting involved. Lawsuits are cropping up everywhere against people who use trademarked terms in their tags in an effort to direct traffic to their site. For example, let's say that you sell a particular brand of stereo equipment. If you use "Pioneer" in your tags, you may be able to get some of that traffic as well. But if you don't sell "Pioneer" stereo equipment, don't do it because if you do you may be caught by the company that owns the trademark *and* by the search engines!

Many large companies have employees who search the Web to see if they can find sites that are using their trademarked terms without permission. When they find such Web sites, their attorney writes a letter warning them of the misuse and generally giving the erring site a certain period of time to get the trademarked terms removed before a lawsuit is filed.

Using the same example, let's say that you don't sell Pioneer stereo equipment, but that within a page of your site you compare your product to Pioneer's. Can you now use the Pioneer brand name in your tags? Probably. However, check with your attorney before implementing any technique that is the subject of current law cases.

While we're discussing trademarked terms, be careful not to use words that, through extensive use, are now often thought to be generic. For example, don't use "Kleenex" because it is a trademarked term. The generic term is "tissues." Another example is "Frisbee."

> Use your tags to bring legitimate, qualified leads to your site. It'll pay off more in the long run.

Don't Use Inappropriate Keywords

Another reason not to use keywords inappropriately is the search engines' possible reaction to such techniques. If you include a particular keyword phrase in your META tags, you had better use that keyword phrase throughout your page. If you don't and some of the engines find out, you could find yourself banned from those engines altogether.

This goes for using trademarked terms but it also is true for sites that employ popular keyword phrases in an effort to illegitimately boost traffic to their site. For example, we all know that "sex" is one of the most searched for terms on the Web. If your site is trying to sell bars of soap, but you're filling your tags with "sex" just to increase traffic, you're taking the risk of angering the search engine gods. Just as important, if your "sex" technique works and you've attracted a visitor looking online for something related to sex, what are the chances that you'll sell him soap?

Use your tags to bring legitimate, qualified leads to your site. It'll pay off more in the long run.

Let's Develop a Strategy for Choosing Keywords

Because it's crucial to choose the right keywords for each important page of your site, let's look at a step-by-step approach for choosing keywords.

As you work your way through this approach, write down all the keywords and keyword phrases that you think of. Don't try to analyze whether those keywords are totally appropriate—simply write them down. You can analyze their merit later.

1. Write out a focused description of your business for your home page or the purpose of each individual Web page.
2. Do you sell a product or service? Product names can be excellent keywords for some of your pages if you sell those products. Do you provide information? What type of information? Do you provide free services to your Web visitors?
3. Does your business have any quirks or unique aspects? What are your objectives?
4. Think of as many ways as you can to describe what you do in your business. Brainstorm! Write anything and everything down!

> ## *Need More Info?*
>
> Search Engine Watch offers a page that discusses the potential problems with using trademarked terms:
>
> *searchenginewatch.internet.com/sereport/9805-metatags.html*

Extra Hints and Tips

In an effort to get found under the more general keywords, be sure to use individual keywords from your keyword phrase throughout the page and in the tags as well.

Need More Info?

These Web sites will help you consider additional keyword phrases:

Roget's Internet Thesaurus:
www.thesaurus.com

Plumb Design Visual Thesaurus:
www.plumbdesign.com/thesaurus

WordNet:
www.cogsci.princeton.edu/~wn

5. Start with a main word; then add other words to that main word. Compile a list and consider other descriptive words based on your business.
6. Keep a listing of your keyword ideas because you'll want to add to that list as you consider new keyword phrases. As you continue working on your site, you can consider creating new pages that will use some of the keyword ideas on your list.
7. Visit some of your competitors' Web sites. What keywords do they use? Don't use your competitor's name as a keyword, however, and don't use product names if you don't sell those products.
8. Make a list of at least fifty keywords or keyword phrases.
9. Place those keyword phrases in order of importance to you and your business.
10. Visit one of the major search engines and search for each of your phrases. Write down how many results you get when searching for each of your important keyword phrases.
11. In the beginning, narrow the competition by choosing keyword phrases that produce ten thousand or fewer results. Once you are ranked high under those keyword phrases, branch out to the keyword phrases that produce more results, and increase traffic to your site in this manner.

    After all, your goal is to get top rankings under keyword phrases that will bring you the most business. If you choose keyword phrases that produce only five hundred results when searching for them, you're probably not going to bring in much Web site traffic through those phrases.
12. Determine if those keyword phrases are ones that searchers are actually using by visiting GoTo's Search Term Suggestion page, which we'll discuss later in this chapter.

Other Places to Get Keyword Ideas

Look up your keyword in a thesaurus or dictionary. Many word processing programs have a thesaurus that you can use. Or look in magazines or trade journals for your industry. Find your products. How are they described? You also can use online thesauruses and dictionaries.

How Many People Are Searching for Your Keyword Phrase?

Besides looking at the competition you'll have when choosing a certain keyword phrase, it's also very important to learn if people are actually searching for that particular phrase.

To get an idea of how many people are searching for your keyword phrase, visit GoTo's Search Term Suggestion List and type in your keyword phrase. You'll learn how many people actually searched for that term at GoTo for the previous month: *www.goto.com/d/about/advertisers/othertools.jhtml*

Though this won't tell you how many people are searching for your keyword phrase at the other engines, it will give you an idea of how popular the keyword phrase is.

Search Engine Watch, one of the best Web sites for search engine information, offers a page titled, "What People Search For." You'll find a listing of Yahoo's top 200 search words as well as the top search words from Dogpile, WebCrawler, Magellan, and more: *searchenginewatch.internet.com/facts/searches.html*

One Final Word

When choosing keywords, remember, that your ultimate goal is to increase traffic to your site.

Choose Keywords That Will Give You a Chance at Success

Don't make the mistake of targeting very general keywords and getting frustrated when those keywords don't make it into the top ten.

If you pick a keyword phrase that produces two million search results, consider fine-tuning that phrase considerably. Remember that it's much more difficult to get into top-ranking positions if you target generic keywords. And the chances that you'll attract *qualified leads* through such a technique are slim.

However, once you've achieved top-ranking positions for several of your keyword phrases, have increased your Web site's *popularity*, which we'll cover in Chapter 13, and have become more experienced

> ### Extra Hints and Tips
>
> WordSpot is a subscription service that is a helpful source of information about what keywords people are actually searching for. WordSpot will generate a customized report based on six of your primary keywords and will show the top 500 words that are most often used with your primary words: *www.wordspot.com*
>
> Another subscription service, WordTracker.com, has a database of over thirty million results that is updated every 2 hours. Enter a phrase that describes your business, and you'll learn how many people are actually searching for that phrase: *www.wordtracker.com*

in search engine positioning, then go after more general keywords. After all, if you can get ranked high with very general keywords, you'll certainly bring in traffic to your site. It's much harder to do, but if increasing the number of hits to your site is important, such as for attracting more advertisers, then go for it.

By the same token, don't make the mistake of going after a keyword phrase that produces just forty-two results. How much traffic do you think you'll get out of that keyword phrase? Not much.

Try to reach a happy medium, and you'll be able to watch your site traffic improve dramatically.

> One of the most crucial steps to promoting your site on the search engines is choosing the proper keywords to target

From an Expert
Choosing the Right Keywords Is Crucial!

We asked Brent Winters, president of First Place Software, creator of the popular WebPosition Gold software, the following question:

"If you had one piece of advice to offer someone who wants to get their site positioned in the engines, what would that advice be?"
Here's his response:

One of the most crucial steps to promoting your site on the search engines is choosing the proper keywords to target. If you choose keywords that few people search for, all your optimization work will be in vain. Choose good keywords and you could see several times the traffic someone else would receive for the same amount of work. That's why we set up a free resource to help people through this critical process at www.marketposition.com/keywordgenerator.htm.

For more information on this topic, visit our Web site at www.businesstown.com

Chapter 5

I've Got My Keywords, Now Where Do I Put Them?

Once you've determined your keyword phrases, it's important to learn how to get the best mileage out of them. Having the best keyword phrases in the world won't bring you traffic if the placement of the keywords isn't done strategically. Just sticking your keyword phrase in here and there won't get you a top ranking.

It's also important to understand the importance of "relevancy" and what factors come into play when determining relevancy.

Factors That Can Affect Relevancy

Search engines send their spiders to crawl the Web, and the spiders index certain areas of your Web page. Then, the engines sort those pages in their databases by the keywords contained in the tags and body text of each Web page. Therefore, you need to make sure that the keywords you've chosen are implemented throughout your page.

When people visit the engines and search for a keyword phrase, they expect the engines to return a listing of relevant Web sites based on the keyword they entered. Search engines sort the Web pages in their index by the keywords contained in a Web page to produce the search results.

In other words, which keywords each individual search engine determines your Web page is relevant to and how often those keywords are searched for will determine your Web page's ranking in that particular search engine. As we said before, the ranking criteria differ from search engine to search engine.

If you organize your keywords consistent with a search engine's ranking criteria, your ranking with that particular engine will go up. That's the reason it's so important to study what each particular engine considers relevant.

How Can You Improve Your Relevancy?

Study the following ways of boosting your relevancy, and watch your Web page's rankings go up!

Prominence: How Early Do Your Keywords Appear?

How early in a Web page's title, description, body text, and so on, does a searched-for keyword appear? Make sure your title or description begins with your most important keyword phrase. By using your keyword phrase early in your tags and in the body text, you're increasing its prominence, thus improving your relevancy.

So, do you need to use your keyword phrase as the first words in each of those tags? Generally, yes. But it's a good idea to analyze top-ranking sites in each engine for your keyword phrase. Where did they use their keyword phrase? Is it the first words in the title? In the description? How soon did they use it in the body text? If you see a definite trend, fashion your tags accordingly.

Further, periodically, many of the engines offer boosts in relevancy to keywords that appear as the third or fourth keywords in a title or description, versus the first. Or it may be the second or third keywords. Don't be afraid to test the waters here. Try your keywords as the first words in the tags. If you don't get the rankings you want, put them as the third or fourth keywords and see if that makes a difference, and so forth.

Frequency: How Often Have You Used Your Keyword Phrase?

How frequently did you use your keyword phrase in your tags or in the body text? How many times did you use the phrase in your title tag? Your description tag?

Many engines don't like to see your keyword phrase more than once in the title tag, but they'll let you get by with using it twice in the description tag.

Be careful about repeating your keyword phrase in any tag, however. If you repeat your keyword phrase too many times, you could be accused of "keyword stuffing," which we'll cover in Chapter 17.

Don't use your keyword phrase more than three times in the META keyword tag.

Need More Info?

What exactly is "relevancy"? Relevancy is the ability to retrieve information that satisfies the needs of the user. The more relevant your Web page is, or the extent that it satisfies the needs of the user, the higher your ranking will be.

Extra Hints and Tips

If you're working with very competitive keyword phrases, try inserting the keyword phrase in the middle of the description tag instead of at the very beginning. It sometimes helps boost your ranking a little.

In many cases, "less" is better than "more" in this business. If you're using your keyword phrase twice and aren't getting the rankings you want, drop back and use it only once and see if that makes a difference.

Site Popularity: How Many Web Sites Link to Yours?

One measure of a site's "value" is the number of other Web sites that have agreed to link to it. Therefore, do whatever you can to get other sites to link to yours. These days, having a very popular Web site can make a huge difference in the rankings with many engines, particularly GO/InfoSeek, Snap, and AltaVista.

The importance of site popularity is discussed in detail in Chapter 13.

Keyword Weight: How Many Times Did You Use Your Keyword Phrase in Relation to the Total Number of Words on Your Page?

Each engine likes to see a particular keyword weight and assigns more relevancy to pages that use that keyword weight. For some engines, it might make sense to keep the total number of words on the page down, thereby increasing the "weight" of the keyword phrase that you're using. Other engines like a lot of text, so in these cases, you'd want to increase the number of repetitions of the keyword within that text.

We'll discuss keyword weight in greater detail in Chapter 6.

Proximity: Keep Your Keywords Near Each Other

Keyword proximity is the placement of keywords on a Web page in relation to each other. For example, the connected phrase "children's playhouse" will outrank the phrase "children's wooden playhouse" when the searched-for phrase is "children's playhouse."

So, keep your keywords together!

It's also beneficial to use the individual words from your keyword phrase throughout the page. This will increase your chances at getting a good ranking for your keyword phrase without using

> Just as how you use your keywords is important, so is where you place your keywords.

quotes when searching for it because you're also working toward optimizing the page for those individual keywords.

Strategy: Place Your Keywords in All Important Places

Just as *how* you use your keywords is important, so is *where* you place your keywords. If you place your keywords in the title and heading tags, and if a particular engine attributes more relevancy to keywords in those tags, your page will get a boost in the rankings for that engine. In some engines, placing keywords in the link text or in the URL can add more relevancy to those words. Again, the chapters on the individual engines will provide information on the preferences of each engine.

Root Domain: Don't Put Important Pages in Subdirectories

Don't put your pages in a subdirectory that's two or three directories away from the root domain. In most cases, pages that are closer to the root domain are deemed more relevant than pages farther from the root domain.

For example:

www.spiderfood.net/directory/subdirectory/mynewpage.htm

This page (which isn't a real URL) generally won't get ranked as high as:

www.spiderfood.net/mynewpage.htm

Even if both pages are identical in every other way.

So, give your page an automatic edge over the competition by placing it as close to the root domain as possible.

What Are META Tags and Why Are They so Important?

META tags are HTML tags that give information about a Web page. There are many different types of META tags that perform various

> ### More Hints and Tips
>
> Some experts believe that the degree of difficulty in getting your Web site ranked in the top ten is determined by the spread of percent relevancy between the top ten sites rather than the total number of pages in the search results. If there is more than a 10 percent difference between the number 1 site and the number 10 site, your keyword will get placed fairly easily. As the gap narrows, the difficulty increases.

Need More Info?

For detailed instructions on META tags, see:
    "How to Use META Tags" at Search Engine Watch Web site:

searchenginewatch.internet.com/ webmasters/meta.html

    "Search Engine Design Tips" at Search Engine Watch Web site:

searchenginewatch.com/webmasters/ tips.html

Extra Hints and Tips

Sometimes you can achieve good results by including multiple title tags with AltaVista, Excite, and the Inktomi engines. Don't use two title tags with GO/InfoSeek, however. In any event, use this technique with care and monitor your rankings closely.

Extra Hints and Tips

Remember that all META tags should go in the <head> </head> section of your page and beneath your <title> tag.

tasks, but the most common are those that help a Web page to be found by search engines. Important META tags include the META keyword, META description, and META robots tags.

Many engines consider the content of META tags when determining relevancy. Therefore, with those engines, it's crucial to use your important keyword phrase toward the beginning of your META tags.

Many HTML editors, such as FrontPage and GoLive, insert unimportant META tags on your page, which will serve only to confuse the engines. The only important META tags are the keyword, description, and robot tags. Any others can be deleted.

All META tags should go in the <head> </head> section of your page, and all META tags should be beneath the <title> tag. The <title> tag must be the first tag on your page.

Which Engines Consider META Tags When Determining Relevancy?

AltaVista	Yes
Excite	No
HotBot	Yes
GO/InfoSeek	Yes
Lycos	No
Northern Light	No
WebCrawler	No
Yahoo!	No

Where You Can Put Your Keywords

Keywords in the <TITLE> tag
Example:
<TITLE>Educational children's software</TITLE>

Keywords in the <meta name="description"> tag
Example:
"<meta name="description" content="Educational children's software makes learning just plain fun!">

Some of the engines, such as Lycos and Excite, don't consider the content of the description tag when determining relevancy and ranking, but they sometimes use the tag to describe your site in the search engine results.

Keywords in the <meta name="keyword"> tag
Example:
<meta name="keywords" content="educational children's software, educational software, childrens software, EDUCATIONAL CHILDREN'S SOFTWARE">

Remember that sticking in a bunch of keywords in the keyword META tag won't get your page ranked high for all those keywords. In order to get a top ranking with a keyword phrase, you have to use that phrase throughout your page, in your title tag, and in other tags as well.

Keywords in the <meta http-equiv="keywords"> tag
Example:
<meta http-equiv="keywords" name="keywords" CONTENT="educational childrens software">

The engines do not make this an easy situation for positioners because, as usual, there is no "one size fits all" approach to the use of this tag, either. For example, AltaVista considers the content of http-equiv keyword tags for relevancy, but GO/InfoSeek does not.

Keywords in the headline tags (h2, h3, etc.) tag
Example:
<h3 ALIGN="CENTER">Educational Children's Software is Fun!</h3>

Many of the engines place considerable relevancy on headline tags, so use them frequently, especially toward the top of your page. You may also want to try putting your entire body text in a small headline tag.

Keywords in the link text
Example:
<A HREF=yourWeb site.com/keyword-phrase.htm></A>Click here for more educational children's software programs.

Note: When you put your keyword phrases in your URLs, be sure to separate those phrases with a "-" or a "_" instead of running the keywords together. By breaking the words up in some way, the engines will see them as individual words in a phrase. If the words are not broken up, the spiders will see the words as a single term.

Example:
www.yourWeb site.com/web-optimizing-techniques.htm
instead of:
www.yourWeb site.com/weboptimizingtechniques.htm

Keywords in the body text
Remember the importance of keyword prominence, and make the first twenty-five words in the body of your page keyword rich. Further, since some search engines retrieve the first few lines of your Web page to use as the description of your site in the search results, be sure to not only put a number of important keywords in the first few lines of your introductory text, but to also make that text inviting. Craft the beginning text so that it is a great description of your site.

Spread your keyword phrases throughout the body of the page in natural-sounding paragraphs, keeping some of them fairly close together for proximity's sake. Put a keyword toward the end of your body text as well.

Whenever possible, begin your page with text, not an image. The engines can't "read" images, though many of the engines can read ALT tags describing those images.

Keywords in the ALT tags
Example:
<IMG SRC="images/box.gif" ALT="educational children's software" WIDTH="415" HEIGHT="100">

> Since some search engines retrieve the first few lines of your Web page to use as the description of your site in the search results, be sure to not only put a number of important keywords in the first few lines of your introductory text, but to also make that text inviting.

The purpose of an ALT tag is to describe the contents of a picture that hasn't loaded yet for the benefit of Web surfers who surf with the images turned off. Many surfers with older computers or browsers surf with the images turned off because it takes too long to load the images.

However, instead of merely describing the graphic, you can choose to insert your keyword phrase in your ALT tag—or you can do both, describe and keyword-stud. For example, if your keyword phrase for this page is "green widgets" and the image is of a factory worker on a lunch break, your ALT tag copy could be:

<IMG SRC="images/worker.gif" ALT="green widget worker takes a break" WIDTH="415" HEIGHT="100">

This can give this keyword a boost in relevancy with many of the engines.

Of course, there are always those engines that decide not to fit a particular mold. In this case, it is Excite, HotBot, WebCrawler, and Northern Light that don't consider the content of ALT tags when determining relevancy.

Use clear single pixel images with ALT tags

If your page doesn't contain graphics, or if you'd like an extra boost in relevancy, consider using clear single pixel images.

Download this small clear gif:

www.robinsnest.com/clr.gif

When you go to this page, it will be totally blank because the graphic is clear.

To download the gif, click on File on the top toolbar; then choose Save As (since you can't see it on the page).

Then, insert that tiny, transparent graphic preferably near the top of the Web page for the best effect:

<IMG SRC="clr.gif" BORDER="0" ALT="educational children's software">

Notice that the height and width tags are left off. Without those tags, the engine can't easily determine the size of the graphic, so nothing about this strategy will send up a "red flag."

Extra Hints and Tips

Try putting your keyword phrases in boldface in your body text. Sometimes this boosts relevancy.

Extra Hints and Tips

Another idea that works quite well, especially with AltaVista, is to create a bulleted list on your page. Use tiny bullet graphics with ALT tags, and insert your keyword phrase in each of those ALT tags.

To download a tiny bullet graphic, visit this Web site:

www.robinsnest.com/circle1.gif
Click on File, then Save As.

You can use single pixel gifs even if you use other graphics on your page.

Keywords in comment tags
Example:

<!–educational children's software>

The only major engines that consider the comment tags for relevancy at this time are HotBot and other Inktomi engines. InfoSeek and AltaVista don't, so there's no reason to use this tag with those engines.

Keywords in hidden links
Example:

<A HREF="educational-childrens-software.htm"><IMG SRC="clr.gif" BORDER="0" ALT="educational children's software"></A>

When would you want to use hidden links?

Maybe you want to include links from your home page to your doorway pages so that the engines can find and index them, but you don't want your home page human visitors to find your doorway pages. Using the single pixel graphic properly allows the spider to find your doorways while your other visitors cannot see the single pixel links on your main page. Including your keyword phrase in the URL, in the ALT tag of the hidden links, or in both also allows you to boost your relevancy.

Again, notice that we've left off the height and width tags. In the future, spiders may decide not to spider links from images that are known to be only one pixel in size. Without those tags, the engine cannot easily determine the size of the graphic, so nothing about this strategy will send up a red flag to the engine.

For many of the engines, it's advantageous to include hidden links on your home page to all of your other pages so that the engine's spider can crawl through your site following link after link. But if your site has a large number of links, this may not be practical. In that case, you can create a table of contents or site map that has links to all the pages you want indexed. Then, on each of your

> Including your keyword phrase in the URL, in the ALT tag of the hidden links, or in both also allows you to boost your relevancy.

pages, put a hidden link to the site map. This helps get more pages into engines like AltaVista and Excite.

This provides the added benefit of giving the engines' spiders a way to index those pages themselves without submitting them. This will give you a boost in relevancy with some engines, such as AltaVista and GO/InfoSeek.

Keywords contained in the URL or site address
Example:
www.spiderfood.net/educational_childrens_software.htm

In this example, you name your HTML page after your keyword phrase.

Keywords contained in the names of images
Example:
"childrens-educational-software.gif"

Sometimes renaming your images after your keywords can give you a boost in relevancy.

Keywords in the domain name
Example:
EducationalChildrensSoftware.com
Or:
Educational-Childrens-Software.com

If you're in the market for additional domains, be sure to purchase domain names that have your keywords in them. You'll get a boost in relevancy, plus an index page for each domain. Most of the engines give a boost in relevancy to an index page of a domain.

Do you need to use hyphens between your keywords in your domain name? There are advantages to using hyphens, but there's a disadvantage, too.

If you use hyphens, the engine may recognize the domain name as a keyword phrase and give you a boost in relevancy. But it's much easier to tell customers your URL and have them *remember* it if you don't use hyphens.

> For many of the engines, it's advantageous to include hidden links on your home page to all of your other pages so that the engine's spider can crawl through your site following link after link.

For example, let's say your Web site is:

DietFoodForFun.com

It would be simple to tell someone to go to your Web site at "diet food for fun dot com." But if you have hyphens in the middle of the domain name, it wouldn't be quite as easy:

Diet-Food-For-Fun.com

In that case, you'd have to say, "diet hyphen food hyphen for hyphen fun dot com." Chances are your customers wouldn't remember to put the hyphens, so they probably wouldn't find your site.

Further, since both Internet Explorer and Netscape use technology that allows you to enter a domain name in the search box without listing the full URL, the Web site that you're taken to is always the one without hyphens.

For example, if you enter "robinsnest" in the browser window, you'll be taken to *www.robinsnest.com* and not *www.robins-nest.com*, though both are working sites.

> Whether or not to use hyphens (or underscores) between keywords in the domain name can often be determined by the use of the domain.

Whether or not to use hyphens (or underscores) between keywords in the domain name can often be determined by the use of the domain. If you'll be giving out the name of the domain and expecting people to find it, consider leaving out the hyphens. But if you're in a highly competitive business, you may want to use the hyphens to make sure that the engines recognize the keywords as a complete phrase.

Because domains are inexpensive, many companies purchase numerous domains and use them for various areas of their company. The other domains, also called "doorway domains," will link from the main domain and serve as "doorways" from that domain.

For example, let's say that you have a jewelry store that's named Pandora's Box. Your main domain could be PandorasBox.com. Then you could purchase additional domains for various areas of your company, such as Jewelry-Cleaning.com, Gold-Bracelets.com, Costume-Jewelry.com, and Infant-Jewelry.com. Those additional domains are doorway domains, and you'll link to those domains from your main domain, PandorasBox.com.

You'll notice in this example that we didn't use hyphens in the main domain because that's the domain name we'll be giving out to customers. But in order to gain a boost in relevancy with the engines, we did use hyphens in the doorway domains. After all, we probably won't be giving out those domain names.

If you use multiple domains, however, don't use a technique known as "pointing." With pointing, you route all business through one domain. If you do, you'll be able to get only the main domain indexed because the engines pass through the pointing domain and index only the main one. Further, if you use pointing, you'll lose the benefits of all those additional index pages.

> Additional domains are doorway domains, and you'll link to those domains from your main domain, *PandorasBox.com*.

Keywords in a <noframes> tag even though you're not using frames

Example:

<noframes>
<body>
<h2> Educational Children's Software offers Learning under the Guise of Fun! </h2>
<p>Can't get your child to play educational games on your computer? No problem! Our educational children's software is designed to be just plain fun, so that your kids don't even realize they're learning.</p>
<p>Purchase educational children's software in subjects such as foreign languages, math, and English.</p>
<a href="educational-childrens-software.htm"></a>
<a href="sitemap.htm"></a>
</body>
</noframes>

You can use the <noframes> tag on a nonframed page to place text, and some of the engines will "find" and index it. It will index the page, plus any content within the <noframes> tag. You can place links to other pages of your site, text, tags, etc.

You can place the tag anywhere on the page that you want. Text within this area does count toward your total keyword weight.

Keywords in a <style> tag
Example:
<style>educational children's software</style>

A few of the engines will index the content of <style> tags and consider the content for relevancy. AltaVista is one of those engines, as is Excite/WebCrawler.

How Many Keyword Phrases Should You Use per Web Page?

In most cases, you won't be able to optimize each page for more than one or two keywords. But with Excite, you can try optimizing pages for five to six keywords, and you might be successful.

Do You Need to Make Changes in All the Preceding Categories?

No! Remember what we said about the engines preferring simplicity. Don't try to optimize all of your pages with all these techniques for all the engines. Start with a few techniques and one engine at a time and build from there. Test the waters by making changes in a few areas, then see how those changes affect your ranking before making additional changes. Then you can easily see what works and what doesn't.

Again, take good notes about everything you do!

Do You Need to Include META Tags on All Pages of Your Site?

If a Web page is important, add META tags to it. And don't rely on the search engine spiders to find all of your important pages. Submit your important pages yourself. There are a few exceptions to this rule that you'll read about in the chapters on the individual engines.

Factors That Won't Affect Your Rankings

In Chapter 19, we'll discuss various techniques that could negatively affect your rankings, such as using frames, dynamically delivered pages, and javascript.

But let's briefly look at factors that won't affect your rankings.

No! Remember what we said about the engines preferring simplicity. Don't try to optimize all of your pages with all these techniques for all the engines.

The size or types of graphics you use won't present ranking problems. However, try to start your page with text instead of a graphic because the engines can't "see" the graphic itself but can read only the ALT tag with that graphic. Using graphics that spell out your keyword phrase won't do you any good because the engines can't read the graphics.

Your site's overall design or layout won't affect your rankings in the engines but may affect your success in the directories. More on this later. Remember that simplicity is the key to good design for the engines, so try to keep your pages simple. Your choice of colors doesn't matter to the engines, but don't ever "hide" keywords by using the same color font with the same color background. Further, be careful when using similar font colors to your background. Many of the engines are getting wise to that trick, which they consider to be spamming.

We'll discuss spamming and how to prevent problems with the engines in Chapter 17.

An Example of a Well-Optimized Page

As of the writing of this book, the page that follows ranked 4 out of 10,296,035 pages in the GO/InfoSeek engine.

Keyword phrase: home mortgages

www.wholesalemortgageinc.com

Credit: George Penev of TotalDesignz.com (*totaldesignz.com*)

> ## *Extra Hints and Tips*
>
> Include words that are related to your important keywords in your META tags. If your keyword phrase is "genre fiction," include related keywords such as "mystery fiction," "romance fiction," and "historical fiction."

Keyword Weight—"Heavier" Is Not Always Better

Keyword weight, also known as keyword density, refers to the total number of words on your page in relation to the total number of keywords on the page. A standard approach to achieving keyword density is to keep the overall word count on your page down, while increasing the number of times you used your keyword phrase. This is a smart approach for general optimization but can be problematic for some individual engines.

Tips for Keeping Your Word Count Down

Optimize your home page for a keyword phrase that describes your Web site as a whole. Don't provide detailed information about each of your products on your main page. Instead, use your home page as a kind of annotated table of contents; briefly mention your products there, then provide links to interior pages that describe those products in detail.

This will allow you to be more specific with your keywords for each individual product or service page and increase the "weight" of the keywords on those subpages. For example, if you sell flower arrangements, don't provide a lot of information about the different types of bouquets on your main page. Instead, provide a brief description of each with links to interior pages. Each interior page can be optimized for a particular keyword phrase, like "red roses" or "spring flowers."

Keyword Weight Stumbling Blocks

The engines have put a couple of stumbling blocks in our path when it comes to keeping the word count down to a minimum. For example, GO/InfoSeek generally won't index a page that doesn't have at least seventy-five words in the body text, and Lycos won't index a page that doesn't have at least one hundred words. This is their way of preventing people from creating dozens of doorway pages with little body text and dominating the rankings. We'll discuss doorway pages in Chapter 10.

AltaVista, GO/InfoSeek, and Lycos tend to like even longer pages—as long as nine hundred words. That doesn't mean that

> By analyzing the pages that are scoring high in relevancy on the various search engines, you collect the statistical data that makes it a simple job to duplicate the keyword density mix of the top-scoring Web pages.

shorter pages won't be indexed by these engines. It simply means that longer pages appear to do better in the rankings at this time.

How Do You Determine Your Keyword Weight?

To determine your keyword weight manually, you simply cut and paste the viewable text of your Web page into a word processor. Have the program count the total number of words. Then, run a find and replace, putting your keyword phrase in both areas. The program will search for your keyword phrase and replace it with the same keyword phrase, and it will tell you the number of times it replaced the phrase.

Then, take the number of times you used your keyword phrase and divide it by the total number of words on your page to determine your page's keyword weight. For example, if you used your keyword phrase 5 times, and if there are 100 words on the page, your keyword weight is 5 percent.

Software Programs Can Be a Big Help

A couple of software programs are available that can determine your keyword weight for you. Some will even tell you your keyword weight for specific areas, such as link text, body text, and ALT tags.

Keyword Density Analyzer is an excellent program that many professional search engine positioners couldn't do without: *www.grsoftware.net/grkda.html*

From the Experts

Roberto Grassi, president of GR Software, which produces Keyword Density Analyzer, had this to say about his program:

> The most powerful function of the program is the "compare" feature. GRKda allows you to easily compare your own Web page's keyword density with that of your competitor's pages. By analyzing the pages that are scoring high in relevancy on the various search engines, you collect the statistical data

---

Extra Hints and Tips

Another way to determine the keyword weight of a page is to visit:

keywordcount.com/keys/search

that makes it a simple job to duplicate the keyword density mix of the top-scoring Web pages.

What Should Your Keyword Weight Be?

As we've said, there isn't one "magical" keyword weight that works across the board. Instead, when optimizing a page for a particular engine, it's important to arrive at the keyword weight preferred by that engine.

As of this writing, these are the keyword weights that appear to be most effective with these major search engines:

Approximate Keyword Weight of Visible Text as Preferred by the Individual Engines

AltaVista	5 percent
Excite	3 to 8 percent
HotBot	2 percent
GO/InfoSeek	2 to 5 percent
Lycos	1 to 2 percent
Northern Light	Unknown
WebCrawler	3 to 5 percent
Yahoo!	Not applicable

An important thing to remember is that "less" is sometimes better than "more" in this business. So, if you can't get top rankings using a particular keyword weight, try decreasing the keyword use rather than increasing it.

> With every positioning technique, one of the best ways to determine what's working is to study top-ranking pages in each engine.

Study Top-Ranking Pages

With every positioning technique, one of the best ways to determine what's working is to study top-ranking pages in each engine. Look for trends so that you don't waste time imitating isolated instances where the Web site owner seems to be getting away with techniques that are probably a one-time fluke or an illegal technique that you don't want to replicate.

To periodically update this keyword weight technique, search for your keyword phrase in each of the major engines. Go to the top ten sites and determine their keyword weight. Adjust your keyword weight accordingly. Try going up just a little in your keyword weight to see if it helps you get better rankings. If it doesn't, or if your rankings go down, reduce your keyword weight a little and see if that helps.

Appropriate Keyword Weight for More Than One or Two Keywords

It's very difficult, if not impossible, to arrive at an appropriate keyword weight for more than one or two keyword phrases per page. This is why it's best to optimize each page for one or two keyword phrases only, then optimize other pages for your other keyword phrases.

If you want to optimize a page for two keyword phrases, it isn't necessary to arrive at the same keyword weight for both keyword phrases. For example, let's say you're creating a page for AltaVista, and you know that keyword weight should be around 5 percent. Make sure your primary keyword phrase for that page has a keyword weight of 5 percent, and then try to deliver about a 4 percent keyword weight for the secondary keyword phrase.

Extra Hints and Tips

Be sure to spread your individual keywords throughout your page besides using them together as a keyword phrase. This can sometimes boost your rankings, as well as give you a better chance at good rankings with the more competitive and general individual keywords that make up your keyword phrase.

For more information on this topic, visit our Web site at www.businesstown.com

The Importance of Captivating Titles and Descriptions

Overview of Section III

If your site's title and description aren't appealing, you'll lose out to other sites that are.

Section III explains how you can create title and description tags that will rake in traffic to your site.

You'll also learn tips on how to use keyword META tags.

Chapter 7

Creating Titles That Command Attention!

Your <title> tag is the most important tag on your page. Notice that we're talking about the<title> tag that appears in the <head></head> section of your Web page.

Why is it so important? When you go to a search engine and search for a particular keyword, you're given a set of results from your search. Almost all the engines use the contents of your title tag in those search results, and they use it exactly as you've written it.

Keep in mind that, while wanting to craft a title and description that will appeal to the search engines, you also want to appeal to the humans in your audience. Try to strike a balance: if you present a keyword-studded title and description designed to achieve top rankings in the engines that can also entice visitors to click to your site, you will get more traffic than a higher-ranking site that doesn't present an attractive title or description.

When discussing your title tag, remember that we're not talking about the title that you may have put on the top of your Web page. We're talking about the contents of your <title> tag. When you visit a site, the <title> tag is displayed across the top of the browser window before the tool bars.

You can also see it in any page's source code. Both the <title> and META description tags are in the <head></head> section of your Web page, along with your other META tags. However, the only way most visitors see the title tag is when it is displayed across the top of the browser window or when it is included in search results. The engines, though, see the title and consider it when determining relevancy.

> Your <title> tag is the most important tag on your page.

What Makes an Effective Title?

An effective title:

- Is appealing, captivating, compelling, or eye-catching
- Exhibits professionalism
- Uses your keyword phrase early
- Is simple and easy to read and understand
- Solves a problem
- Makes a reader curious to know more

Is your title appealing, captivating, compelling, and eye-catching?

Getting ranked number 1 for your most important keyword is a goal we all aspire to. However, if your title is dull and boring, you won't get the traffic this top ranking should deliver.

When searchers glance over the search results, they will click to the sites that have the most appealing titles and descriptions. So, start things right with a title tag that sells the merits of your site. Encourage the searcher to skip over sites that are ranked higher than yours to visit *you* because *you've* taken the time to create an effective title and description.

Let your title and description sell them on the honest benefits of your site—loud and clear! But make sure to avoid "snake oil salesman" marketing hype because no one believes it (not even the Web site's owner!).

A few years ago, InternetDay published a list of compelling words to use in an advertising campaign. The list is no longer available on their site, but here are some of those suggestions, plus some suggestions of our own.

breakthrough	announcing	secrets	dazzling
incredible	overwhelming	imagine	acclaim
prosper	in depth	ingenious	succeed
success	impressive	admirable	powerful

Does your Web site exhibit professionalism?

Before a customer will purchase any of your goods or services, you must make him or her feel comfortable in doing so. In other words, your Web site must be professional and exhibit trustworthiness. Your consistent message to your potential customers must be that they can trust you and your online business.

Let's face it. When customers visit your site, they may know nothing about you or your business. They're simply looking for the products that you sell. If they don't feel comfortable ordering from you, they'll find a different site that gives them that feeling.

Extra Hints and Tips

InternetDay is an excellent source of information about online marketing and promotion. Visit this URL to subscribe to their free newsletter.

internetday.com

This also applies to titles and descriptions. If your title isn't professional, the viewer may not even visit. And, of course, in order to make a sale, the viewer must visit!

Simply listing keyword after keyword isn't very professional. Coming across as a snake oil salesman isn't professional. Making promises that you can't keep isn't professional.

Have you used your keyword phrase early in your title tag?

As we discussed in chapter 5, prominence, or how early you use your keyword phrase, is very important. The more prominent you make your keyword phrase, the better chance you have at a higher relevancy or ranking.

Try to begin your <title> tag with your keyword phrase, which isn't always easy to do while also achieving a compelling and professional title.

A way around this problem is to begin with your keyword phrase followed by a couple of dashes, and then the rest of your title. For example:

Virus protection—Protect your hard drive from malicious computer viruses.

Exceptions to beginning with your keyword phrase

An exception to using your keyword first in your title or description tags can be seen with Excite, AltaVista, and Lycos. At the time of this writing, those engines placed more relevancy on keywords found in particular spots other than the first word. For Excite, try putting your keyword phrase as the third word in the title. With AltaVista, put your keyword phrase as the second or third words. Put your keywords toward the beginning of the title tag for Lycos pages, but avoid having them as the first words.

Study what top-ranking sites are doing right now to get those excellent ratings. Search for your keyword phrase and see who's on top. Where are they using their keyword phrase? Is the phrase first in the title tag? Third? Adjust your title accordingly. And don't be afraid to try new things with one major exception: **don't spam**, which we'll discuss in Chapter 17.

For More Info

Be sure to keep up with the changes by visiting Search Engine Watch and subscribing to their free newsletter or their subscription service.

www.searchenginewatch.com

Is your title tag simple and easy to read and understand?

Don't use all capital letters in your title tag. On the Internet, this is considered "shouting," and it's very annoying. Capitalizing all of the letters won't help improve your relevancy by any means.

Also, it's more difficult to read words that are in all capital letters. Most people don't want to read them!

Here's an example:

HOME PAGES SEEM TO CARRY SLIGHTLY MORE WEIGHT WITH MOST OF THE MAJOR ENGINES.

Is that easy to read? No. Do you want to read it? No!

Now, read this example:

Home pages seem to carry slightly more weight with most of the major engines.

Much better, and it's not at all annoying. (Plus, it's true!)

Did you know that most people don't read text? Instead, they simply *recognize* words. And they recognize words by looking at the tops of the words.

We want our titles to be easy to read and understand. So, start your sentences with one capital letter and follow with all lowercase letters. The words in your title or description will be easier to recognize and will get read first.

Here's an example:

Video game tips—Discover the latest tips and tricks for mastering those tricky video games!

That's very easy to read and understand. Is this example?

Video Game Tips— Discover the Latest Tips and Tricks for Mastering Those Tricky Video Games!

It's not as easy to read, is it? We can read the first example much faster, which is what we want. Keep in mind that Internet viewers are like the rest of the world—very busy. Give us the information we want in the easiest possible way and we'll reward you by visiting your site!

Don't make the mistake of using a listing of your keywords as your title. Again, a listing of keywords isn't as easy to read and certainly isn't as professional. For example:

fresh garden vegetables, hand-grown vegetables, hand-picked vegetables

Extra Hints and Tips

Remember that most people search using all lowercase letters. If you use all capital letters in your all-important title tag, you'll lose out with the engines that are case sensitive.

Instead, make your <title> easy to read as well as a selling point to lure viewers to your Web site, such as:

Fresh garden vegetables, hand-grown and hand-picked right from the garden and delivered straight to your door!

Does Your Title Solve a Problem, Whether from a Monetary, Time, or Other Standpoint?

If you can prove to the viewers that you can solve a problem for them, they'll certainly want to visit your site.

Here's an example:

High-risk automobile insurance at no-risk prices will get you back on the road!

If you've had several car wrecks and have been unable to get car insurance, wouldn't that title and description appeal to you? The prices are competitive, and you should be able to drive your car again soon.

Obviously, if your prices aren't competitive for whatever reason, you don't want to mention price in your title or description. Instead, you'll want to capitalize on your superior service, customer support, or return policy.

> Give the viewers a captivating glimpse of your products or services and make them want to rush to the site to learn more.

Does Your Title Make the Viewers Curious to Learn More About Your Company, Products, or Services?

Give the viewers a captivating glimpse of your products or services and make them want to rush to the site to learn more.

In our "high-risk automobile insurance" example, wouldn't it make you curious to learn more?

However, what about this example:

High-risk automobile insurance will help you.

How boring, and it certainly doesn't make you very curious, does it?

Create dynamite title tags to "sell" your company to your potential customers. Give them enough information to entice them to visit and look around. By doing so, you'll knock out your competition that may be above you in the rankings.

How Many Times Should You Use Your Keyword Phrase in Your <title> Tag?

Most of the time, you'll want to use your keyword phrase in your title tag only once. With some of the engines, you can try using it twice. But if you need a boost in the rankings, drop back to using it once and see if that helps.

Do's and Don'ts for Writing Effective Titles

Do's

- Create longer titles when possible. A longer title is generally more effective because you have more words to persuade the reader to visit your site.

  An exception to this rule is with AltaVista, where top-ranking pages commonly have very short <title> tags—sometimes just the keyword phrase itself.

  In any event, always keep your most important keyword or phrase near the beginning of all of your tags.

  Some top-ranking pages seem to put a string of keywords at the end of the title. The title tags are long, with those keywords at the end. This is something you might want to try. However, be sure to check each engine's limits on the length of titles in the following chart.

  Note: The title limits include spaces between words.

Extra Hints and Tips

Remember that "more" isn't always better in the search engine business.

Title Guidelines

AltaVista	78 characters
Excite	70 characters
HotBot	115 characters
GO/InfoSeek	70–75 characters
Lycos	60 characters
Northern Light	80 characters
WebCrawler	60 characters
Yahoo!	5 words or 40 characters

- Start your sentence with a capital letter and follow with all lowercase letters.
- Place your most important keyword phrase near the beginning of the tag.
- Place your <title> tag as the first tag on your page.

Take time to view your source code on the Web. Click on View, then Page Source. If your <title> tag isn't listed first, you need to move it first, followed by the description and keyword META tags.

If you use FrontPage or any of the WYSIWYG HTML editors, check this carefully because those editors generally list unimportant META tags first (such as the generator tag), followed by the description and keyword tags, and finally the title tag.

Other editors will place a comment tag above the <head> section (like HotMetal Pro).

The comment tag probably doesn't hurt your rankings, but try removing it anyway. You want the engine to see your <title> tag first in the most prominent position on your page.

When you remove the tag, your HTML editor may automatically put it back in every time you open the page. So, try to get in the habit of viewing the source code right before you close the HTML editor to remove the tag.

- Try using multiple title tags with AltaVista, Lycos, and HotBot.
- Get the opinion of others. When analyzing your page's title and description, ask others for their opinion.

Extra Hints and Tips

WYSIWYG stands for "what you see is what you get." WYSIWYG HTML editors allow you to create a Web page as if you're working in a word processing program, without viewing any of the tags. The program handles the tags behind the scene.

Don'ts

- Don't use just the name of your business in the <title> tag. Here's an example:

    <title><Robertson's Software Warehouse></title>

    Think of it this way. How many people are going to be searching for your actual business? Does the name of your company provide instant name recognition? Are you a company like Sony or Microsoft?

    If not, you'll be much better off creating a title tag that uses keyword phrases that your customers will use when searching for your site, like this:

    <title><Educational software programs at rock bottom prices!></title>

    In other words, if you want your site to be found, you must use your most important keyword phrase in the <title> tag. By using keyword phrases rather than the name of your business, you'll get more traffic unless the name of your business provides instant name recognition.

    Most businesses feel that it's also important to create a page that is optimized for the name of their business, which is an excellent idea. So they create a "doorway page" (which we will discuss in Chapter 10) and use their company name as the keyword phrase.

    Another alternative is to use both your keyword phrase and your company name, like this:

    <title><Bulldog puppies—Best of the breed at Riverside Bulldog Kennels></title>

- Don't begin your title with symbols such as !! or even @. Using symbols in the title to try to capitalize on the way that computers alphabetize really doesn't help because very few of the engines alphabetize in order to determine rankings.

    The search facilities that do alphabetize, like Yahoo!, will more than likely remove the symbol before indexing your page unless the symbol is part of the official name of your company or Web site, like $$Lenders USA. Using symbols

> Don't use just the name of your business in the <title> tag.

inappropriately could cause a delay in getting your site indexed, or even get it rejected totally.

- Don't use dull and boring titles. Your title and description may be the only things that determine whether a viewer will visit your site, so they must be compelling!

    Consider using questions in your title or description tags. Questions can be very powerful because they make us stop and think (probably because we're subconsciously trying to answer the question).

Here is an example:

Has income tax season gotten you down? (title)

Visit the income tax specialists at TaxesRUs, and let us take the dirty work out of preparing your tax forms. (description)

- Don't repeat your keyword phrase in your <title> tag. Don't overdo your use of keywords and get labeled a spammer.
- Don't put your <title> tag in all capital letters.
- Don't use just a listing of keywords in your title tag.
- Don't use "yellow page" tactics when creating your title. In other words, don't stick A's in front of your title tag in order to get ranked higher, like this:

<title>AAA Software Warehouse</title>

    Remember that most search results aren't alphabetized. However, if the actual name of your company or Web site is "AAA Software Warehouse," it's fine to use it, of course. An alphabetically superior title can help you in directories like Yahoo! or the ODP that capitalizes Web sites under the category listings. We'll learn more about these two directories in our Meet the Search Engines section.

Let's Look at Some Examples of Effective Titles and Descriptions

If you were presented with these two Web sites in the search results, which one would you visit first?

> Consider using questions in your title or description tags.

Web site Promotion, the Web site promotion specialists (title)

Web site promotion, graphics, design, graphics design, Web site promoter, Web page designer, design experts, Web site promotion specialists (description)

Web site promotion by Web optimization experts (title)

Web site promotion designed to boost traffic to your Web site within record time. What will you do when your traffic doubles or triples due to our Web site promotion tactics? (description)

Let's Analyze the Examples

Both would score high in a search engine's rankings based on the keyword phrase, "Web site promotion." But the second choice has, by far, the most effective title and description.

Further, notice that the first example is rather difficult to read since it just lists keyword after keyword as the description.

In the second example, "Web site promotion" is listed as the first word of the title, the first word of the description, and repeats the phrase one more time. This description is captivating, solves a problem (fast Web site promotion), and asks a question that will cause any Web site owner to stop and think.

The actual name of the business was not used as the title. However, the business could write a doorway page and optimize it for the name of the business, which is always an excellent idea.

Notice also that a synonym of our important keyword phrase could have been used, such as Web site optimization. Instead of using the keyword phrase twice in the description, we could have substituted it with the synonym with the hope of getting the page optimized for both.

Though the first example lists "Web site promotion" twice in the title, twice in the description, and once as a variation of the keyword phrase, it's not very businesslike or appealing, and it's more difficult to read. It's also pushing the limits of the engines by using the keyword phrase that many times in those two tags.

Additional examples of effective titles and descriptions can be found in Chapter 8.

> Remember that most search results aren't alphabetized. However, if the actual name of your company or Web site is "AAA Software Warehouse," it's fine to use it.

Writing Description Tags That Rake in Traffic

Your META description tag is the second most important tag on your page. Why?

Just like the <title> tag, the META description tag is presented in the search results for most of the engines. If you present a captivating description, designed to achieve top rankings in the engines while enticing visitors to click to your site, you can actually get more traffic than a higher ranking site that isn't using an effective META description tag.

Like the <title> tag, the META description tag is found in the <head></head> section of your Web page. In fact, all META tags are found in the <head> section of your page.

Unlike the <title> tag, however, not all search engines use the META description tag. Instead, to describe your site within their rankings, some of the search engines use the first lines in your body text, so keep that in mind when developing your pages.

To see if an engine uses the META description tag or the first few lines in your body text, search for your site manually and view the description in the search results. Or use this chart as a guide.

AltaVista	Uses META description tag
Excite*	Uses META description tag
HotBot	Uses META description tag
GO/InfoSeek	Uses META description tag
Lycos	Doesn't use META description
Northern Light	Doesn't use META description
WebCrawler*	Uses META description tag
Yahoo!	Doesn't use META description

*Excite and WebCrawler use the content of META description tags in the search results, but the content of those tags doesn't count toward relevancy and won't help your rankings.

What Does a META Description Tag Look Like?

The following is an example:

"<META NAME="description" CONTENT="Virus protection programs will protect your valuable hard drive from malicious computer viruses.">

> Your META description tag is the second most important tag on your page.

Again, like all META tags, the META description tag goes in the <head></head> section of your Web page.

An Effective META Description Tag Can Contribute Greatly to the Success of Your Site

The description tag can create success for a site, or it can keep people from visiting it. Quite simply, an effective description tag can compensate for a slightly lower ranking if the Web sites above yours have unimpressive tags. People will scan past an unappealing description to find something that's a better fit for their needs.

Writing a strong description tag takes the same kind of marketing thinking as does creating the concept for a top-notch advertising campaign. After identifying your target audience, what can you tell that audience that will attract them to your site? Choose each word carefully, and be sure to use compelling words like those we discussed in the previous chapter on titles.

> The description tag can create success for a site, or it can keep people from visiting it.

Keep in Mind the Components of an Effective Advertising Campaign

Ad campaigns should:

- Solve a problem
- Solve it at a reasonable cost
- Make the reader curious to learn more
- Observe the KISS (keep it simple stupid) rule

Apply those components to creating your description META tags, and traffic to your site will increase dramatically.

The same principles for effective titles apply to creating winning META description tags. So, review those principles in detail from Chapter 7. We'll briefly mention them here.

- Watch your word count and don't go over the limit. Each engine has a limit for the description of your site in the results.
  Note: The limits shown here include spaces.

AltaVista	150 characters
Excite	395 characters
HotBot	249 characters
GO/InfoSeek	170–240 characters
Lycos	135–200 characters
Northern Light	150–200 characters
WebCrawler	395 characters
Yahoo!	25 words or 200 characters

If your description is longer than the engine's limit, your description will be cut off in midsentence or midword, which isn't very impressive.

- Create a captivating META description tag using compelling words that are professional yet easy to read and that make the reader curious to learn more.
- Use your important keyword phrase early in your description tag.
- Use your keyword phrase no more than three times in your description META tag. In many cases, once is best, or twice at the most.
- Start the sentences with one capital letter and follow with all lowercase letters. Don't use all caps.
- Don't use just a listing of your keyword phrases.

Let's Look at More Examples of Effective Titles and Descriptions

Here are two examples that emphasize the importance of attractive titles and descriptions. Decide for yourself which would be more attractive to you if you were in the market for a Web site.

Extra Hints and Tips

An exception to beginning your description with your keyword phrase is if you're working with a very competitive keyword phrase. Sometimes inserting your keyword phrase toward the middle of your description tag helps your rankings.

Web Experts (title)

Web-experts.com innovative design content development internet marketing solutions hosting services shopping carts maintenance clients (description)

Custom Web site design tailored to your specific needs (title)

WebDesign 2 is your complete solution for development of your Web site, from custom Web site design to Web site marketing, hosting, maintenance, and programming. Let us work for you! (description)

Which of those Web sites would you visit?

The first example's description is just a listing of keywords. This approach is not an easy read, nor is it an appealing one.

The second example, on the other hand, is quite readable. It solves a problem, does it quickly, and shows several advantages. Note that the keyword phrase "Web site design" is the second, third, and fourth words in the title instead of the first, which is AltaVista's preference at this time. If this example needed a boost in the rankings of the other engines, the important keyword phrase could be moved closer to the beginning of the META description tag. Note also that several other important, related keywords that a person may be searching for in this context are also included in the description: development, hosting, maintenance, programming, and marketing. This inclusive approach can broaden your reach in the algorithms of some engines.

> The same principles for effective titles apply to creating winning META description tags.

More Examples

Here are more examples taken from an AltaVista search in November 1999 for the term "effective advertising campaign." Look at the titles and descriptions. Did these Web sites create effective advertising campaigns with their titles and descriptions? Do they appeal to you and make you want to visit the sites? In most cases, no!

Tri-County Network Services Page (title)

Services. Commerce On the Internet. Your Business On the World Wide Web. What a Web Presence Can Do For Your Company. What Can We Do For Your... (description)

TVP Promotions (title)
ADVERTISING ADVISORY PROGRAM CLIENT ADVISORY BOARD COMPETITIVE ANALYSIS PROGRAM (CAP) INTERNET REVIEW SERVICE (IRS) Advertising Advisory Program. On... (description)

Untitled Document (title)
Welcome to a magazine now in its fourth year and as such has well and truly established itself on the ...... (description)

Not very impressive are they?

The first example has a misspelled word, and it's very difficult to read with almost every word capitalized. Would you visit the site? Is their description very professional?

Also notice how difficult it is to read the words that are written in all caps in the second example. It stops many people cold, and they have to force themselves to read it.

In the third example, the submitting site didn't even use a <title> tag which is why "Untitled Document" appears in the search results.

In every one of these examples, the description tags were too long so they were cut off in midsentence.

In Conclusion

Spend as much time creating captivating <title> and META description tags as you did when choosing your important keyword phrases. The time you spend will be well worth it when your traffic increases and your online sales jump!

> Spend as much time creating captivating <title> and META description tags as you did when choosing your important keyword phrases.

For more information on this topic, visit our Web site at www.businesstown.com

Chapter 9

Tips for Keyword
META Tags

The META keyword tag doesn't have nearly the importance of the META description tag because it's not shown in the search results and because many of the engines give it a low priority when determining relevancy. In fact, not all the engines index the content of META tags or consider the content when determining relevancy.

To complicate matters, many of the top-ranking sites in the engines that do consider the content when determining relevancy don't even use the META keyword tag. With GO and AltaVista in particular, you'll want to check competing Web pages to see if they're using the tag because many top-ranking sites in both of those engines don't use the META keyword tag.

However, for those engines that consider the content, it's a good idea to use the tag. After all, all META tags are in the <head> section, which places them in a prominent position on your page. You can enter your keywords in the tag, which will place them directly in front of the engines as they index your site.

Like all search engine positioning tactics, use the META keyword tag as part of your overall strategy. But if you're having ranking problems, consider removing it and see if that makes a difference.

Let's take a look at a list of the major engines to learn which of them consider the content of the META keyword tag.

> After all, all META tags are in the <head> section, which places them in a prominent position on your page.

AltaVista	Yes
Excite	No
HotBot	Yes
GO/InfoSeek	Yes
Lycos	No
Northern Light	No
WebCrawler	No

Of course, none of the directories consider the content of META tags.

What Does a META Keyword Tag Look Like?

Here's an example:

    <meta name="keywords" content="bulldogs, Bulldogs, English bulldogs, health problems dogs, caesarean section dogs, bulldog puppies, artificial insemination dogs, BULLDOGS">

How Long Should a META Keyword Tag Be?

The length of the keyword META is defined by many of the engines differently.

As a general rule, though, limit the number of characters and spaces in a keyword tag to one thousand. You'll also want to limit the particular words you use in the keyword META to only your main keyword phrase, different variations of that phrase, and synonyms. What you don't want to do is add so many keywords that you dilute the effectiveness of your main keyword phrase.

Remember that in order to achieve top rankings for a keyword phrase, you'll need to use that phrase throughout the body of your page and in the tags. Simply sticking a keyword phrase in the keyword META tag and no where else generally won't give you a top ranking for that keyword phrase because the keyword weight is virtually nonexistent. You've got to use the keyword throughout the page in order for the engine to give it a high relevancy ranking.

Remember that it's always an excellent idea to see what your competition is doing. Are competing Web sites using keyword META tags? How many keywords are in the tags?

Although it's generally a good idea to limit the number of keywords you use in the keyword META tag, you'll also find top-ranking sites that don't adhere to this rule and list keyword after keyword. So test the waters here and see what works for you with your particular keyword phrase.

With highly competitive keywords, you'll want to fine-tune the page to where you're pointing everything toward that one keyword phrase. This is one case where you'll want to limit the number of keywords in the tag to just the keyword phrase itself and variations and synonyms of the phrase.

> Remember that in order to achieve top rankings for a keyword phrase, you'll need to use that phrase throughout the body of your page and in the tags.

Do You Need to Use Commas to Separate Your Keywords or Phrases in the Tag?

If you are doing a general optimization of a page to be submitted to all the engines, it is a good idea to use commas because GO specifies that you do so. With most of the other engines, it doesn't matter.

Many search engine optimizers don't want to waste the space in the tag with commas, so they don't use them.

And there are some advantages to not using commas. When you use commas, you're telling the engine that the phrase itself is what's important to you. But you're also preventing the engine from putting together other word combinations and determining other phrases on its own.

For example, let's say that this is your META keyword tag:

<meta name="keywords" content="discount coupons, shopping bargains, saving, free, consumer, deals, professional, services, discounts">

Let's take out the commas and see what phrases the engine could find:

<meta name="keywords" content="discount coupons shopping bargains saving free consumer deals professional services discounts">

The engine could find these phrases, among others:

discount coupons
coupons shopping
shopping bargains
bargains saving
free consumer deals
professional services
services discounts

Does this mean that you'll get top rankings with those keyword phrases? Nope. This is simply a strategy that you can try to see how it works for you with your particular keyword phrase.

Another reason not to use commas is to avoid using the same keyword over and over again, which can be interpreted as keyword

> If you are doing a general optimization of a page to be submitted to all the engines, it is a good idea to use commas because GO specifies that you do so.

stuffing. This is because the engine may link one keyword to the same keyword before and after it.

Here's an example:

<meta name="keywords" content="writers resources, resources for writers, writing links, writers workshops, workshops genre fiction">

By removing the commas, we can eliminate some of the duplications found:

<meta name="keywords" content="writers resources writing links writers workshops genre fiction">

This prevents the engine from seeing all those instances of "writers" and considering this to be a spamming attempt.

Do You Need to Space After the Commas?

Again, many search engine positioners choose not to space after the commas because they don't want to waste the space in the tag. But it's a personal preference, and the engines don't care one way or the other.

Try This Tactic!

Try putting a <BR> in the middle of your META keyword tag. This strategy may cause the engine to pause, thus giving your keyword phrase more prominence.

Here's an example:

<meta name="keywords" content="
writers resources, writing links, writers workshops">

Be sure to check our chapters on the individual engines for specific keyword META tag recommendations.

> Try putting a <BR> in the middle of your META keyword tag.

Warnings!

Don't ever use keywords in your keyword META tag that don't apply to the content of your page or Web site. This is considered a spamming technique and can get you in trouble with the engines.

And don't use the names of your competitors or their product lines in an effort to direct some of their traffic to your site. Lawsuits are springing up faster than the weeds in a garden, and many companies hire people to search for their name and product lines to make sure this isn't being done.

If you're comparing your product to a competitor's product, you may be able to get away with it. Of course, this doesn't mean that you won't get sued. It just gives you a more legitimate reason for using a competitor's product's name in your META keyword tag.

How Many Times Can You Use Your Keyword Phrase?

As a guideline, don't use your keyword phrase more than three times in the keyword META tag. Preferably, use it once, with variations of the phrase and synonyms. If you need a ranking boost, use it twice.

Remember that many of the engines aren't case sensitive, which means they'll see all variations as the same, so don't overdo it!

Need More Info?

What Can <META> Do for You at Web Monkey:

www.hotwired.com/webmonkey/html/96/51/index2a.html

How to Use HTML META Tags at Search Engine Watch:

www.searchenginewatch.com/meta.htm

For more information on this topic, visit our Web site at www.businesstown.com

Doorway Pages: Important Additional Ways to "Get Found" on the Web

Overview of Section IV

What are doorway pages, and how can you use them to boost traffic to your site? Section IV dives into doorway pages and explains in detail how to create them and put them to work to their maximum potential.

Chapter 10

What Are Doorway Pages?

Y ou've probably heard a lot of talk about doorway pages. Or maybe you've heard of "bridge," "splash," "gateway," or "entry" pages. Those are all other names for doorway pages. In fact, we prefer calling them "information" pages.

But what exactly *are* doorway pages?

Doorway pages are simply other "doorways" into your site.

Let's say that you've created your Web site, and you have a main page and ten other pages. You've optimized those pages for various keyword phrases that are important to your business.

But what about other keyword phrases that are important as well? You learned that you can't effectively optimize one page for more than one or two keyword phrases because it's virtually impossible to arrive at the appropriate keyword weight for each phrase. Further, in all likelihood, you won't be able to achieve top rankings with all the important engines because any one page rarely achieves top rankings for more than a few engines.

So, how can you get top rankings with other keyword phrases for other engines?

By creating *doorway pages*.

> Doorway pages are simply other "doorways" into your site.

How Are Doorway Pages Used?

Doorway pages have many important functions. They can be used to:

- Add additional pages to your site for your other important keyword phrases
- Create engine-specific pages
- Keep from having to rewrite the content of important index and interior pages
- Bring in traffic for important keyword phrases when your client won't let you touch the main page
- Bring in traffic to Web sites that use techniques that can cause ranking problems, such as frames and java

The Story Behind Doorways

The doorway page technique is highly popular, not only for its effectiveness, but because it allows busy webmasters the chance to optimize a page for an important keyword without having to work within the design constraints of an existing Web page. Sometimes, it is simply easier to build a set of doorways than it is to redesign what you've already got.

Professional Web positioners are often given a Web site and told to bring in the traffic for certain keyword phrases, but they can't make any changes to the main pages. Many companies have worked hard to create their main pages, and they want them left just as they are. However, it's impossible to optimize a page without changing the tags and generally the body text.

The Web positioners' solution is to create doorway pages that will bring in traffic, then route the traffic through the main pages.

> Sometimes, it is simply easier to build a set of doorways than it is to redesign what you've already got.

Are Doorway Pages a Viable, Professional Option?

Like many other effective search engine positioning techniques, doorway pages have been abused. Spammers have used them to create hundreds of entry pages to their sites, and the engines have retaliated by implementing tactics to stop the spammers.

The result is that doorway pages have gotten a bad name, in a sense, and many positioners are almost afraid to use them for fear of getting on the wrong side of the engines.

However, if you follow the guidelines as outlined in this book, you won't get in trouble with the engines for using doorway pages, and you'll achieve success with them. Keep in mind, however, if you abuse or overuse doorways, you run the risk of getting in trouble and possibly even banned from the engines.

Let's take it a step further. Let's call our doorway pages information pages because that's a better description of them. Creating content-rich information pages leading into your site will boost your traffic and greatly benefit your site, and you're doing nothing that could possibly get you in trouble with the search engines.

Warnings When Using Doorway Pages

Keep these warnings in mind, and you'll stay out of trouble with the search engines.

Keep in mind that if you follow this book's doorway page guidelines, your doorway pages will be content-rich information pages that will look like any other pages of your site. And you won't be using any spamming techniques whatsoever.

- Link doorway pages to different pages of your site. Make sure that your doorway pages link to different pages, information, or products. Don't point all of your doorway pages back to your main page.
- Don't create more than a couple of pages for each keyword. None of the engines like to see a Web site dominate the rankings. Have you ever run a search and found the same Web site in seven or eight of the top-ten rankings? That's considered dominating the rankings.

  Rather than creating more than a page or two for each keyword phrase, create pages that are optimized for other keyword phrases, and bring more traffic into your site through those additional doorways.
- Be sure to vary the content of each doorway page. Don't create fifty doorway pages with the same content with only the keywords swapped out. It just won't work. You may get away with it for a while, but chances are the pages will drop from the rankings.

  Most search engines consider the act of creating dozens of nearly identical pages spamming, and your pages could be permanently removed from the engine altogether.
- Don't create copies of your index page! In the past, it was a common practice to create numerous copies of your index page, make changes to the page to emphasize different keywords, and name the pages index1.htm, index2.htm, and so forth. In fact, software submission programs actually created those duplicate pages for you and submitted them to the engines.

  This practice is long out of date and can only get you in trouble. Remember that anyone seeing index5.htm knows that you have five other copies of your home page floating around out there.

- Like all pages of your site, don't use spamming techniques with doorway pages. Don't do anything that will bring unwanted attention to the pages. Don't stuff keywords in tags; don't use the same or similar color of font on a similar-colored background; don't use keywords in your tags that don't apply to your pages. Be honest and be professional.

What Happens if Your Doorway Pages Get Dropped from an Engine's Index?

Many times you've work very hard to get your doorway pages indexed, only to find that they've been dropped from the index or their rankings dropped. Does this mean that the engines have kicked them out of the index or that they don't like doorway pages?

Probably not.

Keep in mind that if you follow this book's doorway page guidelines, your doorway pages will be content-rich information pages that will look like any other pages of your site. And you won't be using any spamming techniques whatsoever. You're not doing anything that could possibly get you in trouble with the engines, so that's not a concern.

The bottom line is that the engines aren't perfect. They lose submissions. Sometimes those submissions reappear after a day or two, and other times they don't reappear until you resubmit them.

With AltaVista, results checked a few times just minutes apart will be different, with the pages having different rankings. Further, when certain engines index a page, it appears as though the page is put through an initial ranking algorithm and placed one way in the index, and later placed elsewhere by a second algorithm.

So, if your doorway pages disappear or drop in the rankings, simply resubmit them. This is another reason why it's so important to keep track of your rankings, that is, so that you can do something about it whenever they slip.

Need More Info?

Search Engine Watch has an excellent page about doorway pages. It's called, "What is a Bridge Page or Entry Page":

searchenginewatch.internet.com/ webmasters/bridge.html

The Importance of Site Maps

What *are* site maps?

A site map is simply a page that lists links to all pages of the site, similar to the index found at the back of this book. They're excellent for navigating a large site because you can glance through the alphabetical listing of pages and find what you're looking for quickly and efficiently.

Using Site Maps Can Help You Place Your Doorway Pages in Front of the Engines Without Individually Submitting Them

If you create 30 doorway pages for your Web site, you'll certainly want the engines to index those pages. But submitting all thirty pages won't guarantee that the pages will be indexed. For one thing, many of the engines are beginning to index only the main page of your site through submissions, then spidering that main page to find other links. Therefore, it's very important to provide links on your main page to other areas of your site so that the spiders can find them.

One very effective way to place your doorway pages in front of the engines is to create a "site map" of your doorway pages. A site map used in this manner is also referred to as a "hallway page" for your site. You may already be using a site map for your site, which is an excellent idea, especially now that many of the engines are not accepting any submissions other than the main page of a site. But the site map that we're referring to here is slightly different.

On the site map you're already using, you probably aren't including links to your doorway pages. After all, doorways are intended to be one-way streets; you only want to pull in traffic only through those doorways, not direct traffic from your site to those pages.

On your doorway page site map, however, you will list all the doorway pages that you've created for your site. Submit that list of links to the engines or add a hidden link to the page on your main page, and the engines will crawl, or spider, the links and pick them up in their indexes.

Need More Info?

For an example of an effective site map, visit eBay Auction. Look at the top of the page for the Site Map link:

www.ebay.com

This doorway page site map can be an "orphan" file, meaning that you won't link to it from any other page on your site. It is known in the industry as a *hallway* page. However, for engines that will accept only your main page through their submission process, you'll have to add a link to the page from your main page in order for the site map to be found. Your visitors will never see this doorway page site map unless they find it through the search engines. However, since it is not optimized for any particular keyword phrase, it will not pop up high enough in the rankings of the engines to be very "findable."

Do You Have to Optimize Your Site Map Page?

No, it's not necessary. You aren't interested in getting a top ranking for the page. You simply want to get it indexed so that the engines' spiders will visit the page and spider through it, thereby indexing the rest of your doorway pages without your having to submit them yourself.

Actually, you don't want a top ranking—because you don't want the page in competition with your other pages!

Is There Any Special Format to a Site Map Page Listing Your Doorway Pages?

No. You simply want to list your doorway pages. You could certainly include a descriptive title of each link containing your important keyword phrase as well as the URL, but there's no need to go into more detail than that. If you do, again, you may run the risk of the page competing with your doorway pages for some of your keyword phrases (as strange as that sounds).

So, keep it simple and to the point—just a no-nonsense list of links to your doorway pages with a little descriptive text.

However, keep in mind that depending on the eventual ranking of the site map page, you could get some traffic to the page. In this regard, be sure to make the page presentable so that you won't be embarrassed if you get visitors through that page.

You can title the page "Links" or whatever, and prominently display a link to your main page.

Need More Info?

For an example of a hallway page, visit:

www.whootnews.com/atlantic-city-links.html

Another Option

Instead of creating a doorway page site map, you can always include hidden links to all of your doorway pages on your main page. If you don't have many doorway pages, this may be a better option for you.

How Can You Create Hidden Links?

In Chapter 5, we discussed how to create hidden links, but here's a quick example:

"<A HREF="doorwaypage.htm"><IMG SRC="clr.gif" BORDER="0" ALT="insert your keyword phrase here"></A>

The height and width tags were left off to be on the safe side. In the future, engines may decide not to spider links from images that are known to be only one pixel in size. So, without those tags, the engine cannot easily determine the size of the graphic, and nothing about this strategy will send up a "red flag" to the engine.

Notice that in this example we've taken further advantage of the tag by adding another instance of the keyword phrase in the ALT tag.

Do You Have to Limit the Doorway Page Site Map Links to Just Doorway Pages?

No! You can certainly include links to your important interior pages on the site map page, as well as a link to your main page.

In fact, as we mentioned earlier, since many of the engines are allowing you to submit only the main page of your site, you have to figure out a way to make sure that your pages are found by the spiders. To do this, you can create a site map and link to that site map from your main page, or you can create hidden links to all important pages of your site on your main page. These links can be to interior pages of your site or to content-rich doorway pages.

Since you generally won't want to send customers to your doorway pages from your site map, you can always create hidden links to all doorway pages on your site map. The engines will see those links and spider them, but visitors to your site who are viewing the site map won't.

If your Web site spans several domains, why not put all of your doorway pages for all the domains optimized for that one particular engine on that one page? Submit it to the engine or add a link to it on your main page, making sure that it gets indexed, and those doorway or interior pages will get indexed when the spider visits.

You can even post the same doorway page site map to every one of your domains. This is another good way of boosting Web site popularity, which we cover in chapter 13.

Do You Need Separate Site Maps for Each Engine?

Yes, it's a good idea.

As you know, the engines don't like to see identical or almost identical pages. If you've created eight doorway pages for your important keyword phrase, you certainly don't want the engines to think you're trying to dominate the rankings.

So, create separate doorway page site maps for each engine, only including links to doorway pages optimized for that particular engine. Submit the site map page only to that one engine, and you'll solve the problem.

Of course, you can also create a robots.txt file to keep certain engines out of certain pages.

Using robots.txt Files Can Keep You out of Trouble

Let's say that you create seven different doorway pages, optimized for the same keyword phrase, but for seven different search engines. Will AltaVista find GO/InfoSeek's and Excite's pages, for example, and think that you're spamming their index by creating similar pages optimized for the same keyword phrase?

It's a possibility.

Keep in mind, however, that you won't be submitting GO/InfoSeek's and Excite's pages to AltaVista. But if you have links

In fact, as we mentioned earlier, since many of the engines are allowing you to submit only the main page of your site, you have to figure out a way to make sure that your pages are found by the spiders. To do this, you can create a site map and link to that site map from your main page, or you can create hidden links to all important pages of your site on your main page.

to those doorway pages from any of the pages that AltaVista spiders, it will find the links.

Your solution is to create a robots.txt file and place it on your server. With this file, you can keep certain engines out of certain pages and prevent any problems from happening.

In Chapter 22, we'll discuss in detail how to use robots.txt files.

> Create a robots.txt file and place it on your server. With this file, you can keep certain engines out of certain pages and prevent any problems from happening.

Slight Disadvantage to Using Site Maps to List Doorway Pages

Truthfully, the only real disadvantage to using site map pages and not submitting your URLs individually is that you'll experience a delay in getting your pages indexed. Why? Because you're depending on the engine's spider to find and index those pages on its own. The engines tend to place a somewhat higher priority on indexing pages that are submitted to them and will index those pages faster.

Therefore, it will probably take longer for your pages to get indexed if you've used site map pages than if you'd submitted the individual pages yourself.

But if you're working with a very competitive keyword phrase, this small disadvantage is well worth it. You want every edge you can get, and this is an important step in gaining that edge.

If your site map pages don't get indexed, resubmit them again. If worse comes to worse, you can submit the individual pages themselves to those engines that will accept submissions other than the main page of a site.

Doorway Pages at a Glance

Keep these important doorway page facts in mind.

Doorway pages should be:

- Fine-tuned pages that are optimized for one or two keyword phrases only. The content of the page is crafted solely to highlight and support your important keyword phrase(s).

- Content rich and full of information about your important keyword phrase. Think of them as information pages.
- Kept as simple as possible. They are primarily text pages, with the length of text dependent on the preferences of the individual engines.

Remember that the Engines Like Simplicity!

Don't use frames, java, image maps, or other techniques that make it difficult for the engines to index the content of your pages.

- Link *to* your home page or to an interior page of your site rather than linking *from* your main page. You don't have to and shouldn't link all of your doorway pages to your main or index page.
- Use the same techniques as every other page on your site, such as effective titles and descriptions, META tags, and keyword weight.

Build a page that looks as if it belongs with your site. You want visitors to know they're on your site. "Cardboard-looking" doorway pages are not appealing and therefore not as effective.

Doorway pages should be:
- Optimized for one or two keyword phrases only.
- Content rich and full of information
- Kept as simple as possible.

For more information on this topic, visit our Web site at www.businesstown.com

What's in a Doorway Page?

You know what a doorway page is, and you've learned some important reasons for using them. You've learned how to submit your doorway pages to the engines, and you've discovered ways to avoid getting in trouble with the engines for using doorways.

But how on earth do you create a doorway page? A doorway page takes advantage of some of the best optimization techniques contained within this book but applies them to only one search engine and generally one keyword phrase at a time.

What Must Be Included in a Successful Doorway Page?

With doorway pages, you'll employ all the basic META and other tags that have been discussed previously. Doorway pages need:

- Title tags
- Description META tags
- Keyword META tags
- ALT tags with images
- Headline tags
- Comment tags, and so on, for those engines that consider them for relevancy
- An appropriate keyword weight for that particular engine
- Keywords in link text

Remember to optimize each doorway page for generally one particular keyword phrase for one specific engine only. If your keyword phrase is "Spanish tutorial software," you'll write your title, keywords, description and other tags for *that* keyword phrase, using the keyword phrase in the beginning of every tag.

Be sure to check your source code, and if your HTML editor sticks in relevant tags, delete them immediately, or cut and paste them below your important META tags. Again, WYSIWYG editors sometimes place several different META tags before the <title> tag. Move that title tag to the top!

Extra Hints and Tips

Remember that no other tag should come before your <title> tag. As we've mentioned before, some HTML editors stick in tags before the important META tags. Here's an example of such a tag:

<!DOCTYPE HTML PUBLIC "-//W3C//DTD HTML 3.2//EN">

As with all other pages of your Web site, capitalize on the existence of graphics by adding an ALT tag with your keyword phrase in it. If you're optimizing your page for an engine that considers the content of comment tags, put in one of those, also.

Keep the text on your doorway page down to a minimum, and use your keyword phrase as many times as you can, watching your keyword weight carefully. Don't use huge graphics on your doorway page to where it takes too long to load. And *begin* your page with text, not an image.

Emphasize a single keyword phrase on the page, keeping the primary emphasis of the page on that one topic. Fine-tune!

Provide a link to another page on your site from your doorway page. This can be your main page, or it can be an interior page. Try not to point all of your doorway pages to your main page.

Take the concepts we've discussed in earlier chapters and in the chapters on the individual engines to create a highly fine-tuned doorway page for each engine.

> ### Extra Hints and Tips
>
> At this time, the only engines that use the contents of comment tags are HotBot and other Inktomi engines.

Can You Use Frames or Java on Doorway Pages?

Remember: KISS (Keep it simple stupid)! With doorways, Java and frames are the kiss of death!

If you use frames on your site, create doorway pages that don't use frames. Since using frames, tables, or java can cause ranking problems, keep your doorway pages simple, get them ranked high with the engines, and watch your Web site traffic soar!

Use Doorway Pages to Get Your Web Site Found Under Important Keyword Phrases!

Remember that if you want your Web site to be found under several keywords or keyword phrases in all the major engines, you'll have to create additional pages that are optimized for all those other important keywords and engines. Regretfully, a single Web page will not accomplish this because it cannot rank well for all of your chosen keywords in all the engines.

Doorway pages help you solve that problem. With doorway pages, you can create many pages, each optimized to rank well for a different keyword in a different engine. This means that if you targeted 3 keywords across 8 search engines, you could end up with 24 pages pointing to various pages of your site.

What Should Be Left out of a Doorway Page?

Since doorway pages need to be fine-tuned for one keyword phrase for one engine only, generalized pages don't work well as doorway pages. Creating a page that doesn't focus on any particular keyword phrase or any particular engine won't be successful.

By the same token, don't try to optimize a doorway page for several keyword phrases. Fine-tune!

All spamming techniques should be left out of doorway pages and from all other pages of your site! Don't take a chance at getting in trouble with the engines. It's not worth the consequences. We'll discuss spamming techniques in detail in Chapter 17.

If you use tables, make sure that you use your keyword phrase high up in the tables. Don't use any techniques that will push your important keyword-containing text farther down on the page. Check your source code carefully.

Specific Guidelines for Doorway Pages

Some of the engines have specific guidelines for doorway pages, so let's look at some of those guidelines here.

Extra Hints and Tips

Yahoo! and many of the directories don't allow you to submit more than one URL. So, doorway pages isn't a concept that will help you in Yahoo!.

AltaVista	No minimum word count limit	Prefers you to submit just one page and their spider will find the rest
Excite and WebCrawler	No minimum word count limit	Sometimes won't accept doorway page submissions, so use site maps of doorway pages with this engine
HotBot	No minimum word count limit	Can submit individual doorway pages to this engine
GO/InfoSeek	Won't index a page unless it has at least 75 words in the body text	Will accept only your main page, so use site maps of doorway pages with this engine
Lycos	Won't index a page unless it has at least 100 words in the body text	Can submit individual doorway pages to this engine
Northern Light	No minimum word count limit	No limit
Yahoo!	No minimum word count limit	Submit only your main page to this directory; don't submit any doorway pages

In the next chapter, we'll look at examples of effective doorway pages, and we'll analyze those examples to learn what other things we could have done to achieve additional boosts in ranking.

For more information on this topic, visit our Web site at www.businesstown.com

Chapter 12

Let's Analyze Effective Doorway Pages

We've learned what doorway pages are, and we've learned what's needed in an effective doorway page.

So let's analyze some successful doorway pages and see what we can learn.

Example 1: Excite
Orange county bail bonds
Optimized for Excite
Keyword phrase: "orange county bail"
Results as of the writing of this book: 1 out of 1,946,256
www.bindersbailbonds.com/orange-county-bail/as/index.htm

When you can get a page ranked number one out of almost two million results, you know you're doing something right! We can learn a lot by studying this page.

Example 1: Excite
Orange county bail bonds
Optimized for Excite
Keyword phrase: "orange county bail"
Results as of the writing of this book: 1 out of 1,946,256
www.bindersbailbonds.com/ orange-county-bail/as/index.htm

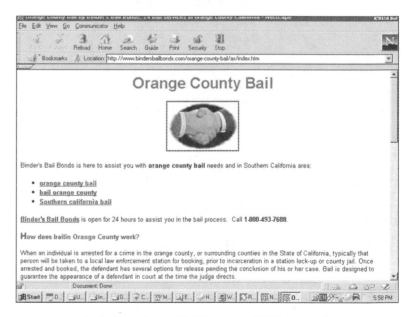

Credit: George Lenev of TotalDesignz.com (*totaldesignz.com*)

- **Very simple page**
  Notice how simple the page is. It doesn't contain frames, javascript, or tables. It's a simple text page with one graphic.
- **Starts out with text**
  The page begins with a headline tag, using the keyword phrase in that tag. Then, the graphic follows. The page begins with the keyword phrase.
- **Keyword phrase in bold in the first paragraph**
  You can sometimes get a boost in relevancy by putting your keyword phrase in bold.
- **Keyword phrase in all lowercase letters and capitalized**
  Remember how we learned that most searchers search in all lowercase letters? This search engine optimizer took that fact into consideration and used the keyword phrase in all lowercase letters throughout the page. But the optimizer also capitalized the phrase. Excite isn't case sensitive, though it's best to search for your keyword phrase in all variations to know for sure.
- **Individual words in keyword phrase used as well**
  Besides using the keyword phrase in its entirety, the search engine optimizer also used the individual words in that phrase throughout the page.

Now, let's look at the source code for the page:
(For the sake of brevity, we haven't included the entire source code here, but you can view it on the web.)

A successful doorway page:
- Very simple page
- Starts out with text
- Keyword phrase in bold in the first paragraph
- Keyword phrase in all lowercase letters and capitalized
- Individual words in keyword phrase used as well

```
<html>
<head>
<title>Orange county bail by Binder's Bail Bonds, 24 bail ser-
vices in orange county
California</title>
"<meta NAME="description" content="Orange county bail by
Binder's Bail Bonds. Fast reliable 24-hour confidential bail services
serving orange county and throughout southern california. Located
minutes away from orange county jail and courts.">
```

<!—webbot bot="HTMLMarkup" TAG="XBOT" startspan —><INPUT type="hidden" name="hidden" value="orange county bail"><!—webbot bot="HTMLMarkup" endspan —>
</head>

<body vlink="#808080" alink="#FFFF00" link="#000080">

<h1 align="center"><font face="Arial" color="#004080">Orange County Bail</font></h1>

<p align="center"><font face="Arial"><a href="http:www.binder-sbailbonds.com"><img src="../../images/Hands1.gif" ALT="orange county bail" WIDTH="150" HEIGHT="100"></a> </font></p>

<p><font face="Arial"><small>Binder's Bail Bonds is here to assist you with <strong>orange
county bail</strong> needs and in Southern California area: </small></font>

<ul>
 <li><a HREF="www.bindersbailbonds.com/index.html"><font face="Arial"><strong><small>orange
    county bail</small></strong></font></a></li>
    <li><a HREF="www.bindersbailbonds.com/index.html"><font face="Arial"><strong><small>bail
    orange county</small></strong></font></a></li>
    <li><a HREF="www.bindersbailbonds.com/index.html"><font face="Arial"><strong><small>Southern
     california bail</small></strong></font></a></li>
    </ul>

<p><font face="Arial"><small><strong><a HREF="../../AboutUs.htm">Binder's Bail Bonds</a></strong>
    is open for 24 hours to assist you in the bail process.
Call <strong>1-800-493-7688</strong>.</small></font></p>

> Excite doesn't consider the content of META tags when determining relevancy though it uses the META description in the search results.

```
<p><font color="#0000A0"
face="Arial"><strong><big>H</big><small>ow does bailin Orange
County work?</small></strong></font></p>
```

```
<p><font face="Arial"><small>When an individual is arrested
```
for a crime in the orange county, or surrounding counties in the
State of California, typically that person will be taken to a local law
enforcement station for booking, prior to incarceration in a station
lock-up or county jail. Once arrested and booked, the defendant has
several options for release pending the conclusion of his or her case.
Bail is designed to guarantee the appearance of a defendant in court
at the time the judge directs.</small></font></p>

Notice these things from the source code

- **<Title> tag comes first in the <head> section**
- **The <title> tag begins with the keyword phrase, and it is used only one time**
- **The META description tag begins with the keyword phrase, and it is used only one time**
  Excite doesn't consider the content of META tags when determining relevancy though it uses the META description in the search results.
- **No META keyword tag is used**
- **Page namcd after the keyword phrase**
  www.bindersbailbonds.com/orange–county–bail/as/index.htm
    Notice that the keyword phrase is used in the name of the page or URL itself.
    Also notice that the words in the keyword phrase are separated by dashes, which will help the engine recognize it as a keyword phrase.
- **"Index" used in the name of the page**
  The optimizer also used "index" in the name of the page possibly in an effort to make the engine think that this is the index page of the site and because it is the index page of a directory. It's best not to name doorway pages "index,"

> The words in the keyword phrase are separated by dashes, which will help the engine recognize it as a keyword phrase.

Note that hidden value tags are now perceived as spam by many of the engines, so this isn't a tactic you'd want to use.

though, because you could easily have quite a few "index" pages for the same domain, when there should be only one—the true main or index page of your site. A bunch of doorways named "index" may tip off the engine to the use of doorways.

- **Keyword phrase used in both ALT tags, though Excite doesn't index the content of ALT tags**
- **Keyword phrase used in a hidden value tag in the <head> section and at the bottom of the page**
  Note that hidden value tags are now perceived as spam by many of the engines, so this isn't a tactic you'd want to use. At the time this page was created, hidden value tags were accepted by the major engines. This is an excellent example of how fast things change in this industry, so you've got to be on your toes!
- **No irrelevant META tags used**
- **Related pages on the site itself**
  This entire Web site is devoted to bail bonds in the Southern California area. When the engine visits the pages at this site, it finds many related pages using the important keywords.
- **The keyword phrase is used at the very beginning of the page—in fact, the first words on the page—and it is used at the very end of the page as well as being sprinkled throughout the body of the page**
  The keyword phrase is naturally integrated into the body of the page. This tells the engine that the entire page is devoted to the keyword phrase, which may give it a boost in relevancy.
- **Links to other pages on the site**
  The optimizer put in several links to other pages on the site so that when the engine crawls this page, it will find those other pages.
- **The keyword phrase is listed first in all tags**
- **The page doesn't spam the engine in any way**
- **Longer page**
  With Excite, sometimes longer pages with more word count in the body of the page are successful, as in this case.

However, notice that the optimizer broke the page down into manageable chunks of text by using larger font text to describe the information that followed.

- **Doesn't look like a doorway page**
  The page doesn't look like a traditional doorway page. This comment has nothing to do with Web positioning per se, but you really don't want your doorway pages to be so obvious. In fact, it's a good idea if your doorway pages are designed like any other page of your site, with the overall look being similar. You want people to know that they're on your site.

- **Contact information given**
  Again, this isn't a Web positioning tactic per se, but it's crucial for potential customers to be able to contact you. The page lists a toll free number and an e-mail address, with a link to a "contact" page as well.

- **Page optimized for one keyword phrase only**
  Notice that the search engine optimizer didn't try to optimize the page for several keyword phrases. Instead, the optimizer concentrated on one keyword phrase—very successfully in fact.

  However, Excite is the only engine where you can sometimes optimize a single page for five or six keyword phrases and get top rankings.

Obviously, since this page is number one, there's no reason to make a single change to it. After all, don't ever fix what isn't broken!

But let's say that the page's rankings slip. What else could we do in the page to get those rankings back up?

- **Increase keyword weight**
  There are 614 words in the viewable portion of the page, and the keyword phrase in its entirety is used 6 times. This means that the keyword weight for the body text is 1 percent, which is very low. Excite tends to like a higher keyword weight of around 3 to 8 percent.

  However, though the keyword weight for the keyword phrase itself is low, the optimizer used individual keywords

> In fact, it's a good idea if your doorway pages are designed like any other page of your site, with the overall look being similar.

from that phrase throughout the page, and sometimes switched the order of the keywords as well. For example, the optimizer used:

bail orange county

So, the optimizer was smart to keep the overall keyword weight down, and it was certainly beneficial.

- **Put keywords in third position in the <title> tag**
Excite sometimes prefers to see the keyword phrase as the third words in the <title> tag rather than the first words.
- **Try two <title> tags**
- **Reduce length of the <title> tag to just the keyword phrase**
- **Use more headline tags**
Instead of increasing the font size, headline tags could have been used, with the keyword phrase in those tags. Headline tags are generally very effective in boosting relevancy.
- **Use keyword phrase in all caps somewhere**
Excite isn't case sensitive, but it's a good idea to search for the keyword phrase in all caps to see if you get different results when searching in all lowercase letters or capitalized words.
- **Decrease word count in body text**
Excite sometimes seems to like shorter pages.
- **Check your competition**
One of the best ways of gaining tips on what the engine prefers right now is to study top-ranking sites. What is their keyword weight? Where are they using the keyword phrase? How long is the body text? What techniques are they using that could be applied to your site?
- **Hidden links using the keyword phrase**
If you don't want to clutter up your page with more visible links, use hidden links. Name your pages after your keyword phrase. Be sure to add a hidden link to this page from your main page because Excite sometimes allows you to submit only the main page of your site. Therefore, you need to create those hidden links in order to place interior or doorway pages in front of the spider and get them indexed. Or create a doorway page site map as described in Chapter 10.

One of the best ways of gaining tips on what the engine prefers right now is to study top-ranking sites.

- **Use a <noframes> tag**
  This page doesn't use frames, but you can still add a
  <noframes> tag and create a mini-web site in the tag for the
  engine to index.
- **Use a style tag**
  Excite indexes the content of style tags, so the keyword
  phrase could be added to a style tag like this:
      <style>orange county bail</style>
- **Purchase a domain name with the keyword phrase in it**
  If low rankings are a real problem, purchasing a domain
  name with the keyword phrase in it might help. Excite
  assigns more relevancy to keyword phrases found in the
  domain name.
- **Name image files after keyword phrase**
  The first image on the page is named "Hands1.gif." To gain a
  boost in relevancy, the optimizer could have named the page
  "orange-county-bail.gif."
- **Boost link popularity**
  Excite places a lot of prominence on link popularity, so it's
  very important to make this a priority and work on boosting
  your popularity whenever you can.
- **Review latest tips for Excite**
  Visit Search Engine Watch and read Excite's latest tips. Visit
  about.com's Web Search site. If you've subscribed to Planet
  Ocean, be sure to read over their material carefully. Read
  everything you can in order to learn the latest tips for the
  engine. You'll find the URLs for these sites in the Helpful
  Links Section Appendices.

Need More Info?

Another top-ranking Excite page:
Dana Rader Golf School
Number 1 out of 3,719,877 results

www.welcomecenters.com/find/br/
golf_dana_rader_ex.htm

Example 2: AltaVista

Wisconsin Home Builders
Optimized for AltaVista
Keyword phrase: "wisconsin home builders"
Results as of the writing of this book: 3 out of 1,889,630
www.wickhomes.com/wisconsin.htm

Many of the same principles apply as in our other example. But since we're now dealing with AltaVista, there are some differences, too.

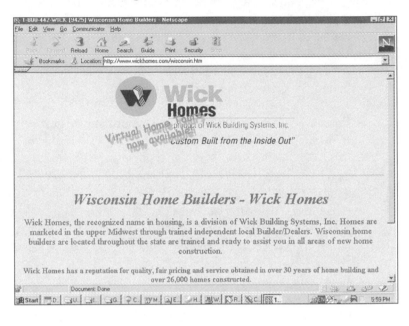

Credit: George Lenev of TotalDesignz.com (*totaldesignz.com*)

Here is the source code:

```
[COD]
<HTML>
<HEAD>
<TITLE>1-800-442-WICK (9425) Wisconsin Home Builders</TITLE>
<META name="description" content="Wick Homes, the Quality
Wisconsin Home Builder has a reputation for quality, fair pricing
and service obtained through 30 years of home building experience
and over 26,000 homes constructed.">
<META name="keywords" content="Wisconsin home
builders,Wisconsin new home construction,Wick Homes,Wisconsin
home construction,home,construction,Wisconsin,builder,Wisconsin
home builder">
```

```
<META name="author" content="Steve Huffman">
</HEAD>
<BODY background="graphics/SweetBackground.gif"
text="#800000" link="#408080">
<FORM>
<P>
<CENTER><!–SELECTION–><!–/SELECTION–><IMG src="graph-
ics/1x1.gif" width="1" height="1" align="BOTTOM" border="0" nat-
uralsizeflag="3" alt="Quality Wisconsin Home Builder"><IMG
src="logos/homes1.gif" width="400" height="158" align="BOTTOM"
border="0" naturalsizeflag="3" alt="Wisconsin home
builders"><BR><EM><STRONG><BR>
        <INPUT type="hidden" name="Profession" value="Home
            Builders">
        <INPUT type="hidden" name="State" value="Wisconsin">
        <INPUT type="hidden" name="Category"
value="Builder"></FONT></STRONG></EM><FONT face="Times
New Roman"><BR>
<HR></FONT></CENTER></P><H1>
<CENTER><EM><STRONG><FONT color="#800000" face="Times
New Roman">Wisconsin
Home Builders - Wick Homes</FONT></STRONG></EM></CEN-
TER></H1>
<P>
<CENTER><FONT size="+1">Wick Homes, the recognized name in
housing, is a division of Wick Building Systems, Inc. Homes are
marketed in the upper Midwest through trained independent local
Builder/Dealers. Wisconsin home builders are located throughout
the state are trained and ready to assist you in all areas of
new home construction.</FONT></CENTER></P>
<P>
<CENTER><B>Wick Homes has a reputation for quality, fair pricing
and service obtained in over 30 years of home building and over
26,000 homes constructed.</B></CENTER></P><H3>
<CENTER><A href="Wick-Homes.htm" onMouseOver="status=";
return true;"><IMG src="graphics/continue.GIF" width="100"
```

Many of the same principles apply as in our other example.

height="25" align="BOTTOM" border="0"
naturalsizeflag="3"></A></CENTER></H3>
<P>
<CENTER>
<HR>
<FONT color="#000000" size="-2">© 1998 Wick
Building Systems,
Inc., Wick Homes Division, 400 Walter Road, Mazomanie, Wisconsin
53560 USA</FONT>
<I><FONT size="-1"><A
href="response.htm">Click here to comment on our Web
site.</A></FONT></I></CENTER></P><!–NOEDIT–><!–
/NOEDIT–>
</FORM>
</BODY>
</HTML>

Let's study the page:

- **Very simple page**
  The page doesn't use frames, tables, or javascript.
- **Keyword phrase used as the first words in the keyword tags**
  Keywords used in title, META keyword, META description, and ALT tags.
- **Keyword phrase used only once in the <title> and META description tags**
- **Keyword weight of 2 percent**
  In the visible text of the page, there are 103 words, and the keyword phrase is used twice, for a keyword weight of 2 percent. With AltaVista, generally a keyword weight of around 5 percent works best.
- **Keyword phrase used in a headline tag**
- **Optimized for one keyword phrase only**
- **Individual words in keyword phrase used throughout the page**
- **The page is named after one keyword:**
  www.wickhomes.com/wisconsin.htm
- **Site itself contains related pages**
- **No spamming techniques are being used**
- **Contact information is provided**

With AltaVista, generally a keyword weight of around 5 percent works best.

What could we do to boost the rankings, if the rankings slip?

- **AltaVista is case sensitive, so search for all variations of your keyword phrase and make sure to use the variations if needed.**
  In particular, you may want to use the keyword phrase in all capital letters somewhere.
- **Move keyword phrase to the beginning of the title**
- **Remove keyword phrase from META description and keyword tags, pursuant to Alta Vista's guidelines.** (See Chapter 23 for more information.)
- **Use hidden links to other pages of the site**
  Name other pages of the site after your keyword phrase, and add hidden links to those pages. Use single pixel images and your keyword phrase in each of the ALT tags. Be sure to add a hidden link to this page from the main page, or create a doorway page site map as described in Chapter 10, because AltaVista may allow you to submit only the main page of the site.
- **Remove irrelevant META tags, such as the generator and author tags**
- **Name images after keyword phrase**
- **Name the page after the entire keyword phrase, with keywords being separated with dashes or underscores**
- **Use <noframes> tag and create a mini-web site in the tag**
- **Try two title tags**
- **Reduce words in the title tag to just the keyword phrase**
- **Begin the page with a headline tag beginning with the keyword phrase rather than with a graphic**
- **Try using your keyword phrase as the second or third word in the title tag**
- **Increase keyword weight of visible text to around 5 percent**
- **Purchase a domain with the keyword phrase in its name**
- **Use additional headline tags, with the keyword phrase used**
- **Put keyword phrase in bold**
- **Add more words in the body text**
- **Try using <style> tags**

Need More Info?

Other top-ranking AltaVista pages:

Hotel Reservations Los Vegas
Number 3 out of 1,154,940 results

www.placesforfun.com/hotel_reservations.htm

Drew University/Roxbury High School
Number 6 out of 1,011,830 results

www.cyberguild2000.com/arv34.htm

The interesting thing about this page is that it has been in the top-ten slots since 1997 and hasn't been modified. The keyword phrases aren't used in the body of the page itself, but only in the tags.

- **Work on boosting link popularity**
- **Sprinkle the keyword phrase throughout the page itself using it in the last paragraph as well**
- **Check your competition**
- **Review latest tips for AltaVista**

Other Examples: Lycos
Virtual flower showroom
Optimized for Lycos
Keyword phrase: "virtual flower"
Results as of the writing of this book: 5 out of 8,300
www.advinfo.com/tropcon/virtual-flower.html

@NetDetective 2000
Optimized for Lycos
Keyword phrase: "netdetective"
    Results as of the writing of this book: 2 in the "Popular" Web sites listing and 1 in the "Web sites"
www.netdetective2000.com/netdetective2000.html

Other Examples: GO/InfoSeek
Hypnosis board
Optimized for GO/InfoSeek
Keyword phrase: "hypnosis board"
Results as of the writing of this book: 1 out of 3,341,022
www.welcomecenters.com/find/hb/hypnosis_board_is.htm

Other Examples: HotBot
Joshua Syna, Clinical Hypnotherapist
Optimized for HotBot
Keyword phrase: "houston hypnotherapists"
    Results as of the writing of this book: 1 in HotBot, and clicking on the "Second Opinion" button going to Lycos shows the page as 1 there as well
www.besttexasbusiness.com/syna/smoke.html

Need More Info?

To review the latest tips for the engines, visit these sites:

Search Engine Watch
searchenginewatch.com

Web Search at about.com
websearch.about.com/internet/websearch

From the Experts:
A Final Word About Doorways

Danny Sullivan of Search Engine Watch answered a few questions about doorway pages.

When creating doorway pages, what suggestions do you have to maximize their success?

I don't really spend a lot of time with doorway pages, in the sense of building them from scratch. Instead, what I suggest people do is look within their sites for existing pages that could be rewritten using more of the key terms they want the page to be found for. I tell them not to lavishly repeat these terms, but to merely use them a bit more frequently than they would if writing normally. Of course, I also recommend the usual usage within the title and meta tag area, and it helps if the page is "normal" in the sense of linking to other pages or even externally from the site.

How do the engines feel about content-rich doorway pages?

Say doorway page to a search engine, and they'll generally say they hate them. Say how do you feel if I have many pages about different topics, and I optimize those pages, and they say great. Generally, what they don't want are pages with redirection or that present something different to their spider than the users. That doesn't mean they ban these pages, but they look upon them with more suspicion. They definitely don't want pages that promise content which they can't deliver. Overall, this is why I advise people to simply concentrate on building content—each page is essentially a possible doorway, whether they realize it or not.

> Overall, this is why I advise people to simply concentrate on building content—each page is essentially a possible doorway, whether they realize it or not.

For more information on this topic, visit our Web site at www.businesstown.com

Search Engine Strategies

Overview of Section V

Site popularity is one of the most important aspects of search engine positioning, but it can also be one of the most difficult to foster. Section V explains how to boost your site popularity, and it also covers additional strategies such as site maps and hidden links in order to improve your site's accessibility.

CHAPTER 13 HOW TO BOOST SITE POPULARITY AND WATCH YOUR SITE SOAR IN THE RANKINGS!
CHAPTER 14 OTHER IMPORTANT STRATEGIES

How to Boost Site Popularity and Watch Your Site Soar in the Rankings!

These days, having a popular Web site can make a huge difference in the search engine rankings. But the popularity of a site can be defined in two ways: site popularity and link popularity.

These days, having a popular Web site can make a huge difference in the search engine rankings. But what do we mean by a "popular" Web site? A site that has a lot of traffic? Not necessarily.

The popularity of a site can be defined in two ways: site popularity and link popularity.

"Site popularity" is determined by the number of visitors who clicked on your site in that engine's search results and stayed at the site for a certain period of time, as opposed to getting to your site and leaving immediately. This might suggest that the visitor didn't find what he or she was looking for.

"Link popularity" is not determined by the amount of traffic a site gets, but by the number of other sites that consider a Web site important enough to link to it. Of course, the more traffic a site gets, the better chance of getting more sites to link to it, so there can be a correlation. With a few of the engines, if you don't have high link popularity, it will be next to impossible for you to achieve a top ranking in that engine. GO/InfoSeek is a good example.

What Type of Link Is Important?

In the past, simply having an abundance of sites that linked to yours could have an impact on your link popularity. However, nowadays, it's more often the "type" of link that's important, not the sheer number.

What's important now is to obtain links from sites that are *related* to yours or links from highly popular Web sites, such as CNET. For example, if you have a site about flower arrangements, you'll achieve the most link popularity by having related sites link to yours, such as flower suppliers, baskets, greenery, "how to arrange flowers" sites, florists, and special occasion sites.

If you're lucky enough to have some highly popular Web sites such as CNET or eBay offer links to your site, you'll greatly benefit in terms of link popularity.

In your business, you may believe that your competitors are some of the only related sites that you can find. However, you should be able to find many sites that are complementary to yours: chambers of commerce and other business and industry associations, suppliers of the different items that you sell, "how to" related sites, and so on.

Having links on your site to related sites also counts toward link popularity these days. So, if you have a page of related links, with a link to that page from your main page or your site map, the engine will see those links and spider them, recognizing that the links are related to yours. This will give you a boost in link popularity as well as a boost in relevancy.

Reciprocity: Creating a Mutually Beneficial "Link Exchange"

Another way to increase "popularity" is to create an informal link exchange. Build a "Favorite Links" or "Helpful Links" page for your site and then ask those sites you list to reciprocate.

Your link page doesn't have to be visibly linked from any other page of your site. They can be "orphan" pages, which means that there are no links to that page from anywhere on your Web site. Therefore, anyone visiting your site won't come across the links page and be tempted away to other sites.

However, since so many of the engines now allow only the submission of the main page of a site, you'll need to be sure to add a hidden link to the link exchange page from your main page, or even a hidden link on your site map.

Keep in mind that we're not talking about adding links for the purpose of building traffic through that link. We're talking about adding links to build Web site popularity only. Of course, by building site popularity, our ultimate goal is to increase Web site traffic. But that will come later after you've boosted your link popularity.

Another way to increase "popularity" is to create an informal link exchange. Build a "Favorite Links" or "Helpful Links" page for your site and then ask those sites you list to reciprocate.

What Search Engines Consider Link or Site Popularity to Be an Important Issue?

Some engines consider link popularity to be extremely important, whereas other engines consider click-through traffic, or site popularity, to be important.

AltaVista	Link popularity
Excite	Link popularity
HotBot	Click-through popularity
GO/InfoSeek	Link popularity
Lycos	Click-through popularity
Northern Light	Link popularity
WebCrawler	Link popularity

One important point to keep in mind: link popularity is not an exact science. Search results can be extremely erratic. To give you an example, we searched for the link popularity of a particular Web site, and we found that the site had 378 links pointing to it in AltaVista. An hour later, we checked again, and AltaVista then showed 158 links pointing to the Web site. Upon checking again a short time later, AltaVista showed 0 (zero!) links pointing to it.

Obviously, a site can't have 378 links at one point and have every single one of those links disappear within a few hours. But that's what the search results showed.

You may know for a fact that links to your Web site can be found in several different places. Yet, when you check on your popularity, those links can't be found. You may check for your link popularity today and get different numbers from those you get tomorrow or even this afternoon.

Keep in mind that in order for a link to show up, the Web page needs to be in the search engine's index. If it isn't, the link doesn't do you any good. To be sure that Web pages offering links to your site are indexed, submit them yourself.

One important point to keep in mind: link popularity is not an exact science.

How Can You Determine Your Link Popularity?

One way is to visit LinkPopularity.com. LinkPopularity.com will determine your link popularity in AltaVista, GO/InfoSeek, Excite, and HotBot, which certainly is an easy route to take.

AltaVista
Go to:
www.altavista.com

Use this command in the browser window: link:yourdomain.com Do not include "http" or "www" in this command. You can check link popularity for individual pages by including the page names in that command, like: link:yourdomain.com/page.htm

To eliminate finding links in your own domain, use this command: link:yourdomain.com/ -url:your domain.com

Excite
Go to:
www.excite.com

Enter your URL in the browser window: www.yourdomain.com

HotBot
Go to:
hotbot.lycos.com

Use this command in the browser window: linkdomain:your domain.com You can also type your URL in the browser window, then choose "Look for" and "links to this URL" on the left side of the page. To eliminate finding links in your own domain, use this command: linkdomain:yourdomain.com –domain:your domain.com

(continued)

Need More Info?

Visit LinkPopularity.com at:

www.linkpopularity.com

You can also check your link popularity at the individual engines.

GO/InfoSeek
Go to:
infoseek.go.com

Works the same as AltaVista. Use this command in the browser window: link:yourdomain.com

Do not include "http" or "www" in this command. You can check link popularity for individual pages by including the page names in that command, like: link: yourdomain.com/page.htm

To eliminate finding links in your own domain, use this command: link:yourdomain.com/ -url:your domain.com

Is there a magic number of links that you need to have? Not really, but try to obtain at least one hundred links pointing to your site.

Is There a Magic Number of Links That You Need to Have?

Not really, but try to obtain at least one hundred links pointing to your site. Use that as your "Phase One" goal. Then build from there as time allows.

Link popularity tends to have a snowball effect. You may find that you'll work hard on it for a while and then slow down. But at that point, you may start getting requests from other Web sites that want you to add a link to their site. What do you tell them? Sure!— but you want a reciprocal link added from their site to yours!

Tips for boosting your link popularity:

• Write to related sites and ask them to participate in a reciprocal linking arrangement with you, where you'll link to their site and they'll link to yours. Include your links pages on your site map so that spiders may find them for indexing.

- Consider linking to related sites before you contact those webmasters. Say you've added a link to their site and would appreciate a link back. You may get better results if you've already done them the favor of linking to them.
- Perform searches to learn which sites have linked to your competitors' Web sites. Write to those sites and ask them to link to yours.
- Visit guestbooks of competing Web sites and see what URLs you can find. Sign the guestbooks with your own URL!
- Offer a discount to those sites that will link to your site and post a small graphic at their site linking back to yours.
- Too busy to search for links yourself? Hire a high school student to do it for you!
- If you know of any Web sites that have linked to yours, but those sites don't appear in the link popularity results, submit the pages yourself to the engine.
- Participate in free classified and free-for-all link areas.
- Add a page of related links on your own site, which now counts toward link popularity as well.

> Offer a discount to those sites that will link to your site and post a small graphic at their site linking back to yours.

Sample E-mail to Use When Requesting Reciprocal Links

You may want to use this sample e-mail as a guide when requesting reciprocal links. In any event, make the e-mail short, professional, and point out the benefits of reciprocal linking.

E-MAIL
Subject: Link request
Dear Web Owner: (list name if you know it)
I enjoyed visiting your exciting/informative/interesting site.
You may know that having a high link popularity can help you in the search engine rankings. Link popularity is defined as the number of Web sites that link back to your site.

For the purpose of link popularity, I have created a listing of relating links, and I've included your site in that listing. You'll find the list at this URL:

www.yourdomain.com/listyourlinkpagehere.html

Would you please consider adding a link to my site from yours?

You don't even have to add a link to your link page from anywhere on your site, so none of your traffic will leave your site. Simply submit the link page to the search engines, as I have done, and we'll both benefit.

Thank you for your consideration.

<signed with your name>

<the end>

From the Experts:
A Final Word About Link and Site Popularity

Stephen Mahaney, President of Planet Ocean Communications, answers a few questions about popularity:

What does it mean when an engine considers "site popularity" to be important when determining relevancy?

Today's engines use one of two methods to determine a site's popularity. At HotBot, for example, site popularity is measured by the amount of traffic that flows through the engine to a site. They simply count the number of clicks a site receives to determine the site's popularity. The larger the number of unique individual clicks (determined by visitor IP numbers), the higher the site's popularity rating.

The other method used by search engines like Goggle and GO/InfoSeek measures how many Web sites outside your domain have links pointing to your site. They also factor in an "importance rating" for each of those referring sites. For example, Yahoo! Is a very important site and gets a high importance rating. Therefore, a link from Yahoo! To your site is worth far more than a link from a free page at Geocities.

What does it mean when an engine considers "site popularity" to be important when determining relevancy?

- The amount of traffic that flows through the engine to a site.
- How many Web sites outside your domain have links pointing to your site.

Does this mean both incoming and outgoing links?

In most cases it means incoming links from other domains. Google does place some importance on out-going links. Our research indicates that pages that are optimized for Google will score best when there are at least a few links to outside sites that are related to your topic.

If a site has one thousand links that aren't related to the site itself, is that more effective than a smaller number of related links?

Our research indicates it's more important to have a small number of links from very important sites such as Yahoo!, LookSmart, Geocities, eBay, and so on, than to have a large number of generic links from less traveled sites pointed at your page. In regards to engines like Google and GO/InfoSeek, these links would ideally also contain related keyword content around the text area of the actual link that is pointing to your site. Other engines, like AltaVista, appear to be factoring in just the gross number of links.

Is there a "magic" number of links to strive for?

Yes, more links than your competition.

What is the best and most efficient way to boost your site popularity?

By getting a listing at Yahoo! in a relevant category, you can significantly boost your link popularity on some engines. Another way is by setting up an affiliate program. Doing so will automatically create link popularity from all of your affiliates linking to your site.

Is there a "magic" number of links to strive for? Yes, more links than your competition.

For more information on this topic, visit our Web site at www.businesstown.com

Chapter 14

Other Important Strategies

In our chapters on the individual engines, you'll learn various strategies that work with each particular search engine. But let's cover some general strategies that you'll want to know and remember.

Content Is King!

The days of creating simple pages with just the keywords stuck in the middle are over. If you want top rankings, you'll need to spend more time developing the content of your important pages.

The engines look for sites that are full of good content for its visitors. By developing rich content, you'll be proving to the engines that your site is truly relevant under your search terms.

What Is Content?

Content is an information-rich page about your particular keyword phrase. It can include things such as:

Links to related pages
Freebies that will get you some traffic
Contests that you can advertise
Polls
Articles
FAQs
Related forums or chat rooms

If much of your Web site is devoted to one overall keyword theme, you'll have a better chance at getting top rankings than single pages optimized for a particular keyword.

For example, let's say that your site pertains to diabetes. If you have various pages optimized for individual topics related to diabetes, such as supplies for diabetics, diabetes research, diabetic complications, and medications for diabetics, you'll have a better chance at achieving top rankings than a site that has only one or two pages devoted to the topic of diabetes.

The days of creating simple pages with just the keywords stuck in the middle are over. If you want top rankings, you'll need to spend more time developing the content of your important pages.

Optimize each page separately, using keywords for just that page in your META and other tags and in the body of the page.

Optimize each page of your site for one or two keyword phrases only. Don't try to list every single keyword that could possibly be related to your site in every one of your META keyword tags. Instead, fine-tune your pages to highlight one or two keyword phrases only, then use those phrases in your META and other tags and throughout the body of your page.

Use Hidden Links to All Important Pages of Your Site

With more and more of the engines allowing you to submit only the main page of your site, it's crucial that you place links to your other pages in front of the engines' spiders.

Create links on your main page to all other pages of your site. These links can be hidden, so they don't clutter up your main page. Here's an example of a hidden link:

<A HREF="educational-childrens-software.htm"><IMG SRC="clr.gif" BORDER="0" ALT="educational children's software"></A>

In this example, notice that no text will appear on your page. But the engine will find that link and spider it, thereby indexing the page.

Also notice that we've used the "single pixel" or "clear gif" tactic and included our important keyword phrase in the ALT tag. In other words, we're making the most out of that hidden link.

> Create links on your main page to all other pages of your site.

Use Site Maps!

Another option to direct spiders to all important areas of your site is to use a site map. Put a link to your site map on your main page. When the engine spiders your main page, it will find the link to the site map and go there, spidering the links on that page as well.

What is a site map?

A site map is simply a listing of all pages of your site. Many large Web sites use site maps to make it easier for their viewers to find what they're looking for.

Let's look at an example of a site map. You may be familiar with eBay auction. eBay provides a link to their site map at the very top of their page:

www.ebay.com

Here is the actual URL of their site map:

pages.ebay.com/sitemap.html

Notice that all important pages of the eBay Web site are included on this site map. When the engines visit eBay's main page, they'll spot the link to the site map and they'll visit, thereby spidering all those linked pages.

> Need a boost in relevancy? Try putting your keywords in bold in your body text. Sometimes it works!

Keywords in Bold in Body Text

Need a boost in relevancy? Try putting your keywords in bold in your body text. Sometimes it works!

Spread Your Keywords Across Your Page!

When working on your Web pages, remember to begin the body text with your keyword phrase, to sprinkle your keyword phrase throughout the page itself, and to use the phrase toward the end of your body text. This will prove to the engines that your page is consistently relevant to your keyword phrase.

Use Short META Keyword Tags

In your META keyword tag, don't try to insert every single one of the keywords that may have a remote connection to your Web site in general. Instead, use finely tuned keyword phrases for each particular page alone. Use variations of those phrases for the engines that are case sensitive, which we discussed in Chapter 4. You can also use synonyms of your keyword phrase.

Revisit Tags Won't Help You

With a revisit tag, you can indicate how often you want the search engine spiders to revisit your page. But will the engines really listen to that request and visit your page every single day if you tell it to do so, or even once a week?

No! Don't waste your time using this tag. It won't help you at all, and it's one of the irrelevant META tags that should be deleted.

Submit Your Pages Often

Many times, it's beneficial to submit your pages often. By putting your pages in front of the engines on a continual basis, you're telling the engine that the material is new and relevant. However, check the chapters on the individual engines to determine frequency of submissions because some engines, like AltaVista, appear to like older pages.

Use an HTML Validator

Many times, your HTML editor will contain a "validation" feature that allows you to make sure your HTML code is correct. It's always a good idea to check your code before placing the page on the Web and submitting it to the engines. This strategy is particularly important with Lycos since Lycos states that inaccurate HTML can hurt your rankings.

> The engines like simplicity! Simple pages that don't use frames, tables, or java will have an easier time getting a top ranking than complicated sites that use a lot of advanced technology.

Keep Your Pages Simple!

We've mentioned this before, but it's worth repeating. The engines like simplicity! Simple pages that don't use frames, tables, or java will have an easier time getting a top ranking than complicated sites that use a lot of advanced technology.

If you use advanced technology on your main page, consider creating simple but content-rich doorway pages to bring in traffic.

Keep Up with the Changes in the Industry

The search engine industry is constantly changing and evolving. Nothing ever remains the same for long. In order to survive and excel in this business, it's imperative that you keep up with changes in the industry.

You do that by accessing our Web site and learning of new developments and by subscribing to services like Search Engine Watch, MarketPosition, Web Search News, or Planet Ocean.

Visit search engine forums; talk with others in the industry; read, read, read.

Try new things (anything but spamming!). Be prepared for pages to disappear from the index altogether or to lose top rankings. Don't be surprised if you have a difficult time getting some pages indexed. Expect the unpredictable and unexplained, and learn to roll with the punches.

It's the most dynamic industry in the world and certainly one of the most challenging. You have the opportunity to succeed in this business and you will, but only if you keep up with the latest developments and change your tactics accordingly.

Help Your Visitors Find What They're Looking for on Your Site

The techniques in this chapter concentrate on search engine positioning strategies and ways to get your page boosted in the rankings.

But once you get visitors to your site, how difficult is it for them to find what they're looking for? Put it this way—if they can't find what they're looking for, they'll leave, and you've lost the business.

An excellent way to combat this problem is to add a search engine to your own site. This tactic is especially important if you have a large site with a lot of pages, but it can be beneficial to any site.

A site search engine offers many benefits, including:

- Improved navigability
- Increased ability to track visitors
- Increased effectiveness of marketing program
- Insight into visitor behavior

From the Experts:

Dan Turchin, process engineer with SearchButton.com, offers this helpful information:

According to *useit.com*, a Web site dedicated to usability and user-friendly site design, search is the most important element on any page. Typical visitors to your site will spend no more than thirty seconds hunting for information. With a site search engine, you can guarantee that they will spend their time using your information—not finding it. Consider this startling figure: though there is unanimous agreement that site search is essential, more than 80 percent of sites currently do have not have a site search engine! But just think of how those that do have benefited.
www.searchbutton.com

A site search engine offers many benefits, including:

- Improved navigability
- Increased ability to track visitors
- Increased effectiveness of marketing program
- Insight into visitor behavior

For more information on this topic, visit our Web site at www.businesstown.com

Learn from Successful Web Sites

Overview of Section VI

One of the best ways to learn what a particular engine likes to see on a Web page is to study competing Web sites. What techniques are they using that may have helped boost their relevancy and ranking in the engines? Why are they ranked higher than your site? Find out what you can learn from studying your competitors.

Checking Up
on Your
Competition

O ne of the best ways to learn what strategies are working in the engines at a particular point in time is to study top-ranking Web sites in your keyword area. By visiting an engine and searching for your keyword phrase, then analyzing the top-ten Web sites for that keyword phrase for that engine, you'll get a good picture of what that particular engine likes to see in the top rankings.

For your keyword phrase, what Web sites are in the top-ten slots? What techniques are they using? Do they use META description and keyword tags? How long is their body text? What is the keyword weight of the page? Why did they succeed? What's so special about their Web pages? Are the pages brilliantly optimized for the keyword phrase; are they using underhanded tricks; is it pure luck, or do they have a high link popularity? Why are they in the top-ten rankings and you're not?

Because each engine's algorithm changes so frequently, if you constantly monitor the top-ranking sites in your keyword area, you'll be able to keep up with the changes much more effectively because you're studying what is working at that very point in time.

So, in this chapter, we're going to concentrate on what your competitors are doing and why they're ranked so high in the search engines.

Sometimes we'll know why the pages are ranked high, but other times, we won't have a clue. It may appear that a site is going against every rule known in the Web optimization business, yet it's still managing to get a top-ten ranking.

However, what we're looking for are trends and not exceptions to the rule. Isolated instances where a Web site managed to get away with something irregular may be a source of frustration but shouldn't serve as a model because it may wreak havoc with your success with that same engine.

Keep This in Mind: Search Results Are Not Always Relevant!

Sometimes you'll find a Web page that's ranked above yours that isn't using your keyword phrase at all and isn't relevant to the search

> One of the best ways to learn what strategies are working in the engines at a particular point in time is to study top-ranking Web sites in your keyword area.

term in any manner. This is one of the most frustrating situations of all, because how can we compete when the other Web page isn't even using our keyword phrase?

The bottom line is the engines aren't perfect. Totally irrelevant search results are a fact of life, and they're impossible to compete against because there's no rhyme or reason for the ranking.

Here's an Example of Totally Irrelevant Results

A year or so ago, a friend of one of the writers of this book wrote to her, impressed at having found one of her Web pages in a search for "recipe rum balls." The page had a top ranking in Yahoo! (though from the supplemental results supplied by Inktomi).

Now, the interesting thing is that the page he found had no mention of "recipe rum balls" on the entire page, in any of the tags, or anywhere on her site. The page was a newspaper column that she'd posted on her site about Mardi Gras resources. She hadn't tried to get it ranked high in the engines, and if she had, she wouldn't have chosen the keyword phrase "recipe rum balls"!

So how did her page get a top ranking in Inktomi's supplemental listings at Yahoo! under a word that isn't used anywhere on her entire Web site? There's no answer to that question. Simply accept that it's happened and move on. Don't try to figure it out because you won't be able to!

> The bottom line is the engines aren't perfect. Totally irrelevant search results are a fact of life, and they're impossible to compete against because there's no rhyme or reason for the ranking.

Is the Page You're Looking at the "Real" Page?

When studying top-ranking sites, be sure that the page you're looking at is the actual page that gained the top ranking.

Before you try to learn from those who have achieved top rankings for one of your keyword phrases, make sure that the page you're looking at is the actual Web page that gained the top ranking.

So what does that mean? Why wouldn't that page be the one that achieved a top ranking if you found the page in the search results?

Several techniques may be employed that will allow the Web site optimizer to substitute a page so that the page that the engine sees is different from the page that the viewer sees. We'll cover those techniques in the next chapter, but for now, let's look at ways we can tell if the page we're viewing is the "real" page.

- Does the page's title and description displayed in the search engine results match what's on the actual Web page?
- Is the file size different?
- Is the file extension something other than .html or .htm?

In Chapter 20, we'll discuss "cloaking" or "food script" techniques, which you can suspect is being used if you find any of the preceding situations when studying a Web page.

For now, just keep in mind that if you find any of those situations, you're not viewing the actual Web page that earned the top ranking, so there's no reason for you to spend your time studying its techniques, or lack thereof.

Step-by-Step Way to Study Competing Pages

Use these steps as your guide to studying your competition.

- Visit an engine and search for your keyword phrase. AltaVista or GO/InfoSeek are good choices because they traditionally index pages faster than the other engines.
- What pages are in the top-ten rankings, or even the top-five rankings? Visit each of those sites and look around. You may even find some *404 File Not Found* pages that are in the top-ten results.

   Check to see if any of the pages contain a <noindex> META tag. If so, the Web master is preventing the engines from reindexing his page, probably because that engine gives a boost in relevancy to pages that have been in its index for a while. Therefore, the page may be old and optimized for an older-ranking algorithm. If the page were reindexed today

> Several techniques may be employed that will allow the Web site optimizer to substitute a page so that the page that the engine sees is different from the page that the viewer sees.

under today's algorithm, its ranking would probably significantly change.

- Resubmit each of those pages to the search engine. Then, wait for a few days to see how the rankings change.

  Since more and more engines are allowing you to submit only the main page of a site, you may not always be able to submit competing sites to the engines. But for those engines that allow multiple pages, this is a solid strategy to keep in mind.

- Search for your keyword phrase again and visit the top-ranking sites, some of which may be different from the ones that you found before.

- Look at the pages themselves, and look at the source code.

- Study their techniques because those are the truly top-ranking sites, unless they're employing "cloaking" techniques, which we'll cover in Chapter 20.

- What kinds of things should you study when analyzing competing pages?

- Where is the keyword phrase being used?

- Is there a title tag?

- Is there a META description tag?

- Is there a META keyword tag?

- Where is the keyword phrase being used in those tags and how many times? At the very beginning of the tags? As the second and third words? The third and fourth words? Not at all?

- Does the page use ALT tags with keywords in the tag?

- How long is the body text?

- What is the keyword weight?

- Is the page spamming in any way? We'll cover spamming techniques in detail in Chapter 17, but we'll briefly cover how to report spammers later in this chapter.

- Are the title and description tags in the search results the same as on the page itself? If not, this is a good indication that cloaking is being used, and there's no reason to study the page.

- Where is the keyword phrase used in the body text?

- Is the keyword phrase being used in header tags?

> Since more and more engines are allowing you to submit only the main page of a site, you may not always be able to submit competing sites to the engines.

- Does the page contain frames? Tables? Javascript?
- Is the entire site centered on the general theme of the keyword phrase?
- Is the page named after the keyword phrase?
- Do links within the page point to related pages?
- Are hidden links used with single pixel images and ALT tags?
- What is the date listed in the search results for the page? Remember to study only new pages because you want to know what the engine likes at that point in time. In AltaVista, for example, the "Last Modified Date" is the date that the page was actually added to the database.
- How popular is the site itself?

Why Would We Want to Resubmit the Top-Ranking Pages to the Engine?

Before you study techniques for a page that is in the top-ranking slots for your keyword phrase in an effort to learn what strategies got that page into the top rankings, you want to make sure that the page has truly earned a top-ten rank.

For example, if a page is using any "underhanded" techniques to achieve a top ranking, you don't want to waste your time studying its techniques because you won't learn anything that will help you legitimately position a Web site.

If the pages got top rankings by swapping codes or pages in an effort to "trick" the engine, their rankings—when you submit them—will plummet, and the true top-ten sites will emerge on top.

You may find *404 File Not Found* pages when you visit the top-ten sites. If you resubmit those URLs to the engine, the engine will remove the pages from its index, and your page may move up in the rankings!

When studying the top-ten pages, you may even find that a particular Web site is dominating the rankings. By that, we mean that the site or pages on the site have several of the top-ten rankings, thereby making it difficult for anyone else to break into the top ten.

> Before you study techniques for a page that is in the top-ranking slots for your keyword phrase in an effort to learn what strategies got that page into the top rankings, you want to make sure that the page has truly earned a top-ten rank.

The engines don't like to see a particular Web site dominate the rankings. So in this instance, you may want to report the pages to the engine as possible spamming, which we'll cover later in this chapter.

Further, if a page received its top ranking under a different algorithm than the one that is being employed at the present time, resubmitting the page could cause its ranking to drop, allowing your page to move up in the rankings.

Once you can view the pages that are truly in the top-ten rankings at that point under the current ranking algorithm for that particular engine, study and analyze those pages because they are the ones that can teach you valuable information that you might be able to use at your own site.

Again, because so many of the major engines allow you to submit only main pages of a site, you may not be able to employ this technique. But you can certainly try it.

Is It Legal to Submit Competing Web Pages for Reindexing?

It is perfectly acceptable to submit another's Web page to the engines. In fact, many of the engines ask you to "suggest" a "favorite" page from any site, not just your own. If the page has not changed since it was last indexed, and if they're ranking high under the current algorithm, their ranking should not change or be affected by the resubmission. So, you're not doing anything devious and it won't boot them out of the rankings if they're legitimately in a top-ranking position.

With many of the engines, resubmitting on a frequent basis can even be beneficial because you're constantly placing the page in front of the engine.

When Will Reindexing a Page Not Work?

There are two occasions when reindexing a page that shouldn't be at the top of the list won't work. If a Web site optimizer uses a CGI script to automatically detect a particular search engine's spider and

> ### Need More Info?
>
> To determine the link popularity of a site, visit LinkPopularity.com:
>
> *www.linkpopularity.com*

then dynamically "serves" a Web page that is different from the one that the viewer sees, there are few ways of knowing that this technique is being used. This technique is called "cloaking" or "food script," which we'll cover in Chapter 20.

Further, if a page contains a <noindex> META tag, resubmitting the page won't work. This META tag prevents all engines from indexing the page. Like all META tags, it's placed in the <head> </head> section.

<meta name="robots" content="noindex">

Resubmitting the page will not remove it from the index if the page is already listed there. It will just prevent the engine from reindexing the page to take into account changes made to the page.

Are You Still Hesitant About Resubmitting Competing Pages?

Some people are hesitant about submitting competing Web sites, so let's discuss it further.

Will you get in trouble for resubmitting a competing page? Will the engine breathe fire down your back, boot you out of the index, or report you to the competition?

If you resubmit pages at either AltaVista or GO/InfoSeek, you don't have to list your e-mail address. You simply enter the URL of the page you want to resubmit. So, you're not advertising to the engine that *you're* the one who submitted the page for reindexing. But do you really think an engine would try to figure out who submitted all the millions of pages submitted to them on a daily basis? Do you think they would care?!

Keep in mind that professional Web designers and optimizers work on clients' sites, so they're constantly resubmitting those third-party pages to the engines.

Remember also that there's nothing illegal or unethical about submitting competing Web sites for reindexing. You're not trying to steal their codes or even boot their Web sites out of the rankings altogether. You're simply trying to even the playing field, so that when you look at who is "really" on top in your keywords, you can

Resubmitting the page will not remove it from the index if the page is already listed there. It will just prevent the engine from reindexing the page to take into account changes made to the page.

learn from those who have actually achieved a high ranking legitimately. You want to learn from the pros.

Most of the time, resubmitting the top-ten pages will cause a decrease in some of the pages' rankings. Not only that, but all the *404 File Not Found* pages will be removed from the index. As a result, you may see an increase in your own rankings, even moving you into the top thirty slots. These are the benefits derived from submitting competing sites, though they're not the only reason for doing so.

The real reason is to study and understand the preferences of the search engines. But if your competitors *are* using underhanded methods, watching their rankings go down while yours goes up is not unpleasant.

Don't Copy Competing Web Pages!

When we encourage you to analyze competing Web pages, we are not asking you to copy those pages or their tags. Rather, we're asking you to examine their techniques. Go to their Web pages and view the source code. How did they write their META tags and title tag? What keywords did they use? Did they use ALT tags containing their keywords? Did they have a lot of links off that main page? Did they name the page after their keyword phrase?

Take notes! Make a simple chart and look for particular areas on every page that you analyze. Then compare the areas in those top-ten sites to see if you can find a definite trend.

While You're at It, Report Spammers to the Engine

When you're studying competing Web sites, you may see some obvious spamming techniques. We'll cover spamming in detail in Chapter 17, but for now, look for any techniques that are obviously questionable.

Are any of your competitors dominating the rankings under particular keyword phrases? Are any of them using the same color font on the same color background? Are they repeating their key-

> You're simply trying to even the playing field, so that when you look at who is "really" on top in your keywords, you can learn from those who have actually achieved a high ranking legitimately. You want to learn from the pros.

Need More Info?

To view the source code on the Web, if you're using Netscape, click on View, then on Page Source. You'll see the HTML coding for the page. In Internet Explorer, click on View, then Source.

Need More Info?

To determine if a page is using the same color font on the same color background, you can highlight the entire Web page and see if "hidden" text is now visible.

Extra Hints and Tips

How often is your competition updating their Web pages? Use javElink to find out—for free!

javElink is a Web site that will monitor 20 other Web sites for you and notify you when those pages change. Enter your competition's Web site, and javElink will let you know when it's been modified:

www.javelink.com

word phrase over and over and over again in the tags, in the body text, or in tiny text at the bottom of the page?

If you see any obvious spamming techniques, report them to the engine.

For AltaVista, fill out a form at this URL:

doc.altavista.com/help/search/report_off.shtml

This form, though not designed for this particular use, can be used to report spammers. Pages are not immediately removed, but they're placed on a list to be reviewed.

For more information about how AltaVista feels about spamming, see Chapter 23, or visit this URL:

www.altavista.com/cgi-bin/query?pg-addurl

To report spammers to GO/InfoSeek, simply send an e-mail to: comments@infoseek.com

GO/InfoSeek says this about spamming:

We will make every effort to resolve reports within 24 hours. To facilitate this process, please include as much detail as you can, such as the query word(s) you used, URL(s) of the page(s) in question, etc.

How Did *That* Web Site Get a Top Ranking?

By studying your competitors' Web pages, you can learn valuable strategies to try at your own site. However, after working extremely hard on your page, you may find that another page waltzes into the rankings ahead of yours and, worse yet, appears to follow no rules. How can this be?

> By studying your competitors' Web pages, you can learn valuable strategies to try at your own site.

Why Does the Page Have a Top Ranking?

Let's look at some specific techniques that could explain why your competitors have top rankings. And let's learn why we do or don't want to use them!

- **Out-of-date pages**

  Maybe the webmaster changed the pages but didn't resubmit them to the search engines. In most cases, resubmitting the pages will put the pages at the ranking they should be, based on today's ranking algorithm.

  Both GO/InfoSeek and AltaVista seem to place more relevancy on pages that have been in their index for a while. So, be sure to check the source code of competing Web sites and look for a META <noindex> tag in the <head> section. This tag will keep the engines from reindexing the page on their next spider run.

  If you're resubmitting competing Web pages to see if their rankings change, could *your* competitors be doing the same thing to your pages? Yes, they could. With GO and AltaVista, you don't want that to happen because you want your pages to "age" to give you an added boost in relevancy.

  To prevent this from happening, add a META robots tag to your page, like this:

  <meta name="robots" content="noindex">

  This META tag will prevent all engines from reindexing your page. Like all META tags, it's placed in the <head> </head> section of your page. Remember, though, that when *you* need to resubmit the page, you'll have to remove the tag.

- **Dynamic page substitution, or cloaking**
  With this technique, webmasters use scripts that can detect the IP addresses of a search engine's spider. When the script detects the spider, it shows a different Web page than the one a human visitor would see after clicking on the link from the engine's results. This is software called *cloaking* or *food script*.

  With dynamic page substitution, the search engines see this generic, very simple, and usually unattractive Web page that is fully loaded with Web optimization strategies. Yet, the viewers see a top-notch, attractive Web page designed to be effective with only the human audience.

  Why would a search engine optimizer want to use cloaking?

  Let's say that the page uses techniques that automatically put it at a great disadvantage in the rankings. Maybe the site is in frames, or maybe it uses a lot of Java. Maybe there's very little content on many of the main pages.

  Or maybe the optimizer is given the Web site to work on its rankings but is told that he or she can't change anything on the site or in the tags. It's impossible to optimize a page for top search engine rankings if you aren't allowed to change anything, and this is a very common problem with professional search engine optimizers.

  Further, if you're working in a very competitive field and if you've managed to get top rankings, you don't want someone to come along behind you and "steal" your hard-earned rankings. You want to "cloak," or hide, those effective techniques in order to try to maintain your top position.

  How can you determine if cloaking is being used? Does the site title and description displayed in the search engine results match what's on the actual Web site? Is the file size different? Is the file extension something other than .html or .htm?

  Another use for cloaking is to hide codes from viewers so that the developer's hard work in getting the page ranked high in the engines can't be copied by others.

> With dynamic page substitution, the search engines see this generic, very simple, and usually unattractive Web page that is fully loaded with Web optimization strategies. Yet, the viewers see a top-notch, attractive Web page designed to be effective with only the human audience.

Read more about cloaking in Chapter 20.

- **Swapping out Web pages**

As you know, the engines like simplicity, so it's difficult to have an eye-catching overall design that lends itself to Web positioning strategies for top rankings. So, some webmasters create optimized Web pages, usually all text with carefully constructed META tags, title tag, body copy, and so on, and submit the pages to a search engine. They'll work with those simple (and not very attractive) pages until they get top rankings under their keyword phrases.

After the webmasters achieve the rankings they're after, they simply switch out the dull and boring Web pages with their "real" pages, complete with graphics, fancy HTML, Javascript, flash, tables, and so on. Now, they've got top-notch rankings to go along with their top-notch pages.

Before your mind begins to whirl in this direction, slow down a little. Keep in mind that the engines send their spiders out to reindex Web sites periodically and without notice. You won't know ahead of time when the spider is going to visit. When that happens, you'll immediately lose those top rankings for which you worked so hard.

Dynamic page substitution, or cloaking, is the same technique as described here but accomplished with software scripting, rather than manually. With dynamic page substitution, you don't have to be concerned when a spider comes to visit because the program will detect the spider and show it the well-optimized page. It's a safer road.

- **Swapping out the code**

In this case, the code of an optimized Web site that has achieved a top-ranked position has been swapped out in an effort to prevent others from imitating the success of the page. Once the webmaster achieves a top ranking, he or she simply removes the winning tags and substitutes them with other tags. So, if you were to study the webmaster's source code, you would never understand how he or she got a top ranking by using those tags.

> As you know, the engines like simplicity, so it's difficult to have an eye-catching overall design that lends itself to Web positioning strategies for top rankings.

This is a variation of swapping out complete Web pages, but the problems associated with the techniques are the same. A page will plummet in the rankings as soon as the spider reindexes it in one of its regular crawls.

- **New ranking algorithm**
As you know, search engines change their ranking algorithms from time to time. Therefore, techniques that worked well last month may not be as effective today.

- **Page popularity**
Your competitor's Web site may rank well because thousands of other Web sites consider it important enough to offer links to it.
Link popularity is extremely important these days, so some pages rank high simply due to that one factor alone.

- **Search engine bugs or problems**
Let's face it, the engines make mistakes. Periodic bugs and disruptions are a fact of life, as are mixed up search returns.

- **A well-optimized page for that particular search engine**
Maybe the reason that the page is ranked so high is that the Web designer has done a superb job of optimizing the page.

- **Human review**
Maybe a human viewed the page and slipped it into the top rankings. More and more of the engines are using editors to review Web pages, which is one more reason to make sure that your Web pages are the best they can be in all respects.

- **Listed in the engine's directory**
Maybe the Web site is also listed in the directory for that particular engine, which may boost its ranking in the search engine results themselves. For example, being listed in GO's directory can cause a significant boost in rankings in the GO engine itself.

> Link popularity is extremely important these days, so some pages rank high simply due to that one factor alone.

For more information on this topic, visit our Web site at www.businesstown.com

Preventing Problems with the Engines

Overview of Section VII

Did you know that certain spamming techniques can get your Web site kicked out of the search engines' indexes? But what exactly is spam? In Section VII, you'll learn about various spamming techniques and why the engines dislike them, and you'll learn how to stay out of trouble with the engines for the continued health and success of your Web site.

Don't Spam!

Chapter 17

What Is Spam?

On the Internet, spam can have several different meanings. In your e-mail box, spam is the equivalent of "junk" mail. When a company or individual sends out thousands of unsolicited e-mail messages trying to sell goods or services, it's considered spam. In newsgroups, spam is created by sending out identical posts to numerous newsgroups in an effort to sell goods or services.

But when it comes to the search engines, spam is a little different, though it still leaves the same bad taste in your mouth. Here spam is using unscrupulous tactics in order to get top rankings in the search engines.

Here's what GO/InfoSeek's says about spam:

> There are unscrupulous Web page designers that try to subvert our search results in an effort to increase traffic to their site. This is called spamming.
>
> The difficulties arise in determining what is "unscrupulous" and what is actually an effective strategy. Even more difficulties surface because the engines don't necessarily agree about what tactics constitute spamming. Techniques that weren't considered spamming several months or a year ago are now "red flag" areas that the engines monitor closely.
>
> As you walk the "fine line" between what you can get away with (that could benefit your site's rankings) and what the engines consider to be spamming, remember to be extremely careful.
>
> More and more search engines are cracking down on what they consider spamming techniques used to gain top rankings. Legitimate webmasters must be careful not to get put in the same category as the small minority of spammers who submit dozens of pages and present off-topic material in irrelevant categories.
>
> Pay close attention to the major "no-no's" here because one thing is for sure: you don't want to get in trouble with the search engines and get banned from their indexes. This could prove fatal to your online business.

But when it comes to the search engines, spam is a little different, though it still leaves the same bad taste in your mouth. Here spam is using unscrupulous tactics in order to get top rankings in the search engines.

Don't Use These Spamming Techniques!

Avoid the following techniques and stay on the good side of the search engines:

- **Keyword stuffing**

  Keyword stuffing is the repeated use of a keyword to increase the page's relevancy. Keyword stuffing refers to repeating keywords over and over again in tags of all kinds as well as body text. Here's an example:

  software soft-ware software software software software software software software software

  Keep in mind that less is usually better. Overuse your keyword phrase, and you'll lose relevancy and your ranking.

- **Tiny text**

  Tiny text is repeating your keywords over and over again in a very small font size usually at the bottom of your page.

  Some webmasters make a Web page look as if it's come to an end so visitors think that they're at the bottom of the page. But if they were to scroll farther down on the now-blank page, they'd eventually find a paragraph or more of keywords used over and over again in very tiny type. Since human visitors won't see it, the text is there strictly for the benefit of the search engines.

- **Invisible text**

  Invisible text is stuffing keywords in a font color that is the same or a nearly identical color as the background of the page. To view the invisible text, you can highlight the entire Web page while viewing it in your browser by hitting Ctrl-A.

- **META refresh tag**

  A META refresh tag is a tag that immediately takes the viewer to another Web page. This tag has some legitimate uses, but regretfully, it's gotten a bad name. Dishonest webmasters sometimes optimize a page for the engines in order to get a top ranking, then use a lightning fast META refresh tag that immediately takes the viewer to the "real" and attractive page of the site. In many cases, the viewer doesn't even realize that he or she has been transported to another page.

If you're going to use a META refresh, make sure that it's set at thirty seconds or above. AltaVista and GO/InfoSeek don't like META refresh tags at all, so it's best to stay away from the tags altogether with those engines.

For an example of a legitimately used META refresh tag, visit this page:

www2.netdoor.com/~smslady

Here's the META refresh tag itself:

<META HTTP-EQUIV="REFRESH" CONTENT="30; URL=www.robinsnest.com" TARGET="_top">

- **META tag stuffing**

META tag stuffing is stuffing your META tags with your keywords, over and over again.

For example:

<META NAME="KEYWORDS" CONTENT="fruit baskets, fruit baskets">

Avoid repeating the same keyword dozens of times in a row on your page, in your METAs, or any other tags. A good rule of thumb is not to repeat your keywords more than three times in any tag. See the chapters on the individual engines for more information.

- **Dominate the rankings**

Optimizing several pages for the same keyword phrase, which may cause those pages to dominate the search results,

> Optimizing several pages for the same keyword phrase, which may cause those pages to dominate the search results, is frowned upon by the engines.

is frowned upon by the engines. For example, let's say that you run a search for "dry skin treatment." Out of the top ten results, seven of them are all pages from the same Web site. That Web site has dominated the top-ten rankings under that particular keyword phrase, which the engine would consider to be excessive.

Rather than letting your Web pages dominate the rankings, take those successful pages and optimize them for other important keyword phrases for your site so as to bring in more traffic through those other doorways.

- **Multiple title tags**

Since the title tag is the most important tag on your page, what about having 5 of them? 15? 40?

No!

Some of the engines allow you to use two title tags, but don't use more than that. Don't use two title tags with GO/InfoSeek. Check the guidelines for each particular engine to see if multiple title tags are an option for that engine.

- **Hidden form tags**

Not too long ago, keywords were placed in hidden form tags as a means of helping to boost relevancy and ranking. However, the major engines now consider the tags to be spamming, and these tags should be used only for the purpose they were created for, as a means of creating an element within a <form> that does not display in the browser. Here's an example:

<INPUT TYPE="HIDDEN" NAME="HIDDEN" VALUE="Placing-Keywords-Here-Is-Now-Considered-Spamming">

- **Extremely high keyword weight**

A keyword weight of 25 percent is certainly a clear indication of spamming. Keep your keyword weight at an optimum level for each engine. See Chapter 6 for more information on keyword density or weight.

> Keep your keyword weight at an optimum level for each engine. See Chapter 6 for more information on keyword density or weight.

Other Techniques That Can Get You in Trouble with the Engines

Keeping these techniques in mind and avoiding them will prevent you from having problems with the engines:

- Never use keywords in your META or other tags that do not apply to your site's content. This is a definite red flag area for the engines. Some unsavory webmasters use porn keywords in an effort to boost traffic to their nonporn site.

  Here's an example. In the Inktomi results from Yahoo! recently a search for "low fat cooking" resulted in five pornographic Web sites in the top-ten results. Those webmasters slid the keyword phrase of "low fat cooking" into their title and other tags in an effort to catch that traffic and bring it to the porn sites.

  Just remember that if the engine(s) catch you, you're in trouble.

- Do not create too many doorway pages. Although it's good to create multiple doorway pages that target different sets of keywords or phrases, don't be excessive. And remember that the important word in the previous sentence is "different."

  How many doorway pages are too many? Though there's no magical number, don't create more than ten doorway pages that link to the same page, such as your home page. Instead, link your doorway pages to other interior pages of your site.

- Don't submit too many pages at one time. Some engines, like AltaVista, prefer that you submit just one page a day.

  Taking this a step further, if you're working with an engine that allows you to submit several pages in one day, try to submit those pages slowly rather than sitting down and submitting every single one of your twenty five pages one right after the other. By submitting your pages slowly and spreading out the submissions a little, you aren't calling attention to your submissions as you would if you submitted fifty pages at one time.

> Never use keywords in your META or other tags that do not apply to your site's content.

- Don't submit the same page twice on the same day.

    None of the engines like to see you submit the same page twice on the same day. You can submit the same page every single day for the next 365 days with no problem. But don't submit that page more than once on the same day.

- Manually submit your pages if at all possible.

    Try to submit your pages manually, at least to the major search engines, rather than using submission software or services.

    Submission software can present problems for a number of reasons. You don't have the flexibility with submission software that you do with manual submissions. It's too easy to forget that AltaVista likes to see only one submission per site per day, or that GO/InfoSeek won't accept submissions other than the main page.

    Some of the major engines won't even accept submissions through submission software. Therefore, if it's important for your site to be indexed, submit your pages manually. Obviously, this can be a problem for someone who needs to submit hundreds of pages every single day. In that case, submission software or services may be his or her only alternative.

Are There Ways Around the Submission Limits?

Let's say that you're a professional search engine optimizer, and you work with clients' pages for ten hours every day. If you're allowed to submit only one page from AltaVista in a day, it could conceivably take you six months to get all the pages submitted. But how can the engines tell how often you submit pages?

Some engines, like AltaVista, will monitor search engine submission activity by placing a "cookie" on your system. This identifies you on each return visit, and your submissions won't be indexed if you submit too many pages too frequently.

If cookies are getting in your way of Web positioning success, it's time to clear unwanted cookies from your browser.

You can disable the cookies in Netscape by clicking on Edit/Preferences/Advanced/Disable Cookies. Then, delete old cookies

Need More Info?

What are "cookies"? Cookies are electronic tags placed on your computer by some Web sites. Cookies can then monitor what pages you visit and generate user profiles of your visiting habits. Cookies aren't always a bad thing because they can sometimes make things easier for you.

Let's say that you make airline reservations online, and you spend several minutes creating a travel profile of which airport you fly in and out of, which airline you prefer, your typical seating preferences, and so forth. The Web site will then create a cookie and place it on your system. The next time you visit, the Web site will hunt for the cookie, and pull up your stored travel profile to keep you from having to enter the same information.

by going to your Netscape directory and searching for a file named "cookie.txt." Open the file in a text editor like Note Pad and delete the contents. With IE, you'll need to get special cookie software to detect old cookies.

If you submit a lot of pages, be sure to change your IP address frequently. When using a dialup service, get offline periodically so that your IP address will change.

Also use different e-mail addresses for each domain that you use. This makes it more difficult for the engines to connect all of your submissions to the same person.

What Each Major Engine Considers to Be Spamming

ENGINE	TINY TEXT	INVISIBLE TEXT	META REFRESH TAGS	IDENTICAL PAGES	KEYWORD STUFFING
AltaVista	Spam	Spam	Spam	Spam	Spam
Excite	No	No	No	Unknown	Spam
GO/InfoSk	No	Spam	Spam	Spam	Spam
HotBot	Spam	Spam	No	Spam	Spam
Lycos	Spam	Spam	Spam	Spam	Spam
NorthernL	No	Spam	No	Unknown	Spam
WebCrawlr	Spam	No	No	Unknown	Spam

What Happens if You Spam an Engine?

If you spam an engine, you could get labeled a spammer. This could cause all of your domains to get banned from the engine and all of your pages to be removed from the index.Or spammers may find that they can't get their pages ranked high no matter what they do. In other words, spamming can mean instant "death" to a successful Web site.

Most of the engines don't have a "lifetime" ban for spamming. Someone who is caught spamming can get back in the good graces of the engines and once again get his or her pages indexed, but only if he or she stops all spamming techniques.

That person may also find that the engine(s) are constantly looking over his or her shoulder to make sure that no more "shady" tactics are employed to achieve top rankings. The spammer may not be able to get away with borderline strategies that other people can get away with simply because the engines need to be certain that he or she is operating totally aboveboard.

Once an engine bans a domain from its index, it's a long and anxious process to try to get the domain back in the engine's good graces and in the index.

It's just not worth it. Don't spam!

> If you spam an engine, you could get labeled a spammer. This could cause all of your domains to get banned from the engine and all of your pages to be removed from the index.

The Art of Groveling

But what happens if someone in your company spammed the engines, and your company's Web site has been kicked out? What can you do to get the pages indexed once again?

The first thing you need to do is clean up the Web site and remove all evidence of spam or anything that could remotely be considered spam.

Get rid of all keyword stuffing, hidden text, irrelevant keywords, META refresh tags, tiny text, and so forth. Employ only aboveboard strategies in a very conservative manner. Visit the engines and read all of their spam-related information. Make sure that your site is ready for a good, close scrutiny.

Then, send an e-mail or snail mail letter to the engine. Be very upfront, and practice the "fine art of groveling." Apologize profusely, and assure the engine that the spamming techniques have been removed and won't be used again. Ask for their consideration in allowing your pages to be indexed in their engine once again.

Don't expect instant results. You may have to write several letters or even place several phone calls before your pages will be allowed back in. But don't give up.

Equally important is not to develop an "attitude" in any way. Don't tell the engine that you've written three letters before and that you "expect" to get back in the index within two days or else. Or else *what?!* You're totally at their mercy here. So, get down on bended knees and get it over with. Grovel!

Then, don't ever spam again!

What if you don't know for sure that your site has been banned from the index?

Your pages may have disappeared from the index, and you can't seem to get them reindexed. Or maybe you have a new site, and you've submitted your pages countless times in vain. Could it be that you've spammed the engine and aren't being allowed in?

If you've used any of the spamming techniques that have been outlined here, then yes, you could be in trouble with the engine. Clean up your act, grovel, and don't spam again.

On the other hand, more than likely your pages just haven't gotten indexed yet for a variety of reasons. The engine could be very slow in accepting new submissions; could be experiencing some major changes, which always creates submitting problems; or could have lost your pages. Simply resubmit once a week until your pages get indexed or reindexed.

If you've tried unsuccessfully for a month or more, then consider writing to the engine and explaining your situation in a very nice way. Many people have been able to get their pages indexed by going this route, but only after they've exhausted other means of getting in.

> If you've used any of the spamming techniques that have been outlined here, then yes, you could be in trouble with the engine. Clean up your act, grovel, and don't spam again.

The Art of Tattling

As you work on your own pages, you may very well find other Web sites that employ blatant spamming techniques—sometimes quite successfully.

How can they get away with it? Well, maybe they can't!

They're walking on thin ice, and if the engine catches them, they'll sink to the bottom of the river.

Many of the engines ask you to report spammers in an effort to keep their indexes clean and more relevant. So, if you spot a spammer when running a search in AltaVista, for example, report the page to AltaVista. If you're in HotBot and find a spammer, report the page to HotBot.

Don't Spam!

Spamming hurts the entire Web, frustrating search engine users and legitimate Web site owners. Help the engines combat spamming, and all of us will benefit from your efforts.

Where Can You Report Spammers?

AltaVista	*doc.altavista.com/help/search/report_off.shtml*
Excite	*www.excite.com/feedback*
GO/InfoSeek	E-mail to: comments@GO.com
HotBot	E-mail to: feedback@hotbot.com
Lycos	E-mail to: webmaster@lycos.com
Northern Light	*www.northernlight.com/docs/gen_help_prob.html*
WebCrawler	*www.webcrawler.com/feedback*
Yahoo!	E-mail to: url-support@yahoo-inc.com

Spamming hurts the entire Web, frustrating search engine users and legitimate Web site owners. Help the engines combat spamming, and all of us will benefit from your efforts.

For more information on this topic, visit our Web site at www.businesstown.com

How to Stay Out of Trouble with the Engines

Chapter 18

As you can see, the search engines are extremely valuable to anyone who wants to conduct business over the Internet. As we discussed in Chapter 17, the last thing you want to do is get in trouble with the engines.

Though not on the same order as spamming, other techniques that need to be avoided, or at least addressed, can present special problems for your Web site.

If you can keep these guidelines in mind when creating your Web pages, you'll be giving yourself an edge over your competition:

Though not on the same order as spamming, other techniques that need to be avoided, or at least addressed, can present special problems for your Web site.

- Begin your Web pages with text rather than an image. The engines can't see images–they can only read the content of ALT tags. So, be sure to use ALT tags containing your keyword phrase for all of your graphics.

  Keyword prominence may be affected if a graphic appears before the body text on your site. So, you should use text before graphics. Some search engines assign weight to the first twenty five words on a page, and the more prominent (higher on the page) those words are, the better for rankings in most cases.

- Engines can't "read" gif or jpeg files that spell out a word or words. In other words, if your company name is spelled out in a graphic on your home page, the engine won't be able to read that graphic. Again, you can use ALT tags containing your keyword phrase that also describe the graphic.

- Make sure that your page loads relatively fast. If the engine sends its spider, and if it takes too long to load your page, the spider may not index all of your page, which can present ranking problems for you.

  Certain engines (like Excite) don't appear to like slow-loading pages since most of the top-ranked pages are not over 60 to 70K maximum.

- Make sure that your pages are accessible. If the engine can't visit the page, the page won't get indexed.

  If an engine's spider tries to visit your site, it may "time out" if it takes longer than sixty seconds to access the page.

- Avoid Javascript, frames, and tables, which we'll discuss in detail in Chapter 19.
- Create static pages for dynamically generated pages, which we'll discuss in Chapter 20.
- Avoid using symbols in your URL for database-driven pages, which we'll discuss in Chapter 20.
- Don't use irrelevant META tags.

    Some META tag generator programs or HTML editors stick in irrelevant META tags like META Author and META Generator.

    Because META tags are found between the opening <HEAD> and the closing </HEAD> tags, if you include too many irrelevant META tags, you run the risk of confusing the engines, making it harder for your Web site to be found.

    The only META tags you need to use are the description and keyword tags, the <noindex> tag, and the <noframes> tag. Eliminate the others since they serve no purpose in search engine placement and could confuse the engine.

- Try to keep things simple! You'll find that most of the top-ranking pages are simple pages without a lot of tags or fancy HTML. Remember that!

If You're Submitting to Directories, Keep These Extra Tips in Mind

Because the directories operate differently than the engines, a different set of guidelines is needed for them.

- Make sure all of your links and graphics work and that your site is in top-notch shape.
- Put contact information (company name, address, phone number, e-mail address) at the bottom of every page.
- Put copyright information at the bottom of the main page.
- If you have a "last updated on" date on your Web site, make sure that it's been updated very recently.
- Submit in the proper category.

Try to keep things simple! You'll find that most of the top-ranking pages are simple pages without a lot of tags or fancy HTML. Remember that!

Other Factors That Can Affect Web Positioning

Overview of Section VIII

Certain Web site design techniques are actually detrimental to search engine rankings, such as JavaScript, frames, and image maps. If your site is database driven, you're also running up against a brick wall when it comes to getting top rankings for your site. Section VIII outlines various factors that can present problems with your rankings, and it offers advice on getting around those problems.

Chapter 19

Frames, JavaScript, Tables, and Image Maps

When you begin to position a new Web site, the page often uses certain techniques that can present ranking problems. So, you need to realize that you have a few strikes against you at the beginning of the game. You'll need to work hard at evening the playing field by incorporating techniques that will allow you to compete, and by understanding and incorporating various workarounds for some of the more detrimental techniques.

After all, you need every edge over the competition that you can get, especially if the page uses techniques that can present problems.

Let's Begin with Frames

Fact: Older browsers, search engines, and Web surfers have problems with frames.

- Older browsers can see only the frameset page, and they aren't able to put the various framed pages together to create the actual site. So, surfers that use older browsers aren't able to see the real site, but only one page that often contains no content whatsoever.
- Search engines have the same problem. They can view the frameset page, but they can't put the framed pages together. The only page that they have to index is the frameset page, which often contains no content that is indexable.
- Web surfers are busy people. They don't like getting caught in someone else's frames, to where the URL in the browser window remains on the framed page, and all pages that are visited from that point on are viewed from within that framed page. It's difficult to bookmark a page, and it's quite frustrating.

Fact: Only extremely complex Web sites need to use frames.

Fact: Very few top-ten ranked sites use frames. Keep that in mind. It's quite difficult to get a framed site into the top-ten rankings.

Fact: Frames increase the file size and the total number of words that make up a Web site. Therefore, they also decrease the overall keyword weight, which can put you at a disadvantage to your competition.

> You'll need to work hard at evening the playing field by incorporating techniques that will allow you to compete, and by understanding and incorporating various workarounds for some of the more detrimental techniques.
>
> After all, you need every edge over the competition that you can get, especially if the page uses techniques that can present problems.

What *Are* Frames?

Have you ever been to a site where the site is split into different sections? One section might be the navigational area of the page; one section might be the title of the site and other standard information; and one section might be the actual content of the page. Those are frames.

What happens is, a visitor clicks on one of the links in the navigational section, and a new page is opened in the content area of the page. The navigational and title frames remain the same, but the content area changes depending on the link you choose.

Every time you click on another link, that page is shown in the content area of the page.

Spiders Can't Read Frames

As mentioned before, many of the search engines' spiders can't read frames. They can read only the contents of the <noframes> tag. The text in the <noframes> tag is often instructions to the readers that they need a frames-capable browser to view the site properly.

Obviously, this type of information on your page does nothing to help you get a better ranking in the search engines.

Is there a way to solve the problem besides not using frames at all? Yes, but remember that as a general rule, only very large, complex sites truly need frames.

If you're working with a framed site, for the benefit of the search engines, you'll need to create an alternative Web page within the <noframes> tag so that the search engines have something to index and so your page can compete in the rankings.

How Do You Create a Page Using the <noframes> Tag?

The frameset page is the master page that actually contains instructions to the browsers on how to put the framed pages together. Because the search engines can see only the frameset page, you'll

---

Extra Hints and Tips

To "break out" of someone's framed page, right click on the page itself. Choose the Open New Window command. The browser will open the new page in another window, and you can close the framed page.

need to use a <noframes> tag on that page in order to give the engines what they need to index your page.

How do you know if a page is a "frameset" page? Frameset pages contain the <frameset> tag. This tag is beneath the <head> section of your Web page. The tag defines the other pages that are used in the framed site.

Under the <frameset> tag, you'll need to add a <noframes> tag. Then, include a <body> tag. Include headline tags and body text as well as links to other areas of your site, including a link back to your home page. In fact, it's very important to add links because the engine won't be able to crawl past the frameset page if you don't put links in the <noframes> area.

On the frameset page, you'll need to add an effective title. For the engines that consider the content of META description and keyword tags, use them. In other words, you'll optimize the page just as you do all other pages, but you'll have to be sure to create text in the <noframes> tag for the benefit of the engines.

An Example of a <noframes> Tag

<noframes>
<body>
<h2> Educational Children's Software offers Learning under the Guise of Fun! </h2>
<p>Can't get your child to play educational games on your computer? No problem! Our educational children's software is designed to be just plain fun, so that your kids don't even realize they're learning.</p>
<p>Purchase educational children's software in subjects such as foreign languages, math, and English.</p>
<a href="educational-childrens-software.htm"></a>
<a href="sitemap.htm"></a>
<a href="index.html" TARGET = "_top">Home</a>
</body>
</noframes>

When adding a link back to your index page, be sure to use the "top" command. This simply ensures that the frames will be viewed

Extra Hints and Tips

When you build doorway or information pages, try to create those pages without frames. Work on getting those pages ranked high in the engines, and you won't have to rely as heavily on the framed pages to achieve top rankings.

the way they're supposed to be viewed when visitors click on the home link from other pages of your site. (See example above)

Are There Any Advantages to Frames?

Very large Web sites sometimes use frames to make it easier for visitors to navigate through the pages. Again, only very large, complicated Web sites truly need to use frames.

Other than that, there are a few hidden advantages to frames.

Some of the engines, like Excite and HotBot, give boosts in relevancy to sites that contain a lot of links with the keyword in the link text and URLs. However, you may not want to clutter your main page with dozens of links to all the pages. One solution is to hide the links in an area that is normally not viewable, but where the engine will still index it.

Both the body area and the <noframes> area of a page that contains the <frameset> tag are hidden to anybody using a frames-capable browser, which includes almost all recent browsers.

So, the way to use frames to your advantage is to create a Web page to look exactly like you want it to look, then make it a "framed" page. The framed area could be zero columns wide, effectively becoming invisible.

Add links to the rest of your site, and you're using frames to your advantage.

Of course, another way of adding a listing of links to other areas of your site is to use hidden links on your main page, which keeps you from having to use frames at all.

> Very large Web sites sometimes use frames to make it easier for visitors to navigate through the pages. Again, only very large, complicated Web sites truly need to use frames.

An Additional Use for the <noframes> Tag

Since the engines consider the content of the <noframes> tag, you may want to use the tag even if you're not using frames. Simply add the <noframes> tag to your page, and create a content-rich page using your keyword phrase. In this manner, even if your actual Web page contains little text, you can add content for the benefit of the engines through the <noframes> tag.

> *JavaScript* is an easy-to-use accessory to the Java programming language. JavaScript can be added to HTML pages to create interactive documents. JavaScript is often used in the creation of interactive Web-based forms.

JavaScript: Another Ranking Problem Culprit

We've discussed how important it is to have all of your keyword-containing tags and text toward the top of the page in order to increase the keyword's prominence, thereby increasing the page's relevancy to that keyword.

Any techniques that push important keyword-containing text farther down on the page can present ranking problems.

Java or JavaScript are such culprits.

What *Is* Java or JavaScript?

Java is a programming language for adding animation and other action to Web sites.

JavaScript is an easy-to-use accessory to the Java programming language. JavaScript can be added to HTML pages to create interactive documents. JavaScript is often used in the creation of interactive Web-based forms.

Workarounds for Java

Some Java is very short and probably won't affect your ranking. But some JavaScript is extremely long, and you have to scroll through several pages of script in the source code to get to the "meat" of the site. Remember that if *you* have to scroll through several pages of script, so does the engine.

Your goal is to put all keyword-containing tags and text at the top of your page in a place of prominence.

When possible, put Java toward the bottom of the page if it's particularly long. If the Java is long, you'll need to create content-rich doorway or information pages for your keyword phrases and bring in traffic through those pages.

How Can You Recognize JavaScript?

Simply look for this tag:
<SCRIPT LANGUAGE="Javascript">
Actual script goes here
</SCRIPT>

On your own page, to determine whether Java might present ranking problems, simply view the source code of your page from your browser. If you have to scroll through page after page of Java, you'll more than likely encounter ranking problems with the page.

An Example of JavaScript

To see an example of JavaScript, visit Search Engine Watch's search page:

searchenginewatch.com/search.html

View the source code, and scroll down until you see this tag:
<script language="JavaScript">

Another Solution for Java

Another solution for Java is to remove the majority of the JavaScript code completely off your pages and into a separate file. By doing so, you will reduce the amount of code in your Web pages, which will boost your relevancy and lead to better search engine rankings. It will also allow you to reuse the code on other pages without duplicating it over and over again.

How can you do this? By placing the code in an external .js file.

By doing so, you will be able to reduce the page size for the search engines, which will help your rankings, and you will be able to modify the JavaScript without changing the date of the Web page, which is an important consideration for engines like AltaVista and GO that give older pages boosts in relevancy.

> ### Need More Info?
>
> For more information as well as an example of a framed page, visit Search Engines and Frames at Search Engine Watch:
>
> *searchenginewatch.com/webmasters/ frames.html*

To do this, any JavaScript code that you would normally place in the <head> section of your Web page can be placed into a separate .js file. This file should contain only your JavaScript code, with no other HTML codes. You can reference it like this in the <head> section of your page:

<Script language-"JavaScript" src="namethisfile.js">
</Script>

When the browser loads the page, it will follow the link to get to the JavaScript code. Keep in mind that some servers may not recognize the .js file type, so experiment on your server to see if it works for you. In order to use the method successfully, your server must be set to map .js files to the MIME type application/x-javascript.

> Tables can "push" your text farther down the page, making keywords less relevant because they appear lower on the page.

Tables Can Present Ranking Problems, Too

Tables can "push" your text farther down the page, making keywords less relevant because they appear lower on the page. Further, tables break apart when search engines read them.

Tables don't present the ranking problems that Java or frames do, but it's still important to understand that they can be an obstacle to a top ranking.

What *Are* Tables?

Tables are used to create columns of text and to divide a Web page into logical sections. Most Web sites use tables because they make the design of the page clean and professional looking.

An Example of Tables

For an example of a page that uses tables, visit the TechEncyclopedia, which is an excellent site for learning the definition of various technology-related terms:

www.techweb.com/encyclopedia/

View the source code, and scroll until you see this tag:
<table border="0" cellpadding="0" cellspacing="0" width="600" align="top">

Looking at the page itself, do you see the sections of the page? On one side is a blue bar with a search box in it. In the center of the page are two columns of text. Those sections and columns are tables.

Workarounds for Tables

One of the main problems with tables is that you often don't use your important keyword phrase in the tables. Instead, the keyword-containing text is farther down on the page underneath the tables.

If you use tables, be sure to include your keyword phrase in the tables themselves.

Consider creating doorway or information pages that don't use tables.

Additional Tip for Tables

Tables across the left-hand side of the page or the top of the page are listed before the body text in the page's HTML. But tables across the right-hand side of the page are listed after the page's body text.

If you're using a lot of tables on your page, and if you're having ranking problems, consider moving your table from the left side of the page to the right. It will push your important body text toward the top of the page.

Make sure the table's width is within common boundaries so that the navigation bar is sure to be seen no matter what width of screen the viewer is using.

Some Web designers feel that a navigation bar on the right is actually clicked on more, possibly because it's closer to the scroll bar. Other designers feel that users are more accustomed to navigation bars on the left.

> If you're using a lot of tables on your page, and if you're having ranking problems, consider moving your table from the left side of the page to the right.

Another helpful solution to solving ranking problems due to tables is to create tables within tables. By doing so, you can keep your relevant keyword phrases early in the body of your page.

To accomplish this, you'll want to treat the entire page as a table, then build tables within the master table, isolating sections of your page. Make your first table within the master table appear above your navigation bar on the left side of the page and include your keywords in that table. That way, your important keyword phrases will appear at the top of the body.

Notes About Image Maps

Have you ever been to a site where you click on various areas of a picture to be taken farther into the site? Those sites use "image maps" for navigation.

What *Is* an Image Map?

An image map is a picture that is logically separated into different areas. You can click on any of those areas to be taken to a different page.

An easy to visualize example of an image map is to consider a map of the world. You could click on Australia, and you'd be taken to a page about Australia. Clicking on Israel would take you to Israel's page. Click on the United States, and you'd be taken to that page. This would be an image map.

An Example of an Image Map

Visit Concierge.com and view the world map:

www.concierge.com/cgi-bin/maps.cgi?link=intro

Click on any area of the map, and you'll be taken to a different page relative to that area.

Need More Info?

Visit HTML Goodies and click on Tutorials, then Tables, for a tutorial on creating tables within tables. In fact, the entire HTML Goodies Web site is excellent:

www.htmlgoodies.com/tutors/tbl.html

Need More Info?

ZDNet also offers a helpful tutorial about using tables:

www.zdnet.com/devhead/stories/ articles/0,4413,1600358,00.html

---

Now, view the source code of the page. Scroll down the page until you see this tag:

<map NAME="map">

The Problem with Image Maps

If image maps are used toward the top of the page, they can push important keyword-containing text farther down on the page.

But another problem with image maps is that the engine can't read or index the links contained in the maps.

Therefore, when using image maps, be sure to include HTML links to all important areas of your site on your page. Those HTML links can be hidden or visible links. By including the HTML links, you're giving the engine something to spider, and the engine will go through other pages of your site and, let's hope, index them.

Or instead of using links, use a site map, and link to the site map from your main page.

When using image maps, be sure to include HTML links to all important areas of your site on your page.

For more information on this topic, visit our Web site at www.businesstown.com

Chapter 20

Dynamically Delivered Pages and Redirections

Dynamically Delivered Pages

Some Web pages are created "on the fly," which means that they're created at that very point in time based on variables identified by a server at that exact moment. This is in contrast to *static* pages that are created ahead of time and simply accessed. The pages created on the fly are called *dynamic* pages because they change constantly depending on who is accessing it and other variables.

Dynamically delivered pages, such as those generated through database programs commonly used by e-commerce and subscriber-only pages, cause several problems for the search engines. For one thing, since the content of the pages changes constantly, there is no consistent content for the engines to index. Further, these pages are essentially invisible to the search engines because most dynamic pages use the ? or a % in the URL, which is where the true problems lie.

Avoid symbols in your URLs, especially the ? symbol. Search engines don't interpret symbols well. Symbols that engines have a difficult time reading include ?, &, %, +, and $.

Symbols in URLs

Avoid symbols in your URLs, especially the ? symbol. Search engines don't interpret symbols well. Symbols that engines have a difficult time reading include ?, &, %, +, and $.

A symbol such as a ? in a URL is like a stop sign to a search engine. The indexing spider stops and won't read past the symbol because they've been programmed to avoid "spider traps." These can occur when a database inadvertently feeds a spider a countless number of URLs, bogging down the spider as it tries to accomplish an impossible task.

Reference to the CGI Bin

URLs that contain a reference to the "CGI bin" also have ranking problems. Again, the engine is trying to keep itself out of a trap where it could be fed a large number of URLs, so it stops indexing when it sees any reference to CGI bin, which commonly occurs in the URLs of dynamically generated pages.

Solution?

One way to work around the problems associated with dynamically generated pages is to create static pages that the engines can safely index and get those pages ranked high in the engines. You could then link these static pages back to your dynamically delivered pages so that visitors could proceed within your site once they discovered it through the search engines.

Further, in some cases, you can still use dynamic pages without using the problematic symbols in your URLs. If you use Apache or Cold Fusion Web server software, both programs offer solutions that allow you to translate URLs containing the ? symbol into engine-friendly addresses.

If you have dynamically generated pages that are generated without special parameters in the URL and without giving any indication that the server is generating them on the fly, you should be able to get the pages indexed. Monitor their performance closely and make adjustments when necessary.

How Can You Tell if Your Page Will Be Able to Be Indexed?

Submit it to a few of the engines and see if you get a message that says that the page can't be indexed. Try deleting everything in the URL from the ? on, and then try to reload the page. If it doesn't work, you'll need a workaround. For example:

www.yourwebpage.com/page?=9843.html

Change it to read:
www.yourwebpage.com/page

Reload the page and see if it works. If it doesn't, you'll need to create static pages for your site.

Need More Info?

A Users Guide to URL Rewriting with the Apache Webserver:

www.engelschall.com/pw/apache/ rewriteguide

What About .asp, .cfm, .shtml, or .pl Pages?

With the exception of pages containing ?'s or a reference to the CGI bin in the URL, the major engines don't have problems indexing active server pages (.asp), Cold Fusion pages (.cfm), or server side includes (.shtml).

Some of the engines have a difficult time with Perl pages (.pl), so avoid them with HotBot or GO/InfoSeek.

Added Note

See the AltaVista chapter, Chapter 23, about reference to dynamic content and keeping the last modified date as "old" as possible.

Redirections

As we've stated elsewhere in this book, most of the engines frown upon *any* redirection, such as META refresh tags and "bait and switch." However, many Web designers have legitimate reasons for wanting to use redirections that have nothing to do with trying to trick the engines or the Web viewers. Of course, the problem here is that you can't "reason" with a search engine spider.

Most of the engines don't have a problem with the use of doorway pages, if they link (not redirect) to relevant material. Yet, Web designers often want to use a redirect to make it easier on the visitors to get into the site. Their concern is that if you make it necessary for your visitors to click too many times, and you may lose them.

Professional Web optimizer Ginette Degner reports that a META refresh can cost ranking if it is under thirty seconds. This is particularly true with AltaVista and GO/InfoSeek. She suggests using JavaScript because it runs faster and is easier to slip by the robots. As she pointed out, there is only one use for a META refresh tag, but there are numerous uses for JavaScript. Java doesn't send up a red flag as META refresh tags do.

> Most of the engines don't have a problem with the use of doorway pages, if they link (not redirect) to relevant material. Yet, Web designers often want to use a redirect to make it easier on the visitors to get into the site. Their concern is that if you make it necessary for your visitors to click too many times, and you may lose them.

Ginette believes that scripts can be useful tools and do have their place. Used with care and good reason, they will continue to be useful tools, but abuse them and all forms of scripts will be suspect to the spiders.

What *Is* a Redirection?

Have you ever clicked on a URL to visit a Web site, but the actual URL where you ended up was different from the one you clicked on? If so, you have been redirected to a different page. If the redirect tag is very fast, you may not even realize that you've been redirected. Or you may find yourself on one page that tells you that you'll be taken to a different page within so many seconds. After that point, you're taken to the new page.

Redirections have gotten a bad name because unsavory Web designers have abused them. For example, a Web designer might copy a top-ranking Web page and put it up on his or her own server. Then, the designer might use a lightning-fast META refresh tag, so the visitors would never see the first page. This way, the designer would have the benefits of a top-ranking page, without getting into trouble for copying a Web page. This is called "bait and switch" because you're baiting the engine with a top-ranking page, then switching the Web surfer to a different page.

However, the engines have gotten wise to this tactic. They often won't index a page that uses a META refresh tag. Further, lawsuits are springing up everywhere against people who have copied Web pages, so this is definitely a tactic to be avoided at all cost.

> When you click on a URL to visit a Web site, but the actual URL where you ended up was different from the one you clicked on, you have been redirected to a different page.

Example of a Java Redirect

```
<script language="javascript">
window.location.href="yourwebpage.com/";
//–>
</script>
```

Example of a Java Redirect with Back Button Working

The following code, compliments of John Heard of Planet Ocean, combines JavaScript with a META refresh tag. It is designed to redirect users to a different page or site without trapping them on your page.

Need More Info?

Visit this site for an example of a script-based toy, Spider Trap:

www.spider-trap.com/trap.html

```
<html>
<head>
<SCRIPT language="JavaScript1.1">
<!–location.replace(http://www.domain.com"); //–>
</SCRIPT>
<NOSCRIPT>
<META HTTP-EQUIV="REFRESH" CONTENT="5;
URL=www.domain.com">
</NOSCRIPT>
<title>Title of page</title>
</head>
```

Please note that the META refresh tag may cause the page with that code not to be indexed. If the page with the code is to be submitted to a search engine, you'll need to leave out the <no script> section. The JavaScript by itself will get indexed just fine.

Example of a META Refresh Tag

```
<HEAD>
<META HTTP-EQUIV="refresh" content="30;URL=bulldogs-
index.html">
<TITLE>ENGLISH BULLDOGS</TITLE>
<META Name="description" content="English bulldogs can make
your life a little happier.">
</HEAD>
```

Special Note About META Refresh Tags

If you use a META refresh tag within a page, GO/InfoSeek will try to index the targeted page, not the page you submit to the engine. So keep that in mind.

Also Keep This in Mind!

Remember that redirection of any kind is frowned upon by the engines; use it only if you have a legitimate reason (not including getting a top ranking!).

Viewing the Source Code of a Refresh Page

Want to view the source code of a refresh page, but the refresh tag is too fast?

Here's the solution!

Prefix the page's name in the browser window with "view-source," as in this example:

view-source:www2.netdoor.com/~smslady

(The above page utilizes a META refresh tag.)

This technique works in both Netscape and Internet Explorer and works for any page, whether it contains a redirect or not.

> Remember that redirection of any kind is frowned upon by the engines; use it only if you have a legitimate reason (not including getting a top ranking!).

Cloaking

Cloaking is a technique that, even if you don't use it yourself, you need to beware of.

What *Is* Cloaking?

Many times, professional Web positioners are presented with a Web site that uses techniques that put them at an automatic disadvantage in the rankings, such as frames, dynamic pages, or techniques such as XML. When the keyword phrase is extremely competitive, it can be a major problem achieving top rankings.

Other times, clients hand a Web positioner their site with the stipulation that they can't make any changes to the pages—they just want top rankings! If you can't optimize a page, there's not much you can do to get a top ranking.

In both cases, a workaround solution is to use cloaking software, also known as "food script." With cloaking, you don't have to optimize the main page of your site. You simply create a simple yet content-rich doorway page for each major engine and get those pages ranked high.

Then, when an engine visits your site, the script detects which engine is visiting by viewing that engine's IP address, and the script immediately "serves" the simple engine-friendly page created specifically for that engine. However, when humans visit the page, they're "served" the beautifully crafted Web page that is using techniques that cause ranking problems.

So, in essence, with cloaking you have unique doorway pages created for each major engine, and when that engine's spider visits your site, it sees only the page created just for it.

> With cloaking you have unique doorway pages created for each major engine, and when that engine's spider visits your site, it sees only the page created just for it.

Cloaking to Protect Your Valuable Code!

Another use for cloaking software is to protect your valuable code from people who might steal it in an effort to take over your top rankings. Just as cloaking can keep spiders from seeing coding meant for others, it can also keep the wrong human visitors from seeing that coding. If you've worked hard on your site and achieved top rankings, the last thing you want is for someone to come along, steal your code, and boot you out of the rankings. Cloaking will prevent that from happening.

Is Cloaking Legitimate?

In the past, cloaking was considered a "no-no" with the engines, but that has changed to some extent. Now, cloaked pages are finding success at the major engines.

Here's what John Heard, of Beyond Engineering and Planet Ocean, says:

> We've used the software at every major search engine in the U.S. with very good success since 1996, and none of our clients have ever gotten a site/page/domain banned because of the software. But again, we haven't used misleading pages or content either. If you're not misleading or causing problems for anyone, it appears the engines take a "don't ask, don't tell" policy with it. There are no automated systems to detect a cloaked page built correctly.
>
> However, part of the problem with cloaking is that cloaking is a rather aggressive form of search engine positioning, and all aggressive forms can be subject to scrutiny. If you use cloaking, make sure that you follow the guidelines presented in this book and at the individual engines, and don't do anything that could be considered suspect.

When asked how the engines feel about cloaking, Heard replied:

> In general, they don't believe it has widespread enough usage to warrant any special attention. However, they do not like any promotion techniques that misrepresent the content of the site. That's the number-one rule, and they will enforce it whenever possible. If you abuse that rule, you do run the risk of getting banned on any search engine, regardless of whether you're using cloaking technology or not.

In the past, cloaking was considered a "no-no" with the engines, but that has changed to some extent.

How Often Is Cloaking Used?

Do most professional Web positioners use cloaking? No, says colleague Ginette Degner. However, says Ginette, "It is a valid solution to problems that can't be solved elsewhere."

However, because cloaking is a relative newcomer to the field of search positioning and, therefore, hasn't a long track record with the engines, she recommends it only to clients who are in highly competitive areas or for sites using technology like XML or JHTM (Java within Hypertext Markup Language). In the latter cases, there's no way that the engine is going to get past the ? in the URL.

Most professional Web positioners do not use cloaking.

Since No Surfers Will See the Site, Can You Get Away with Spamming?

No! A main reason for not spamming is to stay out of trouble with the engines. If you use spamming techniques on cloaked pages, you're presenting those pages to the very entities that can kick you out of the index!

As stressed by John Heard:

Copying someone else's page and "cloaking it" is a big mistake. The company you copied the page from will very likely find that you've copied the page because your pages show up for a "unique" word that was in the page content. If and when they find it, they will likely complain to the search engine, and they will very likely ban your site because of it. There are also copyright and trademark issues, etc. So if you use cloaking, don't expect it to work with stolen pages or content. Sooner or later, you will get caught.

Simply put, the cloaked pages use all the aboveboard techniques that have been discussed in this book. The main difference is that you're not limited to having a "well-designed page" complete with graphics and fancy HTML. Cloaked pages should be very simple, content-rich pages that give the engines exactly what they want to see in order to boost your page's relevancy.

As with all of your other pages, don't do anything that could get you in trouble with the engines. It's just not worth it.

Can You Tell if a Page Has Been Cloaked?

In some cases, yes.

One good indication is when the title and description of the page are different from what appears in the search results, or the size of the page is different.

But as Ginette pointed out, instead of spending your valuable time trying to figure out if a page has been cloaked, simply build a better page.

More from the Experts

An interview with John Heard of Beyond Engineering and Planet Ocean:

Could you explain why it's so important for the cloaking script to be updated constantly, since the updates are obviously exceedingly valuable?

Search engines oftentimes change their spiders IP addresses due to expansion or changes in their systems. If the person is using an industrial strength cloaking software, they depend on these IP addresses to help identify and process the pages correctly for each search engine. If the IP addresses aren't updated often, the user runs the risk of sending the wrong pages to the engines.

What trends do you see in the future for cloaking?

I believe we're going to see worldwide support for international search engines of importance. Also, we're getting more requests to include features such as delivering different Web pages for users in different countries. Another common request is the ability to sense the speed of the user's connection so that cloaking software can deliver the user to a high bandwidth,

---

Extra Hints and Tips

You can also use cloak check to see if a page has been cloaked. (Note: This tool will work with simple "user-agent" cloaking systems. IP-based cloaking systems cannot be viewed with this or any other tool.)

CloakCheck:
se.make-it-online.com

Need More Info

IP Delivery Is an example of cloaking software:

www.ip-delivery.com

> Cloaking won't get you the rankings. You get the rankings by your own blood, sweat, and tears.

regular bandwidth, or very low bandwidth (PDA). I expect the cloaking software to warp into something similar to a personalization system that includes search engine robots, shopping bots, etc.

In Conclusion

Remember that before cloaking can "do its stuff," you have to get the page ranked high in the engines. Cloaking won't get you the rankings. You get the rankings by your own blood, sweat, and tears.

For more information on this topic, visit our Web site at www.businesstown.com

Other Techniques You May Want to Learn

Overview of Section IX

Once you've achieved the level of traffic you want for your online business, how can you further leverage that traffic for increased success? Do you understand which engines are sending you traffic and which keywords visitors are using to find your site? What are the demographics of your visitors? How long are they staying? Where are you losing them? Section IX discusses the importance of studying your log files, and it also outlines how you can keep spiders out of certain pages of your site.

CHAPTER 21 READ YOUR LOG FILES!
CHAPTER 22 KEEPING YOUR WEB PAGE SPIDER-FREE!

Chapter 21

Read Your Log Files!

The best source of information about who's visiting your Web site and how they found you can be learned from your "referrer" log files.

What *Are* Referrer Logs?

Referrer logs, which are also called "common C" logs, help you study traffic to your site. You can learn which engines have sent you traffic, what keyword phrases were used to find your site, which pages are accessed the most or least, the geographic location of your visitors, what type of technology they're using, and much more. You can see why log files can be a gold mine to savvy Web designers and marketers.

Most Internet Service Providers (ISPs) provide referrer logs, so you need to ask yours to provide this information in extended log format. If they don't provide referrer logs, you're missing out on some extremely valuable information about your Web site, and it may even be time for you to switch ISPs.

If your provider captures referrer information, you may want to get a program to read it since the information can be a little difficult to decipher. We've provided URLs to a few software programs later in this chapter.

Why would you care where your traffic comes from?

For one thing, if you know that the majority of your traffic comes from one particular engine, you may want to consider beefing up keyword visibility in that engine by creating additional content-rich doorway pages specifically for that engine.

Or if you know that you're getting no traffic at all from an engine, you'll want to rethink your strategies and create some new pages in order to pull in that traffic. You also may find that you're getting traffic from a keyword you hadn't expected to perform so well. If this is the case, you certainly want to know about it so that you don't make changes that will knock this keyword out of commission.

Further, many Internet users are accessing the Web through older browsers. If you're using technology that isn't accessible in older browsers, you'll want to know what percentage of your visitors

> You can learn which engines have sent you traffic, what keyword phrases were used to find your site, which pages are accessed the most or least, the geographic location of your visitors, what type of technology they're using, and much more.

aren't able to experience the full scope of your Web site. This can have a measurable impact on the financial viability of your site.

What else can you learn through referrer logs?

Although each log program is different, the information that follows will give you a good idea of what is generally available through a referrer log:

- User profile by region, which will also let you know if you're getting any international traffic
- Average length of time someone remains on your site
- Average number of hits or page views per day
- Most and least requested pages
- Top entry page
- Summary of activity by day
- Server errors
- Bandwidth, which is the measure (in kilobytes of data transferred) of the traffic on the site
- Top referring sites
- Top search engines
- Top search keywords
- Visiting spiders

Let's Analyze a Log Entry

Here is an example of some raw data from a referrer log:

208.219.77.29 - - [08/Nov/1999:17:03:36 -0800] "GET /index.htm HTTP/1.0" 200 6923 "http://www.altavista.digital.com/cgi-bin/query? pg=aq&text=yes&d0=1%2fnov %2f99&q=online+marketing%2a
+AND+online marketing%2a&stq=30" "Mozilla/2.0 (compatible; MSIE 4.0; SK; Windows 98)"

As you can see, the raw data is a little confusing, which is why many people use a software program that analyzes the data for them and places it into an easy-to-understand format.

Need More Info?

Read "There's gold in them there log files!" by Charlie Morris of the Web Developer's Virtual Library:

www.wdvl.com/Internet/Management

So what on earth does the raw data mean?
Let's take it apart to find out.

208.219.77.29

The IP address of the visitor to your site, which identifies the visitor's ISP. Think about the ramifications of this for a moment: do you see how your visit to a Web site leaves your footprints in the log file?

> The most important thing of all, however, is simply to compare a site's traffic from month to month, to measure how well your promotional efforts are working.

08/Nov/1999:17:03:36 -0800

The date and time of the visit

"GET /index.htm HTTP/1.0"

The first file requested, which is the index page in the example. However, it might be a graphic file instead of an HTML page.

200 6923

"200" means that the request was completed. "6923" refers to the number of bytes that were transferred.

"http://www.altavista.digital.com/cgi-bin/query?
pg=aq&text=yes&d0=1%2fnov %2f99&q=online+marketing%2a

+AND+online marketing%2a&stq=30"

This is probably the most important area of the raw data because it tells you where the visitor came from. If the visitor came from another Web site, that URL will be listed. In this case, the visitor came from the AltaVista search engine. Notice that the keywords used to find your site are also indicated: online marketing.

"Mozilla/2.0 (compatible; MSIE 4.0; SK; Windows 98)"

This section shows the browser of the visitor, which in our example, is Microsoft Internet Explorer 4.0. It also indicates the operating system, which is Windows 98. If you're using technology that can only be used fully with later browsers, this area will be quite valuable to you since it will inform you of how many visitors are using older browsers.

Again, using a software program to analyze the data will make it much easier for you to review. Most of the programs offer charts and graphs that you can review at a glance.

Helpful Software Programs and Web-Based Services

Your provider may provide a referrer log program for you, or you can download programs like:

FlashStats:
maximized.com/products/flashstats

WebTrends:
www.webtrends.com

Funnel Web:
ctcr.investors.net/funnelweb/Webreport.html

From an Expert:
Comparing a Site's Traffic from Month to Month Is Crucial!

We asked Charlie Morris, managing editor of Web *Developer's Journa*, the following question:

What do you consider the most valuable part of a referrer log?

The first section of a report that I look at is the list of most popular pages. This is something that's easy to act on—whatever content is most popular, simply produce more of the same sort of thing. The list of 404s should also be one of the first sections to look at, as sometimes (though not always) it's easy to find and fix these errors, greatly improving short-term traffic and your long-term reputation. The most important thing of all, however, is simply to compare a site's traffic from month to month, to measure how well your promotional efforts are working. It's surprising how many sites don't do this carefully.

Extra Hints and Tips

How about a free referrer log program? eXTReMe Tracking offers a "free" referrer log that will provide the information you need about the visitors to your Web site. It features percentages, statistics, totals, and averages—from the simple counting of your visitors to tracking the keywords they used to find you:

www.extreme-dm.com/tracking/?home

Still Need More Info?

Visit Search Engine Watch's SpiderSpotting Chart to learn the names of visiting spiders:

searchenginewatch.internet.com/webmasters/spiderchart.html

Keeping Your Web Page Spider-Free!

Throughout this book, we go into detail on how to get search engine spiders to visit your site and how to achieve top rankings with your pages. However, there may be occasions when you'll want to keep spiders out of your pages, believe it or not. There may be other times when you'll want to let one engine's spider in and keep the others out.

Let's say that you have created a page of personnel policies for your employees. You may not want the engines to find that page during their regular spider runs and index it.

Or let's say that you've created some very engine-specific pages for your main keyword phrases. You may have created eight pages that are optimized for the same keyword phrase but are each optimized for a different engine. You wouldn't want AltaVista, for example, to find your pages for GO and Excite because AltaVista may think you're trying to spam it by having a bunch of pages optimized for the same keyword phrase.

Let's Look at a Couple of Solutions!

Listed below are a couple of ways to keep spiders out of your page.

Robots META Tag

The robots META tag can be used to specify that a particular page not be indexed by any of the search engines. The tag looks like this:

<META NAME="ROBOTS" CONTENT="NOINDEX">

Like all META tags, the robots META should go in the <head> </head> section of your page.

If you use a robots META tag, the engines' spiders will spot the tag and not index the page.

The problem is, not all search engines support this tag. Further, when you use the robots META tag, you're keeping out all spiders from your page, even spiders whose visit could be advantageous to your site.

> You may have created eight pages that are optimized for the same keyword phrase but are each optimized for a different engine. You wouldn't want AltaVista, for example, to find your pages for GO and Excite because AltaVista may think you're trying to spam it by having a bunch of pages optimized for the same keyword phrase.

As an alternative, use the robots.txt tag judiciously to block indexing by particular engines. All the major search engines support the robots.txt convention.

Robots.txt File

By using the robots.txt file, you can allow one engine to index the page and keep all other engines out, or use it for any number of other strategies that you may want to try.

Create a text file with Window's NotePad or any other editor that can save ASCII .txt files. Use the following syntax:

```
User-agent: {SpiderNameHere}
Disallow: /{FilenameHere}
```

For example, if you want to tell AltaVista's spider, named Scooter, not to index files called insurance.html and pricing.html, create a robots.txt file as follows:

```
User-agent: Scooter
Disallow: /insurance.html
Disallow: /pricing.html
```

Upload this robots.txt file to the root directory of your Web site just as you do any of your IITML pages.

Voilà! Scooter will spot the robots.txt file on its next spider run and won't index those two pages. But all the other engines' spiders will index the pages.

You can add more lines to exclude pages from other engines by specifying the User-Agent parameter again in the same file, followed by more disallow lines. Each disallow statement will be applied to the last User-Agent that was specified. For example:

```
User-agent: Scooter
isallow: /insurance.html
Disallow: /pricing.html
```

> By using the robots.txt file, you can allow one engine to index the page and keep all other engines out, or use it for any number of other strategies that you may want to try.

User-agent: Gulliver
Disallow: /deadlines.html
Disallow: /agents.html

User-agent: Slurp
Disallow: /life-policies.html
Disallow: /automobile-policies.html

In the preceding example, AltaVista's Scooter wouldn't index insurance.html and pricing.html. Northern Light's Gulliver wouldn't index deadlines.html and agents.html, and HotBot's Slurp wouldn't index life-policies.html and automobile-policies.html.

If you want to exclude an entire directory, use this syntax:

User-agent: Scooter
Disallow: /myowndirectory/*

Other Options for the robots.txt File

Other options are to exclude the page from all spiders with:

User-agent: *
Or to disallow all pages on your Web site for the specified spider use:
Disallow: /*

Word of Caution

Make sure you use the proper syntax. If you misspell something or have a typing error, this technique will not work, and you may never know it. Further, don't put anything else on the page besides the robots.txt information. A colleague added a title to the page, and the engine didn't honor the robots.txt page until he removed the title.

> For engines like GO/InfoSeek and AltaVista that seem to assign more relevancy to "older" Web pages that have been in their index for a while, you can keep nefarious competitors from resubmitting your nicely aged pages by adding a <noindex> tag to your pages.

Names of the Spiders!

Here are the User-Agent names of some of the more popular search engine spiders:

SEARCH ENGINE	ROBOT USER-AGENT
AltaVista	Scooter
GO/InfoSeek	Sidewinder
Excite	ArchitextSpider
Lycos	Lycos_Spider_(T-Rex)
Northern Light	Gulliver
HotBot	Slurp

The following site will analyze your robots.txt file and will report any syntax errors—free!

www.tardis.ed.ac.uk/~sxw/robots//check

Added Use of the <noindex> robots META Tag

For engines like GO/InfoSeek and AltaVista that seem to assign more relevancy to "older" Web pages that have been in their index for a while, you can keep nefarious competitors from resubmitting your nicely aged pages by adding a <noindex> tag to your pages. This will prevent the engines from reindexing the pages.

The next time you want to resubmit the page yourself, you'll need to remove the tag.

Other Parameters for the robots META Tag?

You may have seen other types of robots META tags, such as:
<META NAME="robots" CONTENT="all">
or
<META NAME="robots" CONTENT="index">
or even
<META NAME="robots" CONTENT="follow">

Extra Hints and Tips

Visit Search Engine Watch's Spider Spotting Chart: Robot Agent and Host Names, for more information:

searchenginewatch.internet.com/ webmasters/spiderchart.html

Need More Info?

Read the Robots Exclusion at this Web site:

info.webcrawler.com/mak/projects/robots/ exclusion.html/

The purpose of the "all" parameter is to allow all the files to be indexed. "Index" indicates that the page may be indexed by the spider. "Follow" means that the spider is free to visit all links and index them.

In fact, the robots META tag can be used in all these possible ways:

<META NAME="robots" CONTENT="all | none | index | noindex | follow | nofollow">

So, if you use the "follow" parameter, are you assured that the engine will visit all links off that page? If you don't use the tag, does this mean that the engine won't follow your links?

No on both counts!

The engine will spider links by default, so the "follow" tag isn't necessary. Unless you include a "noindex" tag, the page will be indexed by the spider, and you don't have to use an "index" tag.

On the other hand, you might have need of the "nofollow" tag, if you want the page itself to be indexed but none of the links to be followed. "None" would tell the spider not to index any files and not to follow the links on the page to other pages.

As we mentioned in Chapter 18, use all important META tags, but don't use any that aren't necessary. They can cause confusion with the engines.

> As we mentioned in Chapter 18, use all important META tags, but don't use any that aren't necessary. They can cause confusion with the engines.

For more information on this topic, visit our Web site at www.businesstown.com

Meet the Search Engines

Overview of Section X

How can you create pages that AltaVista will consider highly relevant? What search engines does the Open Directory Project supply results to? How can you get the fabulous Yahoo! to index your site? In this section, you'll learn tips and specific strategies for each of the major search engines and directories, and you'll learn how the engines and directories are related in order to give you the most mileage from your submissions.

AltaVista, Ask Jeeves, and LookSmart

T hese three engines are grouped together in this chapter because of their interrelationships: Ask Jeeves provides the "natural language" results to AltaVista, and LookSmart contributes directory information to AltaVista's search results. Another important facet of AltaVista is its connection to RealNames, which we discuss in detail in Chapter 31, and its connection to the Open Directory Project, which we discuss in Chapter 28.

Do not rely on your site's appearance in the ODP for your AltaVista exposure. Instead, work hard for prominence in the AltaVista search engine because many more people search via the search box of any engine rather than "drilling down" through the directory categories.

> Though Yahoo! is the most popular directory, AltaVista is the most popular search engine.

AltaVista

altavista.com

Though Yahoo! is the most popular *directory*, AltaVista is the most popular *search engine*. According to StatMarket.com, AltaVista in 1999 was responsible for 11.18 percent of search engine referrals. With over 250 million Web pages indexed, AltaVista accommodates over 20 million searches per day.

Founded in 1995, AltaVista was one of the first Internet search services, and it has consistently been one of the most popular. AltaVista now functions as a full-fledged portal, catering on its home page to the human impulses of curiosity (search services), greed (comparison shopping services), and the need for being part of and understanding our community (AltaVista Live). In January 1999, AltaVista was acquired by Compaq Computer Corporation, but later in the year, CMGI acquired 83 percent of its stock, while AltaVista acquired Shopping.com and Zip2 to broaden its offerings.

How AltaVista Works: "Who's Who"

Like many of the largest engines, AltaVista is not a stand-alone engine delivering search results from one database source. Instead, when you run a search at AltaVista, you're presented with results from five sources:

1. *Main search results*, which are matches from AltaVista's Web index built through the efforts of Scooter, AltaVista's Web crawler
2. *Ask AltaVista a Question*, which is powered by Ask Jeeves
3. *The RealNames system*, where you purchase a "real name," which is then matched to your Web site during searches
4. *The LookSmart directory*, which provides directory results under AltaVista recommends at the top of the page
5. *The Open Directory Project*, which provides directory results in the category listing under the search results

Getting ranked well in each of these contributing sources will significantly improve your Web site traffic from AltaVista. Detailed information about these AltaVista contributors will be discussed later in the chapter, information on RealNames is covered in Chapter 31, and ODP information is covered in Chapter 28.

AltaVista also has a link within some search result listings to Company Fact Sheets, which are being produced by iAtlas, a company now owned by AltaVista.

In the past, AltaVista experimented with paid listings, giving top results in search returns to sites that had subscribed for certain keywords. At this writing, that option is no longer available.

How Does AltaVista's Spider Work?

About a month after you submit your Web page to AltaVista, Scooter, AltaVista's spider, will visit your site and search for other pages to add to the index. Every four to six weeks after that, the crawler will return to check for changes and new pages. Generally speaking, AltaVista will index submitted pages in one to three days and nonsubmitted pages within one month.

> Founded in 1995, AltaVista was one of the first Internet search services, and it has consistently been one of the most popular. AltaVista now functions as a full-fledged portal.

Submission Guidelines and Tips from AltaVista

In the following section, we're pasting in (in bold) the most recent information available from the AltaVista Web site regarding AltaVista's submission guidelines and tips. However, when you're ready to complete your online submission form, you should go to *www.altavista.com/cgi-bin/query?pg=addurl* to see if any changes have occurred after this book's publication date that may affect your submission. Our comments about AltaVista's guidelines are printed in nonbold type.

Direct from AltaVista
ADD/REMOVE A URL

> Direct submissions of interior or doorway pages sometimes don't make it into the index and take much longer to get indexed.

- **To have your Web page listed with AltaVista, submit the URL (Web address) to us using the form at the bottom of this page.**
  At the time of the writing of this book, AltaVista had begun to prefer submissions of your main or index page only. Direct submissions of interior or doorway pages sometimes don't make it into the index and take much longer to get indexed. Therefore, it's crucial to add hidden links to all important pages of your site on your main page, or create a site map and link from the main page to the site map. The spider will crawl the main page, find your links to other pages, and index those pages. If you want to try to submit your other pages separately, only submit one page per domain per day. If you use free Web space or share a domain with other sites (Geocities, etc.), you may not get indexed if too many people from your domain have submitted sites that day.
- **Once the URL is verified, it is added to our index. Normally, the page is available for queries in less than a day. It sometimes takes two days for a page to be indexed on our mirror sites.**
  Keep in mind, however, that AltaVista, like every other engine, has periods of delay when systems are being upgraded or revised, so it may take longer to appear in the index. It is a good idea to resubmit every week until your site appears in the index. It may take up to a month or more for unsubmitted sites to be indexed by Scooter.
- **Do not submit a description or keywords when you submit the URL. To provide a summary that appears when some-**

one searches for and finds your pages, use META tags
instead.

- **Remember the URLs are case sensitive. Be sure to double-check your spelling.**
Keep a document file open on your desktop containing your
proofread URL, and then cut-and-paste submission information to avoid errors. Further, submit your pages using
"www" and not using "www" in the URL.

- **We also accept URLs through Scott Danister's Submit It!
Service and Net Creations' Postmaster services.**
You can also help users find your page more easily by subscribing to the Real Name System. Real Name uses ordinary
language instead of complicated URLs to identify your homepage. Register your company name, trademarks, brand
names, or slogans.

After submitting to AltaVista by using their Add URL form,
you'll receive a warning message if there were any problems when
trying to index your page. If you don't receive a message, check back
in a day or two to make sure your site has actually been indexed. If it
hasn't, submit it again.

If at any point your Web page disappears from AltaVista's index,
check it carefully to make sure there's nothing on the page that
could be considered spamming. Then, simply resubmit the page.

To Remove a Page or URL from AltaVista

There may come a time when you'll need to remove a page from
AltaVista's index. If you are trying to remove a bad link, just resubmit the URL. When the spider is unable to find the page, it will
remove it from the index.

These days where some engines are allowing submissions of
only the main index, getting *404 File Not Found* pages removed
from the index may be a little tricky. If resubmitting the bad link
doesn't work, try reporting the bad links at this URL:

www.altavista.com/av/content/helpsearch/report_off.shtml

> Keep in mind, however,
> that AltaVista, like every
> other engine, has periods of
> delay when systems are
> being upgraded or revised,
> so it may take longer to
> appear in the index.

If you wish to remove an active page from the index, you'll need to write a robots.txt file for the page and then resubmit it. More information on this can be found in Chapter 22.

How Can You Tell if Your Site Has Been Indexed?

Enter your URL in the search window in one of these ways:

url:yourdomain.com reveals every page under the root domain

url:members.aol.com/yourwebsite narrows the search to pages within your area if you're under someone else's domain

url:members.aol.com/yourwebsite/yourwebpage.htm finds a specific page at your site

Note: Don't use either the "www" prefix or "http://".

More from the AltaVista Site

www.AltaVista.com/cgi-bin/query?pg=addurl

EXCLUDING PAGES WITH META TAGS

It is possible for you to control how your page is indexed by using META tags to specify both additional keywords to index and a short description. Let's suppose your page contains:

<META name="description" content="We specialize in grooming pink poodles.">

<META name="keywords" content="pet grooming, Palo Alto, dog">

AltaVista will then do two things:

• It will index both fields as words, so a search on either poodles or dog will match.

AltaVista may be placing greater weight on pages it spiders than pages submitted to its directory. Since it prefers that you submit only main pages into its index, you need to be sure to create a site map with links to your other pages, and let AltaVista find the rest.

- **It will return the description with the URL. In other words, instead of showing the first couple of lines of the page, a match will look like the following:**

Pink Poodles Inc.
We specialize in grooming pink poodles.
pink.poodle.org/ - size 3k - 29 Feb 96

AltaVista will index the description and keywords up to a limit of 1,024 characters.

What Does AltaVista Consider Relevant When Ranking Web Pages?

AltaVista may be placing greater weight on pages it spiders than pages submitted to its directory. Since it prefers that you submit only main pages into its index, you need to be sure to create a site map with links to your other pages, and let AltaVista find the rest. It may take a little longer for those pages to appear in the index, but they may appear higher up in the rankings, making this technique a reasonable tradeoff. You can also add hidden links to all important pages of your site on the main page and let AltaVista find the links that way.

With AltaVista, it is important where your keywords appear. In their new guidelines, they claim that only two instances of the keyword are considered when determining relevancy. They also say that keywords found in META tags don't count any more than keywords found in the body text.

So, with AltaVista, try not using your important keyword phrase in your META tags. Instead, use your keyword phrase in your title tag and in a headline tag at the very top of the page. From there, continue using your keyword phrase throughout the body text, link text, ALT tags, URLs, and so forth.

AltaVista's new guidelines can be found at this URL:
doc.altavista.com/adv_search/ast_haw_index.shtml

> With AltaVista, try not using your important keyword phrase in your META tags. Instead, use your keyword phrase in your title tag and in a headline tag at the very top of the page.

For this engine, try putting your keyword phrase as the second or third words in the title tag, not the first. AltaVista also checks the proximity of the search terms to one another in the document itself, how many times the search terms appear in the document or tags, and if the search terms appear early and frequently in the document.

As mentioned earlier, keywords found in titles and headings are assigned the greatest importance. Pages generally rank very well if the title and heading (<h1> through <h6>) tags include important keywords and few other words. Try two title tags with this engine, which sometimes is effective.

Since AltaVista uses automatic phrase searching, try using synonyms of your keyword phrase separated by commas in the keyword META tag, but don't use the keyword phrase itself. Note: Many top-ranking sites in AltaVista don't use a keyword META tag at all. If you don't get a good ranking with this engine, take out the keyword tag, resubmit, and see if it helps.

AltaVista doesn't use word stemming, which means that it won't search for variations of a word based on its stem. For example, a search for "marketable" won't include results for "marketing" or "marketability." Plurals are not recognized as being synonymous with singular words, so use the plural form of your keyword phrase as well as the singular form when possible.

Consider naming your image files after your keyword phrase with AltaVista. Since AltaVista now has a multimedia search, you may bring in some traffic by doing so.

With AltaVista, searches are generally, though not always, case sensitive. Use variations of your keywords once–in lowercase, once in capitalized form, and once in all caps if you want your site to be found in that manner. To see if AltaVista is case sensitive to the keyword phrase that you're using, be sure to search for the phrase in all variations and check the results. Keep in mind that most Web searchers search in noncapitalized form, even when searching for proper nouns, like "new orleans," so if you decide to eliminate one of the cases, eliminate capitalization.

AltaVista appears to be using "exact matching" for popular keyword phrases only. This means that searching for a popular keyword phrase using quotation marks and *not* using quotation marks will

> Keep in mind that most Web searchers search in noncapitalized form, even when searching for proper nouns, like "new orleans," so if you decide to eliminate one of the cases, eliminate capitalization.

give you the same results. So, if you want to be found under popular keyword phrases, make sure that the phrase appears on the page in the exact order as the search term.

For keyword phrases that aren't popular, the searches are still nonexact matching, which means that if your page is optimized well for one particular keyword that is part of a keyword phrase, you can possibly achieve a top ranking with that phrase and variations of that phrase.

Are you thinking of setting up a domain? If so, obtaining a domain name with your keyword in it may significantly affect your score on AltaVista. Including the keyword in a subdirectory name or page name can also help, though not as much. Separate multiple words by dashes or underscores, or slashes in the case of subdirectories.

Note that AltaVista won't index a site submitted as an IP address; you must submit the domain name. Here's what a representative from AltaVista said:

> The spider is doing reverse DNS loopups when an IP site is submitted. You must be registered with Internic and have DNS running to be indexed by the spider.

Older Web pages appear to do better than newly submitted pages when the pages appear otherwise equal in relevancy. Therefore, it's best not to change or resubmit pages to AltaVista unless necessary. The good news for new sites is that newly submitted Web pages may eventually go up in ranking with this engine in time without any changes having been made.

AltaVista prefers long pages these days, with around 800 words in the body text. Also try very short pages with the keyword phrase used only once in the title, in the headline tag, and in the body.

Real-Life Stories

A colleague reported that a discussion in one of the search engine forums is suggesting that AltaVista uses at least four databases, each with a slightly different algorithm. If this is true, it could certainly account for inconsistent ranking results.

> Older Web pages appear to do better than newly submitted pages when the pages appear otherwise equal in relevancy. Therefore, it's best not to change or resubmit pages to AltaVista unless necessary.

Your Title Tag and AltaVista

AltaVista prefers short (3 to 5 words), focused title tags with a maximum length of 78 characters, or 12 words. Try to place the keyword as the second or third words in the tag itself. If you don't include a title tag, AltaVista will list "No Title" in the search results–what a terrific opportunity wasted!

Try two title tags with AltaVista. If you use two title tags, be sure to see how they look on the page itself at the top of the browser window. Sometimes, the two title tags will appear to be "run together" across the top of the browser window, which certainly isn't very professional.

For example:

<title>Educational children's software programs.</title>
<title>Educational children's software programs.</title>

might appear like this at the top of the browser window:

Educational children's software programs Educational children's software programs

So, check to see how it actually looks on the page. To get around this potential problem, try putting one <title> tag at the top of the <head> section and one at the bottom. If that doesn't work, consider writing each tag as if it were connected to the other tag, like this:

<title>Educational children's software programs</title>
<title>are education software programs with your child in mind</title>

which could look like this across the top of the browser window:

Educational children's software programs are educational software programs with your child in mind

AltaVista rewards keywords in the <title> tag. If a keyword isn't in that tag, your site will likely not appear near the top of the search results for that keyword phrase.

Also, try using a regular title tag and a META name=content tag like this:

```
<title>Put your title here></title>
<META NAME="title" CONTENT="Put your title here">
```

AltaVista rewards keywords in the <title> tag. If a keyword isn't in that tag, your site will likely not appear near the top of the search results for that keyword phrase.

Don't repeat your keyword phrase in the title tag. This engine seems to penalize sites that repeat a keyword in the same title tag.

Your Description Tag and AltaVista

In search results, AltaVista will display about 150 characters, or about 22 words, for the description of your site. If you use a META description tag, AltaVista will list that information. For added relevancy and to grab the interest of readers, make sure you put synonyms of your keywords in your description tag. If no META description tag exists, AltaVista will take the first text it finds on the page, not including ALT text, to create your site's indexed description. Again, don't use your keyword phrase in your META tags.

Keyword Weight and AltaVista

AltaVista considers keyword weight as a factor in relevancy. Aim for a 5 percent keyword weight with this engine. If your page is not ranking as high as you'd like, study the competition's keyword weight and consider creating pages with varying keyword weight for resubmission.

Frames and AltaVista

AltaVista is one of the few engines that supports frames and image maps. This is not, however, a recommendation that you use frames in your site because frames are a problem with most of the other engines. If you submit an HTML page that uses frameset tags,

> If your page is not ranking as high as you'd like, study the competition's keyword weight and consider creating pages with varying keyword weight for resubmission.

AltaVista will index the title and any text on the page. AltaVista's spider will index the contents within the <noframes> tags just as it would on a nonframes page. You can move the title and META description from the top of the page down to the <noframes> section, and the engine will use them. However, AltaVista probably won't follow the links that are within the framesource.

You can even use the <noframes> tag on a nonframed page to place keyword-studded text, and the engine will "find" and index it. This may be of help to you in tweaking your keyword weight without altering your visible text.

What Does AltaVista Think About Spam?

AltaVista is very aggressive in its determination to reduce spam, thereby increasing relevant results for its users. In fact, it is the first major engine to announce it is identifying and refusing submissions of "machine-generated pages." Here are a few cautionary notes from the AltaVista site:

doc.altavista.com/adv_search/ast_haw_spam.shtml

Some barriers to being indexed are due to the misbehavior of a handful of webmasters who have tried to fool search engines into ranking their pages high on lists of matches and including them as matches to queries they aren't appropriate for. This is one kind of behavior that is known as "spamming." Spamming degrades the value of the index and is a nuisance for all.

The logic that leads people to try such tricks is rather bizarre. "I figure everybody searches for the word 'sex.' I don't have any sex at my site, but I want people to stumble across my site. So I'm going to put the word 'sex,' three thousand times as comments. And any time that anybody searches for 'sex,' my pages will show up first."

People have actually tried that. They have tried doing the same king of thing in the backgrounds of their Web pages. They have also created page after page of text that is in the same color as the background color so visitors won't see the

> Some barriers to being indexed are due to the misbehavior of a handful of webmasters who have tried to fool search engines into ranking their pages high on lists of matches and including them as matches to queries they aren't appropriate for.

words, but search engine crawlers will. They have tried everything imaginable to fool search engines.

If being found via search engines is important to your business, be very careful about where you have your pages hosted. If the hosting service also hosts spammers and pornographers, you could wind up being penalized or excluded simply because the underlying IP address for that service is the same for all the virtual domains it includes.

What Does AltaVista Consider to be Spamming?

from *www.altavista.com/cgi-bin/query?pg=addurl*

AltaVista's goal is to provide you with the most relevant results when you search. In order to maintain the integrity of the search index and provide relevant search results, we must sometimes exclude submissions that engage in techniques designed to manipulate the search results. Examples of such manipulation include, but are not limited to, the following:

- pages with text that is not easily read, either because it is too small or is obscured by the background of the page,
- pages with off-topic or excessive keywords,
- duplication of content, either by excessive submission of the same page, submitting the same pages from multiple domains, or submitting the same content from multiple hosts,
- machine-generated pages with minimal or no content, whose sole purpose is to get a user to click to another page,
- pages that contain only links to other pages, or
- pages whose primary intent is to redirect users to another page.

AltaVista strives to deliver search results that provide accurate information about the content of Web pages. Accordingly, we reserve the right to remove and/or to disable links to a Web site or Web page to which AltaVista has determined, in its sole discretion, that improper steps have been

Be very careful about where you have your pages hosted. If the hosting service also hosts spammers and pornographers, you could wind up being penalized or excluded simply because the underlying IP address for that service is the same for all the virtual domains it includes.

taken to manipulate AltaVista's search results. If you have any questions or concerns about this policy or its implementation, please contact us by e-mail at: *spam-support@av.com.*

Real-World Stories

More quotes from colleagues:

Here's a good one! After I checked to see what the competition was doing, I visited several sites for my top keyword in AltaVista. Seven of the ten were 404's (indicating dead links)! I, of course, being the good netcitizen I am, immediately resubmitted those URLs to AltaVista and they are being removed . . . just in time for my site to show up in their place <semi-wicked grin>.

One colleague recently wrote a letter to AltaVista about his Web site disappearing from the index. Here's what a representative from AltaVista said:

Our apologies, we have added a new index recently to the search engine, and your site may have inadvertently dropped from the index. We have resubmitted the site. Sorry for any inconvenience.

If this happens to you with AltaVista, simply resubmit your site.

Ask Jeeves

www.askjeeves.com
Ask Jeeves is a natural language search service. Its staff of research editors collect Web sites they feel will be useful to searchers and store them in the Ask Jeeves "knowledgebase." This process allows the inclusion of CGI-scripted pages, unlike many other search services.

Founded in 1996, Ask Jeeves is growing fast. According to StatMarket, Ask Jeeves moved into the top-ten list of search engines according to popularity statistics during 1999, accounting for 0.82

Need More Info?

Visit the Robots Exclusion page:

info.webcrawler.com/mak/projects/robots/exclusion.html

---

percent of all search engine referrals. Although this is small in comparison to the nine other top engines and directories, Ask Jeeves bears watching. As the Internet continues to grow by leaps and bounds, adding millions of Web pages per day, people will continue to look for search services that make searching easier, and Ask Jeeves's natural language approach seems like a natural for continuing success, particularly among the younger demographics.

How Can You Get Your Site Linked to a Question in Ask Jeeves?

There is no "Add URL" form for this search engine. Instead, you should send an e-mail message to url@askjeeves.com. Include in the message your URL and a brief description of your site.

But before you do so, spend time at Ask Jeeves to get a sense of what in particular about your site should be highlighted within your message. Here is the criteria Ask Jeeves uses in considering each submission, from *www.ask.com/docs/about/policy.html*:

Site performance

1. Sites must load quickly.
2. Sites should be polished, easy to read, and easy to navigate.
3. Sites should be well maintained and updated regularly.

> There is no "Add URL" for the AskJeeves search engine.

Editorial criteria

4. Sites should offer thorough, unbiased information that answers a user's question.
5. Sites should offer additional links or information related to the user's question.
6. Sites must be credible sources of information. That is, they should provide author and source citations, and contact information.
7. Sites and site features must be free and available without registration.

If yours is an e-commerce site, go to this URL *www.ask.com/docs/about/policy.html* and review the latest criteria for such sites to be accepted into Ask Jeeves. Read, in particular, the *Ask Jeeves E-Commerce Compensation Policy*. Many of the merchants found in this search service have paid for the privilege, and Ask Jeeves is very upfront in admitting that these paying customers may receive preferential treatment.

LookSmart

www.looksmart.com

LookSmart says that its navigation products reach fifty million unique viewers per month. Now, that's worth paying attention to! Its partners include Excite, Direct Hit, and Inktomi, along with over 280 ISPs which use the LookSmart directory on their sites. LookSmart has also aligned itself with RealNames, so owning a RealNames can help you in this directory. LookSmart also provides directory data to MSN Search.

Like Yahoo!, LookSmart is a directory of Web sites, not a search engine. This means that the information you include in your submissions form is very important; that information, along with an editor's impression of your site, will affect how you are ranked within this directory.

LookSmart also uses AltaVista's Web index to supplement its own listings. So, for any search, users are first shown matches from LookSmart's directory of sites, then matching AltaVista Web pages. If there are no LookSmart matches, only AltaVista Web pages are displayed.

Thus, if you are listed with AltaVista, you may in turn receive traffic through LookSmart.

Submission Guidelines and Tips from LookSmart

In the following section, we're pasting in (in bold) the most recent information available from the LookSmart Web site regarding LookSmart's submission guidelines and tips. However, when you're ready to complete your online submission form, you should go to

> Like Yahoo!, LookSmart is a directory of Web sites, not a search engine.

www.looksmart.com/r?page=/h/info/submitfaq3.html to see if any changes have occurred after this book's publication date that may affect your submission.

Direct from LookSmart

What Criteria Do LookSmart Editors Use for Selecting Sites?
We ALWAYS exclude:
- **pornography and adult-only sites**
- **sites with gratuitous or graphic violence**
- **sites that promote/disseminate illegal activities**

We may exclude:
- **sites with too few pages**
- **sites without any recognizable content**

We are looking for:
- **sites that are rich in original content**
- **sites that are relevant to the work, leisure, and home lives of busy people**

In particular, we prefer sites that are:
- **of high quality and reliability**
- **up-to-date and accurate**
- **easy to use and fast**
- **interactive**
- **unique or original in content**
- **interesting and useful to consumers**
- **visually appealing**

Submitting to LookSmart

Read Chapter 29 on Yahoo! before submitting to LookSmart so that you can fine-tune your title and description for the submission form. If your site is accepted, it will appear within the directory in six to eight weeks. If it isn't accepted, you will not necessarily be notified, nor will you be told the reason or reasons that it was rejected.

> If your site is accepted by LookSmart, it will appear within the directory in six to eight weeks.

As with all directories, take time to find the most appropriate categories for your site.

LookSmart makes it clear that it is in control when it comes to whether your site is accepted or how it is listed:

> The placement of a site in LookSmart is based entirely on its merit as judged by LookSmart editors. The only way to make your site appear more prominently is to improve its content, design, and functionality. If you do make significant improvements, submit the site again and a LookSmart editor will reconsider its placement in the directory.

As with all directories, take time to find the most appropriate categories for your site. You can make site submissions only in complete category paths, not in the general area of a particular topic, such as Entertainment and Media. Make sure you submit your site to as many categories as are appropriate, clicking on the "Submit Link" link and filling out a separate form for each category. Further, editors may list your site under multiple categories on their own. Note that multiple submissions within the same category do not improve your chances for a higher ranking with this directory.

You cannot request that your site be listed in a Best of the Web category. Editors make recommendations for this listing, suggesting sites related to their area of expertise.

Express Submit Service

LookSmart has added an express submission service where you pay in order to get an editor to review your site within 48 hours.

Express Submit requires a one-time processing fee of $199, which does not guarantee acceptance or placement of your site. However, you're notified whether your site has been accepted or declined, and it allows a one-time opportunity to resubmit if your site has been rejected.

Visit this URL for more information:
www.looksmart.com

What If Your Site Is Rejected?

As with any of the directories, this is the best time to take a critical look at your site. Read the chapter about Yahoo! and try to upgrade your site to meet all the criteria. Add more content and make other improvements to your site, and then resubmit it. Since you are dealing with human editors instead of spiders, you must make sure that your site is as appealing and professional looking as possible.

Changing or Updating Your Listing

The form found at *www.looksmart.com/h/info/confirm.html* allows you to update your LookSmart information. You can suggest changes to the description, but the changes will be implemented only if the editors feel that the changes will benefit LookSmart users.

> Since you are dealing with human editors instead of spiders, you must make sure that your site is as appealing and professional looking as possible.

For more information on this topic, visit our Web site at www.businesstown.com

Excite, WebCrawler, and Magellan

Chapter 24

Excite

www excite.com

Anyway you look at it, Excite is a major contender in the battle of the search engines. Excite has gone through some exciting changes, beginning with the breakup of its relationship with AOL. Excite no longer helps fuel the searches of the Netscape search engine and the Netscape Open Directory. But it has garnered an important new relationship, so its power is still significant. The changes are likely to continue at Excite and its associates, making it all the more apparent why search engine positioning is always a "work in progress"!

Anyway you look at it, Excite is a major contender in the battle of the search engines.

How Excite Works

In May 1999, Excite merged with @Home, a cable modem service. For their cable customers, Excite@Home has been using a custom search engine called Scout, which is powered by Inktomi and LookSmart. Since Excite's CEO has been named president of Excite@Home, it is not unreasonable to expect that Excite's own search engine will be used instead of Scout.

Excite's WebCrawler search engine contributes to its own index, which is considerably smaller than Excite's. Until recently, you needed to submit to both Excite and WebCrawler. However, WebCrawler's Add URL page is now feeding into the Excite submission system, so you don't have to submit individually to both places.

Another "two-for-one" deal: Excite's database powers Magellan search results, so when you are listed in Excite, you'll also be listed in Magellan. Since each engine uses a different algorithm, though, your site's performance in the rankings for each may be different.

How Does Excite's Spider Work?

When you submit to Excite, you've made a date with its spider for a visit every two weeks ad infinitum—*or* until Excite's policies change. According to posted information at Excite, its spider will crawl through every page of submitted sites "gathering information to be indexed and noting any content changes you've made." What a handy little helper for the busy Webmaster! As you continue to grow and improve your Web site, Excite should be helping you market your new additions once you're initially indexed. However, you may not want to rely on this spider-assistant completely. This will be discussed later in this chapter.

What Is This Spider Looking for?

Here's a Web design tip straight from Excite:

> Suppose you want users searching for "Hawaiian Bed and Breakfasts" to find your site among the first 20 sites retrieved. Simply adding, removing, or changing a few sentences on your homepage can alter the way our spider indexes you. Our design tip is simple: Relegate unrelated topics to subsidiary pages. If you're advertising your Hawaiian Bed and Breakfast, don't use the homepage to emphasize price, the way the ocean looks from a bedroom window, or your famous pineapple rum concoction. Instead, keep it simple: Emphasize bed, breakfast, Hawaii, and vacation.

Submission Guidelines and Tips from Excite!

When you're ready to complete your online submission form, you should go to *www.excite.com/info/add_url*. From there, you can also link to read detailed information direct from Excite that will provide updated tips for better performance within its databases.

Although Excite states that it needs only one URL submitted for your site and that the rest of your site will be picked up for its index through spidering, you may wish to individually submit the more important pages of your site, especially those that do not have links from your home page. If you have created doorways (Chapter 10) for Excite, you might also wish to try to submit them separately, as well as having invisible links to them from your home page.

Although Excite states that it needs only one URL submitted for your site and that the rest of your site will be picked up for its index through spidering, you may wish to individually submit the more important pages of your site, especially those that do not have links from your home page.

More on Submitting to Excite

Excite takes approximately one week to index a home page, three weeks to index a subpage, and up to six weeks to index a nonsubmitted page. To facilitate this, make certain that the pages you submit have text links for Excite to follow, since its spider doesn't read image maps. In other words, if an image map is all you've got for the spider, it won't be tempted to crawl past your submitted page. For more information on image maps, see Chapter 19.

Excite will accept submissions of up to 25 URLs in one day. Keep in mind that there's some controversy among top search engine authorities about whether the 25 limit is *per day* or *per total Web site*. However, a representative from Excite verified that they allow submissions of up to 25 URLs in one day.

How can you tell if your site has been indexed in Excite? You can enter the URL without the http:// prefix, like this:

www.mydomain.com/green_widgets.html

You might also search for the root domain to find many pages from the same site at once. Enter your root URL, such as:

www.mydomain.com
and choose List by Web Site, which will group your pages together.

When submitting your site to Excite, you will be prompted for the category under which your site should be listed. Just as you must with the directories, make sure you select the most appropriate category for your site. If you have any questions about which category is best, determine where your most important competitors are and follow suit, unless you have a compelling reason not to.

Creating Excite-Friendly Web Pages

Many of the attributes of search engine–friendly pages described earlier in this book hold for Excite, but here are some variations that may prove helpful, along with some reminders of good general prac-

> When submitting your site to Excite, you will be prompted for the category under which your site should be listed. Just as you must with the directories, make sure you select the most appropriate category for your site.

tice. These notes will be particularly helpful for building Excite-specific doorway pages.

Note: As with all of our recommendations throughout this book, keep track of the changes you make to a page and the results when you submit. Because the engines change their algorithms without any notice, you'll want to keep up to date on what techniques no longer work, and which new ones do!

1. Use each page of your Web site to highlight a different keyword phrase. Within each page, use one of the words in your keyword phrase more often than the other words in the phrase so that each word of the phrase will not be repeated exactly the same number of times.

2. Using your most important keywords within the text and making those keywords a link wherever possible will boost your page in the rankings. So, repeat your keywords in your links, even using 20 links or more! Look at the top-ranking sites for your keyword phrase, and use the keywords more often in the link text area than they did. Pages with lots of links with keywords in some or all of them, along with little other text on the page, often do well. Pages with lots of words and links with keywords do well, too.

3. Use your keyword in the title tag. Try creating multiple title tags with keywords. With Excite, don't use your keyword phrase as the first words in the <title> tag, but use the keywords at the beginning of the tag.

4. Words contained in complete sentences appear to be more relevant.

5. Link popularity is a big plus with this engine, especially links from popular Web sites. In Excite, many top-ranking sites are link pages. So, you may want to create a page of "Favorite Links" and then include a listing of resource sites appropriate for your subject matter.

6. Use keywords in the domain name.

7. Using keywords in the URL of subpages also increases relevancy. Naming all of your pages after the keywords you're emphasizing is important.

> Look at the top-ranking sites for your keyword phrase, and use the keywords more often in the link text area than they did. Pages with lots of links with keywords in some or all of them, along with little other text on the page, often do well.

8. Use your keywords in headline tags.

9. Well-constructed doorway pages appear to do well in Excite, at least at the moment. For any doorway pages you're crafting for Excite, highlight each repetition of your keywords and hyperlink it to another page. They can all link to the same page if that is appropriate for your site.

10. Sites that are also listed in Excite's Directory generally rank higher in search results, though a representative from Excite disagrees.

11. Home pages are treated with more respect than subpages in Excite, so make sure you optimize your home page for your most important keyword, which is always a good practice!

12. Try using your keywords in **bold** with Excite. It may make a difference in relevancy.

13. The higher the frequency of keywords, the better. Lengthy pages with the keyword repeated many times in different places can improve your ranking. This may be truer for *single* keywords than for keyword *phrases*. Experiment both ways.

14. Use style tags with your keywords in Excite: <style>keyword phrase</style>

15. Use your keyword phrase outside regular <html> tags, like this:

    keyword phrase
    <html>
    <head>
    <title>Keyword phrase in title</title>

16. Excite "times out" if it takes longer than 60 seconds to access your page when indexing it. Therefore, pages that take longer than 60 seconds to access won't be indexed, though the spider may schedule a visit during its next cycle. Further, Excite doesn't appear to like slow-loading pages either. Most of the top results in Excite are pages under 60K to 70K in size.

> Well-constructed doorway pages appear to do well in Excite, at least at the moment. For any doorway pages you're crafting for Excite, highlight each repetition of your keywords and hyperlink it to another page.

Submit Often to Excite

With Excite, it's crucial to keep your most important pages in front of the engine, since the engine will sometimes allow only a certain number of pages in its index. One Webmaster we know has had good results from submitting her most important pages to Excite every two weeks. It appears to help keep them from getting dropped or replaced by less important pages.

Straight from the Horse's Mouth

Q & A with Jim Reinhold, Excite@Home's engineering manager of Search, and Ron Lange, director of engineering, Search & Directory.

Q. *Regarding submissions, is there a 25-page rule? Please explain.*

A. Our limit is 25 URLs per domain per day. For known ISPs, the limit is 25 per user per day.

Q. *How do you incorporate link popularity into search returns; what impact does it have on rankings?*

A. Popularity metrics (primarily link analysis) are one of the methods we utilize to optimize the precision and relevance of our results; the exact methodology applied is determined based upon constant testing to optimize results' relevance and precision.

Q. *If someone is trying to optimize a Web page, but is dealing with the many difficulties presented by recent design techniques, such as Flash, JavaScript, dynamic HTML, and more, he or she may resort to cloaking. If the content is not misleading, will Excite allow such cloaked pages within its index?*

A. We generally don't like cloaking. It's hard to tell if it's done in order to spam or in order to optimize; when we do find it, it's almost always egregious spamming. We like to index actual documents at their actual locations ("actual" referring to what the user sees).

> With Excite, it's crucial to keep your most important pages in front of the engine, since the engine will sometimes allow only a certain number of pages in its index.

Q. *Do sites with a listing within your directory rank higher in engine search results?*
A. No.

Q. *Do we need to submit to Excite, WebCrawler, and Magellan separately, or may we submit to just one and, if so, which one? What do you see for Magellan's future?*
A. Submitting to one does the trick for all. Magellan will continue to be maintained as a service.

> There's no hard and fast rule on the number of pages allowed in Excite's index.

Robots—Keep Out!

There's no hard and fast rule on the number of pages allowed in Excite's index. However, you may find that Excite has indexed unimportant pages but has overlooked your important ones. One solution used by many is to keep the spiders out of the pages you don't want to have indexed so that they will gobble up those you do want indexed. To orchestrate this, add the following tag to your less important pages that you don't want to have indexed:

<META name="robots" content="noindex">

This tag is placed in the <head> section at the top of the page with other META tags. It tells all search engines that honor this tag (including Excite) not to index this page. The theory is, if you tell it to exclude all pages except your most important doorway or interior pages and your home page, then those important pages stand a better chance of staying indexed within Excite.

Disadvantages to the "Noindex" Tag

Most of the search engines will accept into their database a countless number of pages, so when you use the "noindex" technique, though you may be optimizing your results with Excite, you may be limiting your results in some of the other engines. Ideally, you should create a separate domain for Excite mirroring your current Web site content by using the "noindex" tags on all but your most important pages. At one time, we were recommending the creation of a separate subdirectory of pages for Excite within an existing domain, but it seems that Excite is not treating pages within subdirectories as well as pages within the root directory.

Certain Robots: Keep Out!

Another workaround for Excite's possible limit on page numbers indexed is to use the robots.txt file. This tells particular engines to "keep out" while letting others in.

To do this, create a text file with Window's NotePad or any other editor that can save ASCII .txt files. Use the following syntax:

User-agent: {SpiderNameHere}
Disallow: /{FilenameHere}

To tell Excite's spider, named ArchitextSpider, not to index files called inventory.html and junk.html, for example, create a robots.txt file as follows:

User-agent: ArchitextSpider
Disallow: /inventory.html
Disallow: /junk.html

Upload this robots.txt file to the root directory of your Web site. Although this is a voluntary protocol, most major search engines will honor it.

You can add more lines to exclude pages from other engines by specifying the User-Agent parameter again in the same file, followed by more Disallow lines. Each disallow statement will be applied to the last User-Agent that was specified.

If you want to exclude an entire directory, use this syntax:

User-agent: ArchitextSpider
Disallow: /mydirectory/*

> If you tell it to exclude all pages except your most important doorway or interior pages and your home page, then those important pages stand a better chance of staying indexed within Excite.

Make sure you use the proper syntax. If you misspell something or have a typing error, this technique will not work, and you may never know it.

Other options are to exclude the page from all spiders with:

User-agent: *

Or to disallow all pages on your Web site for the specified spider use:

Disallow: /*

Make sure you use the proper syntax. If you misspell something or have a typing error, this technique will not work, and you may never know it. Further, don't put anything else on the page besides the robots.txt information. A colleague added a title to the page, and the engine didn't honor the robots.txt page until he removed the title.

Here again are the User-Agent names of some of the more popular search engine spiders:

SEARCH ENGINE	ROBOT USER-AGENT
AltaVista	Scooter
GO/InfoSeek	Sidewinder
Excite	ArchitextSpider
Lycos	Lycos_Spider_(T-Rex)
Northern Light	Gulliver
HotBot	Slurp

Visit Search Engine Watch's Spider Spotting Chart: Robot Agent and Host Names, for more information.

searchenginewatch.internet.com/webmasters/spiderchart.html

Traffic Cop: Directing the Spiders via One-Pixel "Hidden" Links

We call them "hidden" links because they are invisible to humans but visible to spiders, their sole audience. To create hidden or invisible links to your doorway pages and other important subpages, submit your home page or another page that includes image links such as the following:

<A HREF="mydoorwaypage.htm"><IMG SRC="myimage.gif" BORDER="0">

The "myimage.gif" file should be a tiny gif file that is only 1 pixel (dot) in height and width and of a transparent color—or so light as to be barely noticeable to the human eye. For more information, see Chapter 5.

> To create hidden or invisible links to your doorway pages and other important subpages, submit your home page or another page that includes image links

Excite and Subdirectories

A colleague's URLs disappeared from Excite's index, and he was unable to get them reindexed. So, he wrote to Excite. Here's what they said:

Thanks for contacting Excite. If you are trying to submit your site for inclusion in the Excite index of Web sites, please only submit the top-level domain name, otherwise know as the root domain. That would be for example:

www.yoursite.com

Unfortunately we will not accept subdirectory pages through the submission process—the site you provided me:

unifiedsystems.com/disney.htm

is a subdirectory page. At this point, we are trying to keep our index to a minimum so we can test new systems and searching techniques.

If you submit your site and it meets our guidelines (please see: *www.excite.com/Info/listing.html*), then it should get indexed in approximately two to three weeks. At that point there is a possibility that another of our spiders may come across your site and index subsequent pages, but there is no guarantee of that.

Your page was most likely grabbed by this spider and brought temporarily into the index only to be rotated out when the next index compiled. Since your page is a subdirectory page, there is no guarantee your page will get listed in our index.

If you have further questions or comments, please feel free to write.

Additional Comments About Excite

To help you work with this engine, review this additional information about Excite:

Frames and Excite—Not!

A framed site, as we have said, is less than ideal. Until you can get around to your next site redesign, here's one technique that can make a difference in Excite, but it's not a total solution.

Add <NOFRAMES> tags to all framed pages. Excite indexes and uses site contents included in the <NOFRAMES> tag to determine:

A site description
Relevancy scores
Keywords to index your site under

If you submit an HTML page that uses frameset tags, Excite will index the title and any text on the page. It will use the META description from the page for the search results, but it will not consider it for relevancy, nor will it index comment tags, ALT tags, or the keyword META.

Frames and Excite—Not!
A framed site, as we have said, is less than ideal. Until you can get around to your next site redesign, add <NOFRAMES> tags to all framed pages.

Excite's spider will index the contents within the <noframes> tags just as it would on a nonframes page. You can repeat the title and META description from the top of the page down to the <noframes> section and the engine will use them.

Excite won't index the content from the frames you link to on this page at the same time. However, it may come back later and try to read the content on the pages. Though it probably won't actually list those pages, it does seem to consider the content of the pages when determining the ranking of the home page. So, if you're trying to get ranked high for a certain word on your home page, make sure that the subpages of your site have your keyword phrase in them, such as in the <a href>keywordphrase</a> link area.

You can even use the <noframes> tag on a nonframed page to place text, and the engine will "find" and index it. It will index the page, plus any content within the <noframes> tag. You can place links to other pages of your site, text, tags, and so on. Construct your doorway pages without frames.

See more about frames in Chapter 19.

Your Title Tag and Excite

If you don't use a title tag, when that page pops up in the search results of Excite it will say "untitled." What a missed opportunity! Don't let this happen to you. Tell your prospective clients what your site is all about and Excite will display seventy characters of it, or six words. If you're crafting a page just for Excite, try using your keyword phrase as the third word in the title, rather than the first. And try creating multiple title tags with keywords.

Your Description Tag and Excite

Excite supports the META description tag, though there is no relevancy boost for using the tag. If you submit a page without the description tag, Excite will create a description for you using sentences from your visible text to represent the content of your page. Therefore, the true benefit of the description tag with this search engine is your ability to control what the description is for the surfer's sake, not the spider's sake. So, unlike the other engines, you

> If you don't use a title tag, when that page pops up in the search results of Excite it will say "untitled." What a missed opportunity! Don't let this happen to you.

> Be sure to check the keyword weight of competing pages and adjust your keyword weight accordingly.

don't even have to worry about starting the description with your most important keyword.

Whichever description is displayed, your META description or Excite's own version, it will pop up in search results with approximately 395 characters of text displayed.

Excite and Keyword Weight

Keyword weight plays a role with Excite. Keyword density should be between 3 to 8 percent, but sometimes as high as 10 percent. Be sure to check the keyword weight of competing pages and adjust your keyword weight accordingly.

Optimizing a page for five keywords has been shown to work with Excite in the past. If you'd like to try this, optimize the first keyword for a weight of approximately 4.5 percent, and then optimize the second and subsequent keywords for a keyword weight of approximately 2.25 percent. Include all keywords in the title tag, but don't begin the tag with a keyword phrase.

How to Determine Keyword Weight

Cut and paste the page's viewable text into your word processor to let the "Word Count" tool count the words. Then, take the number of times you used your keyword phrase and divide it by the total number of words on your page to arrive at your page's keyword weight. If it's a long, text-heavy page, you can use the "Seek and Replace" tool for this. Type in your keyword for "Seek" and type in the same keyword for "Replace." The tool will tell you how many replacements were made, thus telling you how many times that keyword was repeated throughout the page.

Here's an example: if you use your keyword phrase 5 times on the page, and if there are 50 words on the page, your keyword weight is 10 percent.

For another quick way to determine your keyword weight, visit:

keywordcount.com/keys/search

If Your Site Isn't Accepted

After all of your hard work, how can it be that your page isn't indexed? Here is some feedback from Excite:

- **Your server was not connected to the Internet, was malfunctioning, or was busy.**
  Hopefully, it will pick you up during its next spidering cycle, but don't rely on it—resubmit.
- **The search query you entered does not reflect your site's content.**
  Don't rely on your keyword searches to determine if a page has been accepted. You can type in your root domain URL to determine which pages have been indexed. Then it's up to you to troubleshoot why that indexed page didn't pop up in the returns using the keyword search you chose. Maybe it's time to review all the above.
- **A robots.txt file has instructed their spider not to index the site.**
- **Your site uses frames; frames are not indexable.**

Excite's Regional Editions

Individual regional submissions aren't necessary since submitting your Web site at the Add URL form on any of the regional editions or in the main index will get your site added to the main database.

Excite Does Not Consider These Practices to Be Spamming

1. Use of META refresh tag
2. Use of invisible text
3. Use of tiny text

For another quick way to determine your keyword weight, visit: *keywordcount.com/keys/ search*

Excite Does Consider These Practices to Be Spamming

1. Excite attempts to screen out spamming before adding a page to its index. If it finds a repeated series of words such as "boat boat boat boat boat boat boat boat boat boat," it will replace the excess repetition with "boat xxxx xxxx xxxx xxxx xxxx xxxx xxxx xxxx xxxx."
2. If for some reason Excite cannot screen a particular type of spamming, it may penalize the page. The more unusual repetitions that the engine sees, the more heavily it will penalize a page.
3. Excite considers abnormal word densities to be spamming.
4. Excite does not appear to penalize for the use of hidden text unless the hidden text is used to disguise spam content.

In summation, don't spam Excite or any other engine. The engines are upgrading their abilities to screen and thwart spam every day, so why take a chance when there are so many acceptable techniques to help your Web site soar in the ratings?

Real-World Stories

A colleague recently pointed out that while Excite seems to drop pages, the same pages appear in the other search engines that Excite contributes to, and they seem to stay there longer. In addition to creating links, this colleague had the best success having one hidden link at the top of a page that links to a directory or contents page listing all the pages on the site plus a few others that are related to the keywords or theme. For example:

```
<a href="keyword.htm"> <img="1pixelkeyword.gif"></a>
or
<a href="keyword.htm"> *</a>
```

The keyword.htm represents a content page, and you can use a period in place of the wildcard symbol to be less noticeable or use the 1-pixel-by-1-pixel graphic as the anchor.

WebCrawler

webcrawler.com

WebCrawler has the smallest index of any of the major search engines. Because it is owned by Excite, there are many similarities between the two engines. However, there are some differences, too, of which you should be aware. WebCrawler's Add URL page is now feeding into the Excite submission system, so you don't need to submit to both engines individually.

How Does WebCrawler's Spider Work?

WebCrawler uses Excite's spider to create its own database of Web sites. It also does a more thorough crawl through particular sites, probably the more popular sites as indicated by the number of links pointed to them.

WebCrawler's spider crawls the Web about every month or so. It is a creature of habit—if it has spidered subpages of your site in the past, it will probably continue to revisit and reindex those pages in the future.

Submission Guidelines and Tips from WebCrawler

In the following section, we're pasting **(in bold)** the most recent information available from the WebCrawler Web site regarding WebCrawler's submission guidelines and tips. However, when you're ready to complete your online submission form, you should go to *webcrawler.com/Help/GetListed/HelpAddURL.html* to see if any changes have occurred after this book's publication date that may affect your submission.

> WebCrawler's spider crawls the Web about every month or so. It is a creature of habit—if it has spidered subpages of your site in the past, it will probably continue to revisit and reindex those pages in the future.

WHAT WEBCRAWLER INDEXES

WebCrawler indexes every word on your page up to 1 MB of text. The keywords under which your page will be found in a WebCrawler search are thus the words on your page, and nothing else—you don't need to submit keywords or categories along with your URL. We can't guarantee that a particular site will come up at the top or close to the top of our results list for a given search. There are, however, ways in which you can ensure that your site gets indexed as it deserves:

- Use a title uniquely descriptive of your page or site. Since WebCrawler's indexing/relevance algorithm gives slightly more weight to titles than to body text pages with titles containing dead-weight words like "Homepage" or "Home Page on the WWW" don't often get easily found.
- Make sure that the main page of the site describes to the fullest extent possible what the site's about. It doesn't have to be over-long and exhaustive, but as much text with the important words in it as you can possibly have without sacrificing the design/layout of the site will help on the indexing front.

Submit your main URL and those of the main sections of your site

WebCrawler strives to present users with the greatest possible breadth of search results listings, rather than trying to index every document of every Web site we know about. Unlike some others, our robot spider doesn't necessarily "dig down" to index every page on your site, although it does traverse links recursively to save them for future exploration.

We strongly encourage you to submit your main URL (also known as a site's "root" or "index" URL) to us, as well as your site's main subsidiary pages, and not every single document of your Web site.

- **Add your URL**

If WebCrawler does not currently find a URL that you think belongs in our index, you can add that URL to WebCrawler using our Add URL tool. After we verify the existence of the

> Make sure that the main page of the site describes to the fullest extent possible what the site's about.

URL, we'll visit it and add it to our online index during the next update.

Your Title Tag and WebCrawler

Be sure to include your keyword phrase in your title, but don't repeat it within the title. Of course, make your title sound inviting to the human element, too!

WebCrawler will display 59 to 60 characters from your title tag and uses the information within the tag in making its ranking decisions, so it is an important tag with WebCrawler.

Be sure to include your keyword phrase in your title, but don't repeat it within the title. Of course, make your title sound inviting to the human element, too!

Your Description Tag and WebCrawler

Like Excite, WebCrawler uses the META description tag, although it won't affect keyword relevancy. If you neglect to include one, WebCrawler will pull text from your visual page and display about 395 characters of it as your description.

Keyword Weight and Placement

Like Excite, keyword weight plays a role with WebCrawler. Keyword density should be between 3 to 5 percent. Include your keyword phrase near the top of the body of the page itself, but also use the phrase at least once near the bottom of the page as well.

WebCrawler and Spamming

If sites use excessive repetition of keywords in the body text or titles, WebCrawler may ignore this repetition and rank the pages without the repeated words carrying any weight, or it may ignore the submission request.

What's "excessive"? According to WebCrawler, it is when webmasters or designers practice "including unsolicited, extra or irrelevant information on their pages, usually in the form of word lists."

WebCrawler also tends to consider sites that submit a large number of URLs at one time to be spamming. WebCrawler is on the lookout for such submissions, and any site caught doing this may be subject to exclusion from the database.

The use of tiny, unreadable (by humans!) text within a Web page also appears to be frowned upon. WebCrawler considers pages with an abnormally high keyword weight to be spamming, so check your keyword weight carefully.

On the other hand, WebCrawler does not consider the use of META refresh tags and invisible text spamming, as of this printing.

As of this writing WebCrawler hadn't indexed submissions in several months. It is unclear what the future holds for this engine. After all, how viable is the index if the engine hasn't accepted submissions in months?

Magellan

magellan.excite.com

Magellan is owned by Excite, and all search results are provided by the Excite database. If you're listed with Excite, you'll also be listed in Magellan.

To submit a site to Magellan, either visit Excite, or you can use the submission form at Magellan's site itself:

magellan.excite.com/info/add_url

> Magellan is owned by Excite, and all search results are provided by the Excite database. If you're listed with Excite, you'll also be listed in Magellan.

For more information on this topic, visit our Web site at www.businesstown.com

Chapter 25

Inktomi, HotBot, and MSN Search

This chapter focuses on Inktomi and its increasing network of often symbiotic relationships—those engines that Inktomi feeds. What's hardest to understand for new positioners is, as powerful as Inktomi is, you cannot submit your Web site directly to it, which we'll cover later. First, here's how everyone is related.

Inktomi feeds the default search of Yahoo!, GoTo, MSN, AOLSearch, Snap, HotBot, LookSmart (which feeds MSN, Netscape, and Excite@Home), FindWhat, and many other specialty and corporate search engines.

Lycos owns HotBot, but both operate as a separate service from each other.

So, now that you've met the whole family circle, what's the best way to put them to work for your site? Let's start with the core of this group, Inktomi.

> What's hardest to understand for new positioners is, that as powerful as Inktomi is, you cannot submit your Web site directly to it.

Inktomi

www.inktomi.com/products/search

Inktomi Corporation is a technology company founded in 1996 by two UC Berkeley computer scientists, one a professor, Eric Brewer, and the other a graduate student, Paul Gauthier. They named the business, according to their Web site, after "a mythological spider of the Plains Indians known for bringing culture to the people." Its star product is the Inktomi search engine. Inktomi built its company by licensing this product to other companies that wanted their own search engine but didn't have the time or resources to build it themselves. Inktomi customizes search processes so that each engine it builds may integrate the Inktomi listings with client company databases in unique ways.

Named the top search engine by *Internet World* and the Editor's Choice by *PC Computing*, the Inktomi search engine is one of the largest search engines with over 110 million Web pages in its index.

How to Submit to Inktomi

You can't.

But you can get into engines that are powered by Inktomi.

Your best bet in getting listed in all the Inktomi-related engines is to submit individually to all that have their own Add URL form. Here's who and how:

HotBot: This is the more comprehensive approach to getting listed in an Inktomi-powered engine. Submitting your site directly to HotBot may get you listed in the results that Inktomi provides to supplement the listings of Snap, Yahoo!, and GoTo.

Snap: There's no way to submit to the supplemental Inktomi index that Snap uses; instead, submit to HotBot. Submit to the main Snap directory separately. See Chapter 30 for more information.

ICQ iT: This is a search site connected to the ICQ instant message service. To submit to that service, visit this Web site: *www.icqit.com/default.asp?act.addurl=addurl.*

Direct Hit: This is a popularity search engine whose results can be seen at HotBot in the Top Ten listings. Direct Hit works with other search engines to fine-tune their results, based on how popular and how much traffic a Web site really gets. HotBot's top results are being refined by Direct Hit now by default, rather than as an option available to Web users.

Open Directory Project: ODP results are also seen at HotBot and will be discussed later. Inktomi powers AOL Search and MSN Search as well.

Other engines: Inktomi supplies supplemental results to GoTo, FindWhat, and Kanoodle, which are all pay engines. It also provides results to Canada.com and Anzwers.com.

> Named the top search engine by Internet World and the Editor's Choice by PC Computing, the Inktomi search engine is one of the largest search engines with over 110 million Web pages in its index.

The services powered by Inktomi share some similarities, but also have many differences. Some of the important ones will be discussed in this chapter.

Submission Guidelines and Tips from Inktomi

Here are a few tips that can make sure your page can be found by a focused search on the Internet.

> Think carefully about key terms that your users will search under. You'll use them to construct your page.

Think carefully about key terms that your users will search under. You'll use them to construct your page.

Inktomi ranks documents higher if a search term is in the title. Users are more likely to click a link if the title matches what they're looking for. Choose terms for the title that match the concept of your document.

Write your description carefully. After a title, users click on a link because the description draws them in.

Place your key terms in the keyword META tag. This helps, too, although not as much as the title. If possible, customize the keywords for each page on your site instead of using one broad set of keywords on every page.

Keep relevant text and links in HTML. Placing them in graphics or image maps means the search engine can't search for the text and the crawler can't follow links to your site's other pages. An HTML site map, with a link from your welcome page, can help make sure all of your pages are crawled.

Keep your documents reasonably short and make sure that the key concepts appear in the text. Keep words distinctive; abbreviating "opera singers" to "singers" can muddy up a search.

Be judicious with frames, or to be safe, avoid them completely. A complex frame structure confuses many Web crawlers.

How Inktomi Works

About two weeks after submitting a page to HotBot, Inktomi will visit your Web site and look for other pages to add. After that, it is supposed to revisit twice a month to check for changes. Inktomi eventually discerns how often pages change at each particular site and may visit more or less frequently as appropriate to each site. Popular sites probably get visited frequently.

Not all the search engines powered by Inktomi tap into all the information it makes available. Inktomi currently maintains many separate indexes to serve its various partners, so ranking high in one engine won't necessarily mean you'll rank high on another.

Occasionally, people find that a number of their pages disappear for no apparent reason from Inktomi results. This may be due to a refresh of the Inktomi index. Missing pages should automatically reappear during the next refresh when the system tries to find them again. However, don't count on this. Resubmit your important pages to ensure their indexing.

Dynamic pages, problems for most engines, are now indexable by both Inktomi and HotBot. Dynamic pages are database pages that generally have a symbol in them, like the ? or %. To index a dynamic page, submit that page to HotBot or submit a static page that contains the URLs of the dynamic pages on it for later spidering.

See Chapter 20 for more information on dynamic pages.

HotBot

www.hotbot.com

Hotbot, ZDNet's 1999 Editor's Choice for "All-Purpose Search," is an up-and-comer. Acquired by Lycos in 1998, HotBot is garnering praise in the Internet community. ZDNet's award says:

"You can count on getting relevant returns because of its easy and powerful search features and its effective blending of Web, popularity, and directory results."

HotBot says on its site that it "indexes every word, link, and media file on more than 110 million Web documents and refreshes its entire database of documents every three to four weeks."

Extra Hints and Tips

Submitting to Answers.com or Canada.com can sometimes get your site into the Inktomi engine faster than submitting to HotBot. URLs are posted at the end of this chapter.

How HotBot Works

Though it continues to be powered by Inktomi and is owned by Lycos, HotBot operates independently from both. However, in a strange way, having a good ranking in Lycos can help you in HotBot because of the Lycos link at the bottom of the main HotBot page that allows you to search for additional results in the Lycos engine.

Direct Hit is now powering most of HotBot's top results. Therefore, the click-through popularity of a site is even more important. Results from Inktomi are still being used, but when there is relevant data from Direct Hit, those matches are presented on the first page of results, with Inktomi matches listed next.

Can you artificially boost your Web site up in the rankings by clicking on your links over and over again? Direct Hit says it has systems in place to prevent this from happening. You can submit a site to Direct Hit, but that doesn't mean the site will be indexed by the service. Read more about Direct Hit in Chapter 30.

Like Lycos, HotBot is now using directory results from the Open Directory Project. With this alliance, getting listed in the Open Directory is even more important. It appears that HotBot isn't accessing all the listings from the Open Directory Project, but instead selecting particular sites. At this writing, we are not sure of the criteria being used for selection.

> Like Lycos, HotBot is now using directory results from the Open Directory Project. With this alliance, getting listed in the Open Directory is even more important.

How Does HotBot's Crawler Work?

About two weeks after submitting a page to HotBot, Inktomi's spider will visit your site and look for other pages. After that, it will revisit twice a month to check for changes.

Submission Guidelines and Tips from HotBot

Here's what HotBot says about improving your site's ranking with this engine:

> **HotBot's search results are based solely on comparing the user's search query to the content of millions of Web**

pages. There is no list matching certain search terms or keywords with special results.

Basic factors affecting a page's ranking are: the words in the title, keyword META tags, word frequency in the document, and document length.

If you need to know how to structure your META tags, here are a few pointers:

www.hotwired.com/webmonkey/html/96/51/index2a.html
www.searchenginewatch.com/META.htm

If you want to see which of your pages are indexed at HotBot, visit HotBot's main page and choose the "More Search Options" button, which is on the left-hand side of the page right below the Search button. The SuperSearch page will appear. Find the Location/Domain box toward the middle of the page, and enter your domain without the "http://www" prefix in the domain box. You can choose other variables, such as the date, page depth, and the number of search results you'll be shown. Click on Search.

You can submit up to fifty pages per day with HotBot or wait for its crawler, which will index many of your pages for you. It is best, however, to submit your most important pages.

How HotBot Works

Judicious use of keywords is critical in HotBot. Make sure you have your keywords in titles and other META tags as well as in link tags and URLs because pages with these elements are ranked higher than pages with keywords only in the body. Try using multiple title tags with HotBot and other Inktomi engines.

If you consider buying a new keyword-studded URL, separate the keywords by hyphens, such as www.green-widgets.com. Including the keyword in a subdirectory name or page name can also help, although not as much. Consider purchasing additional domain names for this purpose if you've been unsuccessful in ranking well in HotBot for your keywords. Since other engines also appear to

> Judicious use of keywords is critical in HotBot. Make sure you have your keywords in titles and other META tags as well as in link tags and URLs because pages with these elements are ranked higher than pages with keywords only in the body.

> To boost rankings in HotBot, include on your home page links to all other pages on your site.

attribute additional importance to domain names with keywords in them, this strategy may help you in a number of engines. Keep in mind, too, that a home page is considered more important than its subpages in HotBot as well as in other engines, so having multiple home pages can serve you (and your keywords) well.

Pages with a higher frequency of keywords in the body text score better than pages with a lower frequency of keywords in the body. Try adding synonyms for your keywords, too, to cast a wider net without hurting your keyword weight.

To boost rankings in HotBot, include on your home page links to all other pages on your site. And submit your pages frequently, perhaps as often as twice a month since "newer" submissions often seem to fare better than "old" ones.

HotBot's rankings are being influenced by Direct Hit technology, which tracks the number of visitors to a site and how long they stayed. There's no quick fix to making this feature work in your favor. As we say elsewhere many times, a professionally designed, content-rich site will pay dividends over and over again, not only in attracting people through the search engines, but in getting them to be steady customers after they find you.

Additional Comments About HotBot

Keep these important facts about HotBot in mind when working on pages for the engine.

1. HotBot indexes every word on the page and all links from the pages, except certain stop words. Stop words act like wild cards and pull up results that appear to have little or nothing to do with a search. The best way to see if your search phrase includes a stop word is to submit searches with each individual word. If your search yields no results, then you know that word is a stop word, and you need to do some rewriting.
2. HotBot has page clustering, which means it lists only one page per Web site in the top results. This prevents any one site from dominating the search results.

3. HotBot does not support frame links or image maps.

4. A moderate approach to using doorway pages is not considered spamming by HotBot. Limit your doorways to ten or fewer.

5. Searches are case sensitive at times, so it's best to alter your use of capitalized and noncapitalized keywords to be on the safe side.

6. HotBot does not use word stemming, which means it will not search for variations of a word based on its stem. This means you should use every important form of your keywords, including plurals, throughout your visible site and your tags.

7. Include your keyword phrase near the top of the body of the page itself, but also use the phrase at least once near the bottom of the page.

Your Title Tag and HotBot

HotBot will display around 115 characters of your <title> tag, or 15 words. If you don't use a <title> tag, HotBot will list your URL. Keywords in the <title> tag should give you a boost in the rankings although some top-ranking pages do not contain keywords. Try two title tags with HotBot and the Inktomi engines.

Your Description Tag and HotBot

HotBot will display around 249 characters of your META description tag. If you don't write a description tag, the first 249 body text characters after the body tag are used. This does not include text in ALT tags but will include form text. Therefore, it is best to create a strong description tag for each page submitted to HotBot. Be sure to begin the tag with your keyword phrase and to use that phrase only once within the tag. As with every description tag, write a compelling description in support of your keyword phrase and a particular area of your site.

HotBot will display around 115 characters of your <title> tag, or 15 words. If you don't use a <title> tag, HotBot will list your URL.

HotBot and Keyword Weight

Keyword weight plays a role with HotBot, with the preference about 2 percent for the body text. This engine seems to prefer shorter pages.

How Does HotBot Feel About Spamming?

The following information can be found at this URL:

hotbot.lycos.com/help/addurl

> We're aware that some people create pages to maliciously "spoof" search engines. Spoofing a search engine makes search engines return pages that are irrelevant to the search, or pages that rank higher than their content warrants. Common spoofing techniques include the repetition of words, the inserting of META tags unrelated to the document's content, or the use of words that cannot be read due to their small size or color. If HotBot detects search-engine spoofing, it will significantly downgrade a page's ranking.

What Does HotBot Consider to Be Spamming?

Your Web pages will be penalized if HotBot detects spamming techniques, which may include:

1. Keyword stuffing in titles, META tags, and in the body copy. Don't repeat keywords one after the other.
2. Use of invisible text.
3. Use of text too small to read.
4. Submission of identical pages for the same keyword in an effort to dominate the top results.
5. Use of irrelevant keywords in META tags.
6. Same color text on same color background.

Keyword weight plays a role with HotBot, with the preference about 2 percent for the body text.

Note: At the time of this writing, HotBot does not consider using the META refresh tag to be spamming.

Report Obvious Spammers to HotBot

HotBot encourages users to report spammers. If you come across a Web site that ranks higher than yours and appears to do so through disapproved means, feel free to report it by sending an e-mail to feedback@hotbot.com.

How to Use the "robots.txt" File with HotBot

HotBot honors the "robots.txt" file standard, which is documented at:

info.webcrawler.com/mak/projects/robots/norobots.html

This file can be placed on your site to tell search robots which directories they should add to their databases and which they shouldn't index.

If you don't want some of your pages to be indexed by HotBot, ask your webmaster to create a robots.txt file for your site. HotBot's crawler will fetch and obey this command file. It will obey any entry with a user agent of * or containing the word "Slurp" (the name of HotBot's crawler).

HotBot also honors the "robots noindex" META tag, which keeps HTML files out of HotBot's database index. This can be added to the head section of an HTML document, as illustrated below.

<META NAME="ROBOTS" CONTENT="NOINDEX">

Read more about the uses of robot tags in Chapter 22.

> HotBot encourages users to report spammers

MSN Search

search.msn.com

The Microsoft Network is one of the seven largest portal sites on the Web, in the number 7 position with approximately 12.26 million visitors during the month of October 1998. Since MSN Search is this major portal's search engine, you'll want to pull out all the stops when working to get good positioning within this search service.

If your page does well in HotBot/Inktomi and in LookSmart, chances are good that it will do well in MSN Search, too, because MSN Search has integrated both of these search services into its own. Further, MSN recently added a link to Direct Hit Top 10 results from its search results page, so people wanting searches influenced by popularity have that choice. MSN Search also uses the RealNames database in its search results. Obviously, MSN Search wants to have something to appeal to everybody.

> If your page does well in HotBot/Inktomi and in LookSmart, chances are good that it will do well in MSN Search, too, because MSN Search has integrated both of these search services into its own.

Straight from the Horse's Mouth

Q & A with Eric Watson, lead program manager for MSN Search.

Q. *Who are your search partners?*
A. We partner with Inktomi for our full-text results for those queries that are not answered by our own directory.

Q. *Who contributes to your indexes and to whose do you contribute?*
A. We purchase data from LookSmart for our editorially reviewed site listings and then add META data to that for better search functionality.

Q. *Other than offering a link to Direct Hit's Top 10, do you incorporate popularity in any other way into your returns?*
A. Not directly. Our editors rank our directory sites by a number of factors (quality of site, how well known the site is), but we don't do a popularity only listing.

Q. *If someone is trying to optimize a Web page, but is dealing with the many difficulties presented by recent design techniques, such as Flash, JavaScript, dynamic HTML, and more, he or she may resort to cloaking the page, thus delivering up an optimized page for the search engines and showing a different page to human visitors. If the content is not misleading, will MSN Search allow such cloaked pages within its index?*

A. While some people use this for legitimate reasons, this is more widely used for spamming. To get into our directory site listings, the site is editorially reviewed so any technology that is human readable is fine. For full-text listing consideration, we do not recommend this approach either. With changing configurations of search engine crawlers that are used by search engines used to read Web pages into their database, trying to deliver different results to different users often fails or sends less optimized pages to end users. We recommend making some pages that represent your site using page design elements that are readable for search engines and submitting those pages.

Q. *Have you technology to determine when cloaking is done for optimizing purposes versus spamming/misleading purposes?*

A. Often the only way to tell is to have a human look at it. This is why most search engines consider this approach spamming.

Q. *How do you use the LookSmart directory within your returns? Do you apply a unique algorithm to the data, or just incorporate it as is?*

A. We take the raw editorially reviewed sites from LookSmart, and our editorial team at Microsoft adds META data to support our Intellisense search technology. This allows us to give the users what they meant, not what they typed, by understanding common misspellings and synonyms for the same concept and returning the best results in the best order.

> With changing configurations of search engine crawlers that are used by search engines used to read Web pages into their database, trying to deliver different results to different users often fails or sends less optimized pages to end users.

Q Have you technology to determine when cloaking is done for optimizing purposes versus spamming/misleading purposes?

A. Often the only way to tell is to have a human look at it. This is why most search engines consider this approach spamming.

Q. *Do you anticipate making any major changes either in your partnerships or in the way you provide search results in the near future? If so, what are these changes?*

A. We are always looking for partners that can help us provide better results or search functionality for our users. We have several upcoming releases (in 2000) that we believe will further improve the search results we provide, both in the U.S. and internationally.

Q. *How does someone submit their site to your directory? The Add URL form (search.msn.com/addurl.asp?q=&RS=CHECKED&co=20) appears to be the same for both the engine and the directory, yet the limited category choices don't match up with the actual categories the directory offers.*

A. Editors make the final decision on the category. Providing the top-level category information for the site is sufficient for organizing their work.

Q. *What are some of the criteria for ranking sites within the directory?*

A. Sites in the Web directory results are ranked by editors as most relevant to the query. This is done by humans, so word manipulation will not alter relevance.

Q. *How many visitors use the search engine versus the directory for their searches?*

A. One of the unique things about MSN Search is we tightly integrate directory results, directory categories, and full-text results. We treat everything as a search against all three of these search results types.

Submission Guidelines and Tips from MSN Search

In the following section, we're pasting **(in bold)** the most recent information available from the MSN Search Web site regarding MSN Search's submission guidelines and tips. However, when you're ready to complete your online submission form, you should go to *search.msn.com/help_addurl.asp#proc18* to see if any changes have occurred after this book's publication date that may affect your submission. Our comments are in nonbold.

Direct from MSN Search
TO ADD A WEB PAGE TO MSN SEARCH:

If you have a Web page that you want added to MSN Search, you can go to the Add URL page and fill out the form with the following information:

- **Main address for your Web site. Only one page request is needed for your entire site.**
  Additional pages from your site will be spidered. You may also choose to submit one page per domain per day. Expect to see submitted pages indexed in about two weeks, with spidered pages taking somewhat longer. If you're using a shared domain, and if you get a message that says that you've already submitted your site within the last 24 hours when you haven't, send MSN a note and explain the situation.
- **The category in which you think it should be placed.**
  "Drill down" through the categories until you find the most appropriate one for your site.
- **Your e-mail address, which is used if we need to contact you. Your e-mail address will not be used for any other purpose.**
- **The page title as you would like it to appear in the search results.**
- **A description of the site, which is used to find the most appropriate category for your site.**
  On this site, there is no limit indicated regarding the number of words or characters allowed in the description. It is probably best to keep your description brief, perhaps two to three sentences, studding it throughout with your most important keyword phrases.

Q. *How many visitors use the search engine versus the directory for their searches?*

A. One of the unique things about MSN Search is we tightly integrate directory results, directory categories, and full-text results. We treat everything as a search against all three of these search results types.

What Does the MSN Search Engine Consider Relevant When Ranking Web Pages?

Keep these relevancy factors in mind when submitting to MSN.Search.

1. Repeat your keyword phrase six to eight times on the page.
2. Use 330 to 430 total words of text on the page.
3. Use the keyword phrase once in the title, once in the META keyword tag, once in the META description tag, once in the link text, once in an ALT tag, once in a heading tag, and a couple times in the body.
4. Try to link to a page that has the same name as the keyword phrase you're targeting. Most top-ranking pages on MSN normally have at least one link with the keyword included somewhere in the URL.
5. Keep the keywords as close to the front of the tag or text paragraphs as possible.

Need More Info?

Notes on helping search engines index your Web site:

www.w3.org/TR/REC-html40/appendix/notes.html#h-B.4

What Does the MSN Directory Consider Relevant When Ranking Web Pages?

Within the categories themselves, the listings are generally alphabetical. However, there are exceptions to this.

MSN Search Engine at a Glance

MSN Search allows you to submit only one page per site per day. MSN Search doesn't support frames.

Inktomi at a Glance

Here's where you can submit to Inktomi-powered search engines:
Note: Both U.S. and non-U.S. sites should submit to the main Inktomi services as outlined here since sites listed in the U.S. version

are also included in the worldwide indexes. However, non-U.S. sites should also submit to their local Inktomi-powered service.

HotBot—Submit to HotBot (*www.hotbot.com/addurl.asp*)

MSN Search—Submit to MSN Search (*search.msn.com/addurl.asp*)

AOL Search—Submit to the Open Directory Project (*dmoz.org*)

Snap—Submit to Snap (*www.snap.com/<LMOID/resource/0,566,home-1078,oo.html?st.sn.ft.O.surl*) for its directory, and to HotBot (*hotbot.lycos.com/addurl.asp*) for the supplemental results provided by Inktomi

Direct Hit—Submit to *www.directhit.com/util/addurl.html*

Open Directory Project—Submit to the Open Directory Project (*dmoz.org*)

LookSmart—Submit to LookSmart (*www.looksmart.com/h/info/submitfaq.html*)

GoTo—Submit to GoTo (*www.goto.com/d/about/advertisers/;$sessionid$BDO43RAABFLGBQFIEEXAPUQ*) for its paid listings, and to HotBot (*hotbot.lycos.com/addurl.asp*) for the supplemental results provided by Inktomi

ICQ iT—Submit to *www.icqit.com/default.asp?act.addurl=addurl*

FindWhat—Submit to FindWhat *(findwhat.com/static/ab_promote.html)* for its paid listings and to HotBot *(hotbot.lycos.com/addurl.asp)* for the supplemental results provided by Inktomi

Kanoodle—Submit to Kanoodle *(safe.kanoodle.com/client-services/listings)* for its paid listings and to HotBot *(hotbot.lycos.com/addurl.asp)* for the supplemental results provided by Inktomi

> Remember: Inktomi's partners control the relevancy of their results. So, just because you rank well with one Inktomi-powered service, there's no guarantee that you will rank well with any of the other ones.

Canada. com—Submit to Canada.com
(*www.canada.com/search/web/addurl.asp*)

Anzwers.com—Submit to Anzwers.com
(*www.anzwers.com/cgi-bin/print_addurl.pl?*)

Remember: Inktomi's partners control the relevancy of their results. So, just because you rank well with one Inktomi-powered service, there's no guarantee that you will rank well with any of the other ones.

For more information on this topic, visit our Web site at www.businesstown.com

GO/InfoSeek and Search.com

I n December 1998, InfoSeek and Disney debuted the new GO Network. Then, in May 1999, InfoSeek was officially renamed "GO." You can get there typing either *go.com* or *infoseek.com.* InfoSeek has been one of the major and more popular search engines, even though historically its index was rather small in comparison to some others like AltaVista. But its new identity as the core of the GO Network brings it strong partners and the probability of a huge increase in traffic. These partners include ABC.com, ABCNews.com, ESPN.com, Family.com, and Mr. Showbiz. Certainly these major companies and Web sites will ensure the GO Network's growth into a prominent search and portal site. However, GO has indicated its desire to gravitate toward being strictly an entertainment and leisure engine. No evidence of this potential change has been seen as of the writing of this book. Since InfoSeek and GO are now essentially synonymous, we will be referring to the pair as GO throughout this book.

> Infoseek has been one of the major and more popular search engines, even though historically its index was rather small in comparison to some others like AltaVista.

How GO Works

www.go.com

GO is both a search engine and a directory. In the directory, GO Guides organize sites into categories. To create and maintain the engine's database, GO's spider crawls the Web.

When you perform a search at GO, you'll get results from both the engine and the directory. Matching directory categories are listed first under "Matching Topics," which demonstrates the importance of getting listed in GO's directory. Getting listed in the directory also automatically gets your site listed within the engine's results as well. Under "Web Search Results," you'll find the matches from the Web index.

On GO's main page, you'll find the category listing for the GO Guides. Since many searchers start with the directory, rather than initiating a "search box" search, it is important for your site to be listed in the GO Guides system.

CNET's Search.com engine is a branded version of the GO search engine, where it taps into GO's database for general searching but uses its own database for subject searches. So, get your site ranked high with GO, and you may see some nice traffic coming through Search.com as well.

How Does GO's Crawler Work?

After you submit a Web page, GO's spider will generally appear at your site within a week or two to verify the pages and possibly add others from your site. After that, the spider recrawls your site at least every two months, but it may return more often if it has noted that your pages change frequently.

Submission Guidelines and Tips from GO

Unlike some of the other engines, GO is fairly explicit about what it likes and dislikes, and updated information is always posted at the Web site. However, as with most engines, you'll find thousands of Web pages that seem to defy all rules yet still get a top ranking with this engine. A good place to start is always at the engine itself.

In the following section, we're pasting **(in bold)** the most recent information available from the GO Web site regarding GO's submission guidelines and tips. However, when you're ready to complete your online submission form, you should go to *www.go.com/AddUrl?pg=Guidelines.html* to see if any changes have occurred after this book's publication date that may affect your submission. Our comments about GO's guidelines are printed in nonbold type.

Direct from GO.com

InfoSeek takes great pride in providing the best possible search engine experience for our users. By submitting a Web page to InfoSeek, users agree to abide by the InfoSeek Guidelines and Policies for adding a Web page. Adherence to these policies is strictly enforced. Attempts to spam or subvert the InfoSeek index may result in the exclusion of an entire site and/or domain from the InfoSeek index. Repeat violators are subject to legal action.

- **InfoSeek reviews new submissions via the Add URL feature and e-mails as well as regularly examining pages already in our index. InfoSeek is not obligated to index any page. We**

> Unlike some of the other engines, GO is fairly explicit about what it likes and dislikes, and updated information is always posted at the Web site. However, as with most engines, you'll find thousands of Web pages that seem to defy all rules yet still get a top ranking with this engine.

> Submitted pages to GO are generally indexed within one week if submitted through the Add URL form or by e-mail, but it can be much longer.

reserve the right to remove or exclude pages from the index at any time, for any reason, or no reason at all.

- InfoSeek reserves the right to remove or block any site for violation of our submission guidelines via Add-URL or e-mail.
- Words used to describe the pages must accurately represent their content.
- InfoSeek is not responsible for submissions to our index made by third parties on behalf of Web page owners.
- Internet Service Providers (ISPs) of those who attempt to subvert the Infoseek index or violate these policies repeatedly will be contacted. Failure on the ISP's part to act may result in their temporary or permanent exclusion from accessing the Infoseek service.
- A maximum of 50 pages per day may be submitted through Add-URL. If you have 50 or more pages to submit to InfoSeek's index, please send your list of URLs through electronic mail to www-request@infoseek.com. Each entry must begin with http://.
- Pages containing adult-oriented content may be submitted through electronic mail only. InfoSeek regularly monitors certain youth-oriented and other topics to insure that adult sites are not inappropriately indexed in them. E-mail submissions may take up to 7 days or longer. Sites with adult oriented content submitted via the Add-URL feature are subject to exclusion from the Infoseek index.
- At this time, InfoSeek is not indexing Web pages from certain domains through the Add-URL feature. Some larger Web domains are affected by this restriction. We have taken this action because of continued attempts to subvert our index. We recognize that everyone does not use such practices. However, the frequency of abuse requires us to impose it. We apologize for the inconvenience to those inadvertently affected by this policy. Our intent is to insure the highest quality of search results for our users. We will accept submissions from certain domains via e-mail to www-request@infoseek.com.

- **InfoSeek reserves the right to restrict automated or robotic submissions through the Add-URL feature.**
  If you are using a cloaked product like WebPosition Gold, you are probably all right in automating submissions for this engine. However, as with any submission, check and recheck. Do not use online submission services.
- **Web sites that employ practices such as trapping or serving unsolicited files to user systems may be excluded from the index.**
- **Domains/companies associated with e-mail spam received by InfoSeek's email system are subject to being removed/blocked from InfoSeek's index. Note: This rule only applies to email spamming of InfoSeek's e-mail addresses, not for anyone who receives e-mail spam. If you receive e-mail spam, you will have to contact the person(s) who sent it to you and deal with them directly on the matter. Additionally, this rule applies to any of InfoSeek's companies and or Partners.**
- **Infoseek has the right to change its guidelines and policies at any time, without notice.**

Submitting Tips for GO

Submitted pages are generally indexed within one week if submitted through the Add URL form or by e-mail, but it can be much longer. Nonsubmitted pages may take longer still. Although it can be frustrating to wait for inclusion, you run a risk of getting banned if you submit the same page more than once within 24 hours. And resubmitting your page over and over again may actually cause a delay in indexing instead of speeding it up. Stick with a maximum frequency of submitting your page once a week until it is indexed.

Another note on submissions: GO has joined the group of engines and directories that say they will not index anything other than the root URL. If you submit interior or doorway pages, they may be ignored. However, GO's spider will now crawl deeper into your site and index pages on its own. You must include links to all

> Another note on submissions: GO has joined the group of engines and directories that say they will not index anything other than the root URL.

You can stay on top of your GO status by using the Check URL form. It will tell you when the page was added or, if it was rejected, it may explain the problem so that you can rectify the situation.

important pages on your site on your index page, or provide a link to a site map that will direct the spider to your important pages. (It may not be ideal to include visible links to your doorway pages; read more about getting your doorway pages indexed in Chapter 10.) One exception: if you are a GO Guide you can still add individual pages from your site to the directory. So, this is another advantage to being a GO Guide!

There is some evidence that sites found by GO's spider fare better than submitted sites. Further, sites that have been in the index for a while seem to do better than newly submitted pages. If your site is doing well within GO, you might want to take steps to prevent a competitor from adversely affecting your status. To keep someone from resubmitting your top-ranking pages, and thus making your site a "newcomer," add a <meta name="robots" content="noindex"> tag in the <head> section of your page. Then, GO's spider won't be able to reindex the site. Note, however, that the next time you want to submit the page yourself, you'll have to remove the tag.

You can stay on top of your GO status by using the Check URL form. It will tell you when the page was added or, if it was rejected, it may explain the problem so that you can rectify the situation.

www.go.com/AddUrl?pg=CheckURLStatus.html

A quick way to see all of your indexed pages is to type one of the following into the search box:

url:yourdomain.com (reveals every page under the root domain)

url:members.aol.com/yourweb site/ (if you're under someone else's domain, this will narrow the search to pages within your area)

GO, like many engines, turns off its Add URL feature on weekends and holidays. This is because there is no one on duty during those times to monitor submissions, and that is an open invitation to spamming. So, either wait for regular business days or submit by e-mail.

There are a couple of instances when you should submit by e-mail, regardless of the timing: if you have an adult-oriented site; if your Web page is over 64K; and, if you are submitting an IP address instead of a URL.

What Does GO Consider Relevant When Ranking Web Pages?

Keywords in the titles and in the first 200 words on the page are given the most weight. Begin your title with your most important keyword phrase and avoid stop words. Put keywords in META tags, too, such as your description and keyword tags. This gives pages a relevancy boost. Again, try to begin all META tags with your keyword phrase.

Pages with a high frequency of keywords do well. More on keyword weight later.

Pages from sites that are listed in its directory are given a relevancy boost, and link popularity also helps boost some sites to the top. If your pages have many related links pointing to them or even a few links from important Web sites, they may rank better. With GO and the other major engines, it appears that you need a minimum of two hundred links to rank well.

Do links from within your own site count as much as outside links? No, so it isn't likely that you could boost your pages in the rankings simply by linking to them within your own site. Further, having thousands of links in unrelated categories probably won't help you much either. Instead, related, or important outside, links are what will get you a boost in relevancy.

The best way to boost your link popularity is to ask other sites to link to yours. With GO, it also may help to have a number of links from your site to important, popular sites such as CNET or Yahoo! as well as links to related sites. Another idea is to see which sites are linked to yours, then use GO's Add URL form to submit every one of those pages to make certain GO is aware of the links.

Many people have reported that their pages drop in rank significantly a day or two after first being listed. GO may be adding a page rank score *after* a page is indexed, which can cause some recently submitted pages to go down in ranking. One theory for sites

> If your pages have many related links pointing to them or even a few links from important Web sites, they may rank better.

> Remember that the submission of duplicate pages from different domains can become quite noticeable, so you run the risk of being considered a spammer.

dropping in ranking is that GO assigns an initial "link popularity score" at the time of submission. After a day or two, if the site proves in practice to be less popular, it will plummet in the rankings. If this happens to you, submit your page again and see what happens. If the same thing happens again, work on increasing your network of important links, resubmitting again when you've done so.

GO clusters Web results, which means it lists only one page from a particular site, then makes the other pages available through a "grouped results" link. To do this, after a search is performed, GO looks through the top Web index results to see if pages from any site appear more than once.

Some people try to get around GO's clustering feature by running completely different domain names from the same server. Remember that the submission of duplicate pages from different domains can become quite noticeable, so you run the risk of being considered a spammer.

This engine apparently doesn't like more than one page targeting the same keyword or phrase. If you have problems getting a high ranking with this engine, and if you have pages that target the same keywords, remove your old pages and reregister them to remove them from the index. With GO's policy on allowing submissions of only the main page of your site, you may have to send them an e-mail to get those old pages removed. Further, be sure to add hidden links to your new pages on your main page, or create a link to a site map with links to all of your pages.

For some popular keywords, GO editors look for pages of reasonable quality that are relevant to a given topic, then push those pages into top-ranking results, perhaps by assigning extra weight to those pages. Therefore, pages for some keywords may rank in the top thirty positions even though the actual frequency and use of a keyword doesn't necessarily justify its rank.

JavaScript, Frames, Images: Tips from GO

As with most engines, the nice Web site touches delivered by Web designers can hurt your pages in the rankings. GO recommends that you use a META description tag containing your keyword phrase if you use JavaScript in order to guarantee that the description of the page will be useful. If your site uses frames, the frameset page should include a META description tag and a META keyword tag that describe the entire site. It is also helpful to provide a <NOFRAMES> section containing text that completely and accurately describes the entire site. When submitting through the Add URL feature, all pages linked from the frameset have to be submitted since GO's spider does not follow all the links. If your page consists mainly of graphics, use the META description and META keyword tags to describe the page.

More information on JavaScript and frames can be found in Chapter 19.

Your Title Tag and GO

GO considers the prominence of keywords in your title tag for relevancy. So, start your <title> tag with your keyword phrase. The maximum length of title accepted is 70 to 75 characters or 10 words. Don't hesitate to use those 70 to 75 characters, but don't repeat your important keyword in the title tag.

If you don't include a title tag, GO uses the first line of the page as your title.

Your Description Tag and GO

Descriptions for GO are obtained from the META description tag or from the first characters on a page if no META description tag is available. A description can include up to two hundred characters.

Use your keyword phrase only once in your META description tag. You won't get banned for using it more than once, but your rankings could suffer. Start the tag with your targeted keyword phrase.

If you're listed in the GO directory, that description may appear for your page in the search engine results, not the description in

> GO considers the prominence of keywords in your title tag for relevancy. If you don't include a title tag, GO uses the first line of the page as your title.

your META tag. You may also see two listings, one for the actual Web page and the other for your directory listing.

Your Keyword Tag and GO

This information is from GO's Web site:

> When a site is added to GO's index, all the words on the page are included with the exception of any text within a <Comments> field. The META tag keyword field can be used to specify additional keywords or synonyms that describe the contents of a site. META tag keywords are used in the indexing process but will not display on your Web page. The keywords can include up to one thousand characters of text. Be sure that the keywords chosen are relevant to the contents of the page.

Use lowercase only in the META keyword tag, don't use your keywords more than three times in the META keyword tag, and separate each keyword phrase by a comma.

Go figure: some top-ranking sites with GO don't use the keyword tag at all.

Keyword Weight and GO

GO considers keyword weight as a factor for relevancy, so work toward a 5 to 6 percent keyword weight for the visible text and then experiment. You should also analyze the keyword weight of the Web sites in the top-ten slots for your most important keyword and then model your keyword weight accordingly.

Submission to the GO Directory or Guide

Search results for GO start with matching categories from its directory. Searchers can browse through the directory, or conduct a search of the directory. This directory is not as robust as those of Yahoo! and the Open Directory Project. Depending on your site's area of specialty, there may, indeed, not be category that will work

> You should also analyze the keyword weight of the Web sites in the top-ten slots for your most important keyword and then model your keyword weight accordingly.

for you. If this is the case, you may suggest a new category when you submit to the GO Guide.

If you want your site to appear in the GO Guide, you can either become a GO Guide or submit your site for consideration by GO editors. A GO Guide is a volunteer who suggests as few or as many sites for inclusion as he or she wishes. Unlike the Open Directory Project, there is no complex form or "homework assignment" to be completed in order to become a GO Guide. Find out more at *beta.guides.go.com.*

If you choose not to become a GO Guide but want to submit your site for inclusion in the directory, follow these guidelines:

- Make certain your site is of professional quality and offering good content, with no broken links or areas still "under construction."
- Select an appropriate category. From GO's home page, drill down to find the appropriate category. You can also perform a search for terms that are relevant to your site and see in which categories those Web sites are indexed. If there isn't an appropriate category for your Web site, which is often the case in GO, you can request that one be created, but there is no guarantee that your request will be granted.

Submit your site by sending an e-mail message to: url_review@infoseek.com. Include your site title, a very short description, a complete URL, and the appropriate category and subcategories (Kids & Family/Hobbies/Kites, for example). Look back at your submission information for Yahoo! If you followed the specific recommendations of this book, your Yahoo! submission will serve as a template for submission to other directories, including GO Guide.

Keep the e-mail simple and to the point. If your site is a very popular site, tell how much traffic you get. If an appropriate category for your site can't be found, ask them to consider creating a new category to "complete their index," but don't expect it to be done. Check your spelling, don't use marketing hype, and make your request as polite and professional as possible.

> If you want your site to appear in the GO Guide, you can either become a GO Guide or submit your site for consideration by GO editors.

Keep in mind that, even if your site is accepted for indexing, the editors may index it with a title and description different from what you have provided.

After submitting to GO Guide, you'll receive an e-mail that says:

> Thank you for submitting your site to GO. Your site will be reviewed by a Directory manager for possible inclusion in the GO Web Directory. Please do not submit your site more than once. Each site submitted will be reviewed. Please note that we do not review sites that contain "adult" or sexually oriented content.

Your site may be accepted within days, or it may take much longer. If you're submitting to a new category, your submission may not be indexed until enough similar sites have been submitted to justify creating a new category. If your site doesn't get in the directory on the first try, wait a week or two and try again.

Sites are rated Best (three stars), Very Good (two stars) or Good (one star). They are grouped by quality, then listed alphabetically.

Note: You can submit other pages of your site to the channels or directory of GO as long as they offer different content on different topics and are top-notch pages. However, it's best to submit your site in one area, wait to see if you've been accepted, and then submit in another subcategory. Don't try to submit to more than two or three channel areas.

Real-World Stories

This quotation proves the importance of getting in the GO Guide.

> I submitted our site to GO directory and it got accepted. Not only that, our site ranks no lower than number 3 now, for almost all our keywords. It is a page that had a very poor ranking previously. It is very true—once you can get in the business directory, your rankings rocket.

> Even if your site is accepted for indexing, the editors may index it with a title and description different from what you have provided.

Spamming and GO

At this URL, *GO.go.com/AddUrl?pg=Spamming.html,* GO says:

> Spamming is the alteration or creation of a document with intent to deceive an electronic catalog or filing system. Some Web authors use subversive techniques to get their sites to appear more frequently or higher in returned search results. This is something that we strongly discourage and may penalize people for. Searching the Internet is our business, and spamming interferes with providing our users with the best search experience we can.
>
> Those who continually attempt to subvert or spam the GO index may be permanently excluded from the GO index. Extreme or repeated violations may be subject to legal action.
>
> Words used to describe the pages must accurately represent their content. GO's index detects common spamming practices and penalizes pages that use them. Unfortunately, in some cases this may cause valid pages to be penalized as well. For best results, the following Web publishing techniques should be avoided:

(Note: the following details from GO are **in bold**, with our comments in nonbold.)

1. Overuse or repetition of keywords

GO checks for the overuse of keywords in the visible text of the page as well as in the tags. However, the engine isn't going to penalize you if your keywords appear frequently on your page in a legitimate manner. So, don't be concerned that you could accidentally spam the engine. "Overuse" means repeating the keywords over and over again, such as in a nonsensical manner.

2. Use of keywords that do not relate to the content of the site

3. Use of fast META refresh

Some sources say that GO considers any use of the META refresh tag to be spamming, so it might be prudent to avoid using one altogether.

4. Use of colored text on same-color background

> Words used to describe the pages must accurately represent their content. GO's index detects common spamming practices and penalizes pages that use them.

GO checks the background color of a page, then rejects any page using text that matches this color. This can cause a problem for those using tables. Remember that the Check URL feature will warn you of any problems like color incompatibility.

5. Duplication of pages with different URLs

Although this multiple domain strategy has some fans for good reason, it can be problematic with the directories. Read more about this in Chapter 29.

6. Use of different pages that bridge or link to the same URL

Again, most of the directories do not want to deal with doorway pages. Read more about doorway pages in Chapter 10.

If you submit pages with identical or nearly identical content from the same site, only the most recently submitted page will appear, with the other pages automatically removed from the index.

Please note these are only a few examples of what is considered spamming. There are many more types that are not illustrated and will not be permitted on GO's index. Any violation may result in the removal and/or exclusion from GO's index.

Report Spammers to GO!

GO encourages users to report suspected spamming for investigation. Here's what they said:

> There are unscrupulous Web page designers that try to subvert our search results in an effort to increase traffic to their site. This is called spamming. Depending on the content that they provide, spammers can be annoying, offensive or both. GO takes a very aggressive stance against spam. We are constantly upgrading our automated spam filters and have a dedicated staff doing manual spot checks in our most popular query words. We also review sites that you access by going through our channels and Directory pages. Despite our best efforts, we can't ensure that EVERY possible topic you search the entire Web for (via our search box) is spam-free at any given moment.

> Some sources say that GO considers any use of the META refresh tag to be spamming, so it might be prudent to avoid using one altogether.

You can help us and your fellow searchers by reporting all incidents of spam to *comments@GO.com*. We will make every effort to resolve reports within 24 hours. To facilitate this process, please include as much detail as you can, such as the query word(s) you used, URL(s) of the page(s) in question, etc.

What Might Happen if *You* Spam GO?

GO takes strong action against sites it believes are spamming the index. It may remove all of your pages from the index and block all further submissions from your Web site. How might you find out you have been branded a spammer? If you receive a "domain blocked" error message when you try to use the Add URL form, you may be in trouble for spamming the index.

If your site is removed from the index for spamming, you'll need to contact GO and plead your case. They'll ask for a written letter promising that you'll comply with their submission guidelines. If you get back in GO's good graces, behave yourself, because a second offense can cause your site to be *permanently* banned.

> GO takes strong action against sites it believes are spamming the index. It may remove all of your pages from the index and block all further submissions from your Web site.

Straight from the Horse's Mouth

Q & A with Jan Pederson, director of Search, from GO.

Q. *Who are your search partners? Who contributes to your indexes and to whose do you contribute?*

A. GO.com uses purely in-house technology to serve search results. The spidered-based search engine, called Ultraseek, is technology originally developed at InfoSeek (subsequently acquired by Disney) and formed the basis for one of the first Internet search services.

InfoSeek search results are seen on WebTV, CNET, AskJeeves, and MetaCrawler as well as many other small services.

Q. *Do you have a policy regarding the submission of cloaked pages?*

A. We actively discourage SPAM and will ban from our index sites anyone who abuses, in anyway, our primary GO Network users. We do not condemn the use of clocked pages, however, if used responsibly.

> We actively discourage SPAM and will ban from our index sites anyone who abuses, in anyway, our primary GO Network users. We do not condemn the use of clocked pages, however, if used responsibly.

Q. *What is the current size of your index?*

A. 90 million

Q. *May we quote information directly from your Web site about your submission process, and may we include the URLs so readers may go and see your most recent information?*

A. Yes. At this time we are only accepting site submission. We no longer guarantee overnight indexing since this led to abuse by spammers.

Q. *What percentage of visitors prefer to "drill down" through the categories for information rather than rely on the search box?*

A. This is proprietary. However, we can say that our matching topic feature on the search results page is very popular and is selected around 15 percent of the time by our users.

Q. *How many visitors performed searches at GO in 1999; how many do so currently, in an average day?*

A. Currently, we only track unique users for the entire portal. Our current search traffic is around 5.2 billion queries per year.

Q. *What search-related awards have you won recently?*

A. Business 2.0 Top 100 of 1999

Q. *Do you anticipate making any major changes in either your partnerships or in the way you provide search results in the near future? If so, what are these changes?*

A. We recently launched GO Network's Image Search service. It allows users to search for a topic, and the site will produce images on that subject.

Search.Com

www.search.com

Operated by CNET, Search.com is a branded-version of GO. GO technology is also used to crawl selected sites within categories to offer specialty searches. Since late 1997, Search.com has been overshadowed by Snap, also owned by CNET.

If your site is indexed with GO, it will be indexed with Search.com, so you don't have to submit to it separately.

Search.com also has a directory of Web sites called the A–Z List. In order for your Web site to be considered for entry into this list, send an e-mail to *submit@search.com.*

You will be notified if your site gets selected for entry into the directory.

www.search.com
If your site is indexed with GO, it will be indexed with Search.com, so you don't have to submit to it separately.

For more information on this topic, visit our Web site at www.businesstown.com

Lycos and
NetGuide Live

Chapter 27

Lycos

www.lycos.com

Lycos has, according to its own press, gone beyond being a "portal" to become a "hub." Looking at its growing network can give credence to this claim: Tripod, Angelfire, WhoWhere, MailCity, HotBot, HotWired, Wired News, Webmonkey, Suck.com, MyTime.com, and most recently, Gamesville.com. And now, you can even download a free Lycos "browser," so watch out Netscape and IE.

The Lycos search engine is one of the more popular search engines and is one of the oldest. It has an index of one hundred million Web sites, and it claims that seventy million users access the engine day.

At the end of 1999, Lycos bought a 15 percent interest in the Fast Search Engine, and Fast is now providing advanced search results at Lycos.

How Lycos Works: Who's Who

Lycos has followed the trend among search engines and is now both a directory *and* a search engine. In April 1999, Lycos incorporated the Open Directory Project into directory results for both its Lycos.com and Hotbot.com Web sites.

It also has joined the trend of introducing "popularity" as part of the search criteria. Now when you perform a search at Lycos, you may draw information from up to four primary sources:

- Popularity
- Web sites
- News articles
- Shopping

The "Popularity" results appear to be a combination of editor picks and Direct Hit data.

The "Web sites" tab delivers results that begin with Lycos categories, courtesy of the Open Directory Project. Following are individual Web sites from Lycos's database, the listing of which is influenced by the Lycos algorithms.

www.lycos.com
The Lycos search engine is one of the more popular search engines and is one of the oldest. It has an index of one hundred million Web sites, and it claims that seventy million users access the engine day.

The "Articles" results are drawn from Lycos News, Wired News, and other cyber news sources.

The "Shopping" option appears when the editors feel that there is an e-commerce site that might meet your interests.

Not all search options are available in every search return. Some don't offer the "Popularity" listings, for example, and many don't offer "Shopping."

Lycos is also experimenting with "paid-for" listings, as did AltaVista. If there is a paid-for listing for a particular keyword, you will see it at the top of the returned results, with the note: "START HERE" in red.

On the Lycos results page, you'll also find a link for searching on GTE Yellow Pages and a link for searching on HotBot. Remember that Lycos owns HotBot. So, if you're ranked high with HotBot, you could get some visitors through Lycos as well. However, HotBot operates as a separate service from Lycos.

Lycos fuels NetGuide Live, which offers both reviewed and unreviewed listings. For the unreviewed listings, NetGuide Live taps into the Lycos search engine. If you're listed with Lycos, you'll be listed in NetGuide Live's unreviewed listings.

How Does Lycos's Spider Work?

After submitting your Web page to Lycos, it is indexed immediately, but it takes at least two to three weeks or longer for your site to appear in the index. Periodically, the index goes "down." During that time, the spider will still be crawling the Internet, but the new information it finds will not be added immediately to the index. Recently, an associate wrote to Lycos to ask why his site was not indexed in a timely manner. This was the response he received:

> Thanks for using Lycos! The index update process is currently underway, and will be completed as quickly as possible. When the update is finished, all of the sites which have been submitted to us and stored in our off line index will be on line and searchable. This is also when any necessary changes will take place, such as updates and deletions. Thank you for your patience.

Now when you perform a search at Lycos, you may draw information from up to four primary sources:

- Popularity
- Web sites
- News articles
- Shopping

Even when Lycos is actively indexing through crawling, how fast a nonsubmitted page is indexed is influenced, in part, by site popularity. For example, less popular sites may not be subject to as deep a crawl as more popular sites. For that reason, submit all of your key pages.

The spider will revisit your site every four to twelve weeks. If the spider can't connect to your site over a four-week period, it will be deleted from the index.

Lycos's spider will read only the visible text on your page. Then, it will automatically create an abstract based on that information. The keywords and descriptions associated with your page will be generated by the spider, so there is no need for you to use META tags.

However, once in a while, Lycos will use the contents of the META description tag as the description of your site in the search results, so it's always a good idea to include it.

> Even when Lycos is actively indexing through crawling, how fast a nonsubmitted page is indexed is influenced, in part, by site popularity.

Submission Guidelines and Tips from Lycos

In the following section, we're pasting **(in bold)** the most recent information available from the Lycos Web site regarding Lycos's submission guidelines and tips. However, when you're ready to submit your site, you should go to *www.lycos.com/addasite.html* to see if any changes have occurred after this book's publication date that may affect your submission. Our comments about Lycos's guidelines are printed in nonbold type.

Direct from Lycos.com

- **You may submit more than one URL from your site as long as the URLs represent distinct Web pages. Multiple pages that contain the same content will not be added.**
  There appears to be no limit to the number of pages you may submit during any time period. However, if you have a large site, it still might be wise to submit groups of pages at a time, perhaps fifty per day.

Whenever you update the content of your site, consider resubmitting so that critical new information might be indexed.

- **The Lycos spider will try to travel through links contained in the Web page you submit. A good rule of thumb is to count on the spider traveling down one level from the page you submit.**
  To be on the safe side, submit all of your important pages. And, since it appears that Lycos favors new over established pages when it comes to relevancy, try submitting again whenever you see a drop in ranking.

- **Please do not submit Web pages with these symbols in the URL: ampersand (&), percent sign (%), equals sign (=), dollar sign ($) or question mark (?). Our spider does not recognize them.**
  Read more about the challenges of getting dynamic pages indexed, and possible solutions, in Chapter 20.

- **Having trouble entering your URL? Make sure you've typed in the whole address, including appropriate prefixes (i.e., http://www.) and a trailing slash (/) if the URL doesn't include a file name (e.g., http://www.lycos.com/).**
  When two or more sites are considered equal in relevancy, Lycos will rank those sites in alphabetical order by domain. Because of this, omit your site's www prefix when submitting, if allowed by your server. If you're not sure, ask your webmaster or hosting ISP.

Increasing Your Site's Relevancy in Lycos

Where you place your keywords is important in Lycos. Place them in the title tag, repeat them in a headline tag, and mention them very early in the body of the page. Don't hesitate to repeat the keyword, or variations of the keyword, within additional headlines and near the beginning of additional paragraphs throughout the page. Having a keyword in the URL may also help toward relevancy. Whenever possible, don't place an image or an ALT tag before a headline tag.

> Where you place your keywords is important in Lycos. Place them in the title tag, repeat them in a headline tag, and mention them very early in the body of the page.

Lycos does index ALT text and considers it for relevancy, so do use ALT tags, starting each tag with your important keyword.

Add synonyms of your most important keywords. Lycos recognizes synonyms for many words. Try using words that are closely synonymous with your primary keyword, which may improve your page's relevancy.

Because the home page of a site often fares better than other pages, consider using an additional domain strategy with Lycos, building new sites to emphasize each of your most important keyword phrases.

Your Title Tag and Lycos

Lycos will display up to sixty characters of a title tag. If you don't use a title tag, Lycos will use the first line of text from your page. Keywords in the title tag count toward relevancy and are very important. Prominence of keywords in the title tag is important, too, so make sure you use your keyword phrase toward the beginning of the tag.

With Lycos, experiment with multiple title tags if you don't like the ranking you achieve using one title tag.

Your Description Tag and Lycos

Because Lycos sometimes indexes the first text it can find on a Web page and uses it for the description, be certain that the first 135 to 200 words on your page are keyword rich and compelling enough to attract your target audience to your site. However, don't neglect writing a great description tag, too, because text from description tags seems to pop up in Lycos regularly.

Lycos and Keyword Weight

Keyword weight plays a role in the first 270 characters or so on the page. Make sure that your keywords are used frequently in the first 270 characters and that the keyword weight is approximately 1 to 2

> Try using words that are closely synonymous with your primary keyword, which may improve your page's relevancy.

percent of the total number of words on the visible portion of the entire page though some high-ranking pages scored between 4 and 4.5 percent. The majority of the highest ranked pages found in Lycos scored approximately 1 percent for keyword weight. For example, if a Web page contained 300 total words on the page, 3 of them were the keyword.

When You Can't Get Indexed by Lycos

A few people have claimed that Lycos won't index a page unless a robots.txt file is present. As Chapter 22 explains, the robots.txt file is generally used to prevent spiders from indexing a particular page, but in the example shown here, it can be used to invite Lycos's spider to enter.

> User-agent: *
> Disallow:

With this configuration, you're telling the spiders that nothing in the site is disallowed and that they may therefore index anything they find.

> The robots.txt file is generally used to prevent spiders from indexing a particular page. It can be used to invite Lycos's spider to enter.

What Does Lycos Consider to Be Spamming?

Stay on Lycos's good side by staying far away from these spamming techniques:

1. Keywords that are repeated over and over again. If detected, the page will be knocked to the end of the listings.
2. Duplicate pages. If Lycos discovers duplicate pages, it removes them from its index, but you are probably not otherwise penalized.
3. Hidden, invisible, or extremely small text may keep a page from getting indexed.
4. Double word occurrences. Lycos will assign negative relevancy where it detects double words. This penalty is for

adjacent, duplicate keywords, not repeated keywords spread judiciously throughout the document.

You can help keep Lycos uncluttered, and remove a spamming competitor, by reporting spammers to Lycos. Complete the feedback form found at:

echomail.lycos.com/feedback.htm
Or you can send an e-mail to:
webmaster@lycos.com

To Remove a Page or URL from Lycos

If you have an obsolete URL or inactive Web page listed in the Lycos catalog, it is a good idea to submit the URL for deletion on the Add Your Site page.

www.lycos.com/addasite.html

After you have entered the URL and e-mail address, click the submission button, and their spider will try to visit the inactive page. You will see an error message, which means that the spider "learned" that the page is no longer active. Dead links will be deleted from the catalog within two to three weeks.

If you want to remove an active page from the Lycos catalog, you must make use of the robots.txt standard (see Chapter 22).

If your site has moved to a different location on the Web or some of your URLs have new names, you will need to submit both the new and old URLs to Lycos. Dead links will be deleted from the catalog, and the new URLs will be indexed.

Remember to ask all the other sites linked to yours to update the links also. This not only increases your pertinent popularity, but keeps that extra traffic from your linked network coming your way.

If your site has moved to a different location on the Web or some of your URLs have new names, you will need to submit both the new and old URLs to Lycos.

How Can You Get Listed in Lycos's Open Directory?

If you are not already in the Lycos Directory, you may want to submit your site to it at the Lycos site itself versus at the Open Directory site. Lycos lists categories differently than the Open Directory. The same search in both places won't produce the same results because Lycos is applying its own ranking algorithm to the directory listings. So, in order to get the most traffic for your site through the Lycos search results, you may want to submit your site in the Lycos categories.

To do so, run a search for your keyword phrase, and then choose the most appropriate category. Look for the Add Web Site link toward the bottom of the page. Click on it, and you'll be presented with a form for submitting your Web site. You may use the same title and description that you used effectively with Yahoo!.

> If you are not already in the Lycos Directory, you may want to submit your site to it at the Lycos site itself versus at the Open Directory site.

NetGuide Live

www.netguide.com

NetGuide Live is a smaller search service that offers both reviewed and unreviewed listings. There are many fewer categories for your consideration, and there is no site submittal form for reviews. Instead, you can use the feedback form, and if your site is good enough, it may be added.

For the unreviewed listings, NetGuide Live taps into Lycos's database. If you're listed with Lycos, you may be listed in NetGuide Live's unreviewed listings. To ask for your site to be reviewed, follow the guidelines outlined at the following Web site:

www.netguide.com/aboutus/aboutreviews.html

In your e-mail, write the name of the category and subcategory that best describes your site in the subject area. For example, if you sell collectibles, you would write Shopping/Collectibles in the subject line. In the body of the e-mail, write a site review, including the URL. Add a one- or two-sentence description of your site for their reviewers.

For more information on this topic, visit our Web site at www.businesstown.com

---

Chapter 28

Netscape, Open Directory Project, and AOL Search

Netscape Search

search.netscape.com

If you want a presence in Netscape, your best bet is to submit to the Open Directory Project. The human-edited ODP and Google, a popularity engine, power Netscape's search engine, with the ODP the primary database. Netscape Search also uses Netscape's Smart Browsing index. Smart Browsing allows users to enter ordinary words into the search box rather than a complicated URL, similar to the RealNames system (see Chapter 31).

This is how the various layers of information are sorted: when you run a search, if any relevant matches from the Smart Browsing database are found, you'll first see "Official Sites" in the search results with those particular listings. Following that, "Netcenter Pages" may be listed, which is content from within the Netscape Web site itself that seems relevant to your search. After that, you'll be presented with results called "Web Site Categories" provided by the Open Directory Project. Lastly, you'll receive "Additional Results" from the Google search engine.

According to the Netscape Search Web site, visitors using this service can now "search over 800,000 sites well organized into more than 140,000 categories and reviewed by over 14,000 subject experts. Netscape Search offers global coverage of the Web in 229 countries and 44 languages."

home.netscape.com/escapes/search/about.html?cp=nsistatic#betterresults

> If you want a presence in Netscape, your best bet is to submit to the Open Directory Project. The human-edited ODP and Google, a popularity engine, power Netscape's search engine.

What Is the Open Directory Project?

dmoz.org

"HUMANS do it better" is the slogan for this increasingly important directory. The Open Directory Project, formerly known as NewHoo, got its start with the development of a unique editing software in 1994 funded by a grant from the National Science Foundation. In 1998, Netscape bought NewHoo, which was based on the successful approach of Yahoo!, and the ambitious undertaking continued its call for an almost all-volunteer army. The premise was along the lines of what has always built the Internet—people amassing and sorting information to be freely shared with others. The OPD recruits volunteers to edit its categories, which requires many hours of reviewing submissions to determine if and how they should be included in this constantly growing database. According to a CNET news release of September 7, 1999, the OPD currently "has grown from 100,000 sites with 4,500 contributing editors when Netscape acquired NewHoo to more than 900,000 Web sites and more than 15,000 editors."

Today, the ODP remains a volunteer effort, and its importance continues to increase. Here is just a partial listing of the more than ninety search engines currently using data supplied by the ODP:

> AltaVista
> Hot Bot
> Lycos
> AOL Search
> Google Directory
> Thunderstone
> Savvy Search
> MetaCrawler
> DogPile
> InfoSpace

For an updated list of sites that use the ODP, go to this URL: *dmoz.org/Computers/Internet/WWW/Searching_the_Web/Directories/Open_Directory_Project/Sites_Using_ODP_Data*

Of course, the best way to find out more about the ODP is to become an editor yourself. Visit this Web page for more information: *dmoz.org/about.html*

Submitting to Netscape and the ODP

There's no need to submit to both the Netscape Directory and the Open Directory Project. Submitting to the Open Directory will get you listed in the Netscape Directory.

According to a CNET news release of September 7, 1999, the OPD currently "has grown from 100,000 sites with 4,500 contributing editors when Netscape acquired NewHoo to more than 900,000 Web sites and more than 15,000 editors."

To submit a site directly to the Open Directory Project, visit: *www.dmoz.org* and drill down to the category you feel most appropriate for your site. When you click at the bottom of the page to "Submit URL," you'll pull up the screen of the OPD Submission Policies:

Submission Policies

We care a great deal about the quality of the directory. Please be aware that abusive submissions will result in the removal of all sites connected with the abuser.

- **Please only submit an URL to the Open Directory once. If a site has not been listed within three weeks, you may submit it again.**
- **Disguising your submission and submitting the same URL more than once is not permitted.**
  Example: *dmoz.org* and *dmoz.org/index.html*.
- **Please do not submit mirror sites. Mirror sites are sites that contain identical content, but have different URLs altogether.**
- **Sites with illegal content are forbidden in the Open Directory. Examples of illegal material include, but are not limited to, child pornography and sites infringing on copyright.**
- **Please avoid submitting sites with addresses that redirect to another address.**
- **Submit sites to the most relevant category. Sites intentionally submitted to inappropriate or unrelated categories will be removed.**
- **Wait until your site is complete before submitting your URL. Sites that are incomplete, contain "Under Construction" notices, or contain broken graphics or links aren't good candidates for the directory.**
- **Pornographic submissions should be limited to the Adult category.**
- **Non-English sites should be submitted to the appropriate category under World.**
- **Sites consisting largely of affiliate links should not be submitted.**

> Mirror sites are sites that contain identical content, but have different URLs altogether.

Volunteering as editors for the ODP has let us be a "fly on the wall" at ODP, something, as professional positioners, that we'd like to be able to do at all the major engines and directories. It has given us a true appreciation for the complexities of an editor's job and assured our respect for the people and the process. We've also learned that such a patently human effort (unlike the spidered engines) creates both pluses and minuses. For example, as editors, we never know if our decisions will have staying power. Anything that one editor adds or changes, another editor can decide to delete or change again.

Robin recently experienced this situation, much to her consternation. She and a co-editor had determined that their category of more than fifty links was becoming too big and cumbersome. So, following the editors' FAQ that suggests that a category should be split when it exceeds thirty links, she spent two hours creating the subcategory and rebuilding the existing category for postsplit consistency. Shortly thereafter, a third editor came along who didn't like the idea of splitting the subcategory, and he changed it all back again!

Through trial and error, we've learned that communication between category editors can be time consuming and tricky, but the best categories are built by editors who respect and talk to one another. The ODP is a very human work, which means any search results obtained through it will be a mixture of heart, humor, and enlightened subjectivity.

Creating Your Strongest Submission

Choose your category wisely! This is crucial for submission to all directories, and it is examined more thoroughly in Chapter 29.

If you choose the wrong category for your ODP submission, it might kick off this chain of events: After determining that the category on a submission form isn't a good fit, the ODP editor can transfer your submission to another category. In order to do that, he or she will have to visit the ODP main page and drill down looking for the "perfect" category. This is time consuming, and a lot of editors won't do it. So, do the work yourself ahead of time and choose the

> The ODP is a very human work, which means any search results obtained through it will be a mixture of heart, humor, and enlightened subjectivity.

best category for your Web site. You'll stand a much better chance at getting into the index.

Avoid hype and keyword stuffing. Offer the editors a down-to-earth description and title that introduce your site in an accurate and helpful way to Web surfers. Although you'll want to include your most important keywords in both the title and description wherever possible, use those keywords appropriately rather than repetitively. Some editors will automatically delete a submission that contains a lot of marketing hype, and others may rewrite the description in a way that is not in the best interest of your site. Although you cannot control an editor's impulses or biases, you can create a great first impression by approaching the submission process with thoughtful integrity.

Don't put your title or description in ALL CAPS, and don't just list keyword after keyword. Make sure that your title and description are professionally written and effectively describe your site. Always keep in mind that ODP editors volunteer their time and energy to the directory, and they're often overworked. Make it as easy on them as possible and you'll be able to get your pages listed.

> *Avoid hype and keyword stuffing.* Offer the editors a down-to-earth description and title that introduce your site in an accurate and helpful way to Web surfers.

Multiple Categories

The rule of thumb for most directory submissions is and has been—submit to one category only. However, there appears to be some leeway with the ODP. If you feel that your site realistically fits into two categories, submit to both categories. However, keep in mind that some editors prefer not to list sites in *their* category if the site is already listed in *someone else's* category. Therefore, submit to your most important category first and, once that is successful, try submitting to another category.

If you submit in another category but can't get in, and if you have a legitimate reason for needing to be in both categories, try writing to the editor of the second category. Explain your reasoning in a very nice way, and ask if he or she will consider adding your site. One of the benefits of the ODP is that you do have access to an editor, so use that benefit if needed.

Further, you can sometimes get interior pages listed if the content of those pages justifies being listed in a separate category from the main page.

Straight from the Horse's Mouth

Q & A with an Open Directory Project editor, who wishes to remain anonymous.

Q. *Please tell us the process you take as an editor, from the moment you see a submission until the moment you accept it into the index (or reject it).*

A. The first thing I do when I get a submission is to check to see where else in the ODP the page is listed. Because of the importance of the ODP, many people are spamming the index by submitting a lot of interior or doorway pages in addition to the main page. Or they're submitting the same page in numerous categories. If it's listed in several places already, I generally reject the submission unless I see a solid reason for their being listed in that many places.

Then, I visit the site itself. I look through the site, see whether the graphics load, and try to determine whether it appears to have been updated recently. I look to see if there's more than one page in the site, and I click on a few links to make sure they work.

Based on the content of the site, I decide whether the site has been submitted in the proper category. If it hasn't, I move it to that category. If I don't edit that category, then the site has to go through yet another editor before being accepted into the index.

If the site has been submitted in the correct category, I review the title and description on the submission form and make changes if needed. From there, if I approve the submission, I accept it into the category.

> You can sometimes get interior pages listed if the content of those pages justifies being listed in a separate category from the main page.

> If the site has been submitted in numerous categories, or if it's already listed several places in the ODP, I'll reject it.

Q. *Do you inform the Web site owners that you've accepted or rejected their submission?*

A. No, regretfully, I don't have time for that. Most editors don't.

Q. *What, if anything, would make you automatically reject a submission?*

A. If the Web site has a huge "Under Construction" sign on the first page, or a note that the page hasn't been updated in a quite a while, I'll reject it. If the page isn't ready for traffic, I won't put it into the index. If the site has been submitted in numerous categories, or if it's already listed several places in the ODP, I'll reject it.

I've had some submissions that were 404 File Not Found pages when I visited them. Obviously, I don't put them in the index!

However, with 18,000 editors, others have much more stringent rejection policies than I do. Some editors will reject a site if it's been submitted in the wrong category. If the Web site owner simply lists keyword after keyword in the title or description placed on the submission form, they'll reject it. Or if they blatantly use marketing hype, it might get rejected.

Q. *You said that you review titles and descriptions. Do you change them? If so, why?*

A. I never like to see submissions that simply list keyword after keyword. That's not professional, and I don't want it in my category. So, yes, I'll change it. I correct misspellings or grammar errors. I remove marketing hype. I cut down descriptions if they're too long. Some people write their titles and descriptions in all caps, which is horrible!

Really, I prefer to leave the titles and descriptions as they've been presented because the Web site owners know better than anyone else how to describe the content of their sites. But if they don't present professional titles and descriptions, I won't let them go through like that.

Q. *Do the editors exchange notes about Web sites in their categories?*

A. Certainly. If someone submits a site over and over again, the editors will make a note of it, saying something like, "Repeated submissions—rejected." Therefore, other editors will know the history of the site and are better informed.

Also, we have several forums, and we do discuss problem Web sites there as well.

Q. *What advice do you have for our readers on how to get their sites indexed in the ODP?*

A. Make sure that your site is ready for traffic. If it's not, don't submit it to the ODP or any engine or directory. Finish your site, and then submit it.

Then, find the best subcategory for your site. Don't choose an upper-level category. Click down until you find the subcategory that's most appropriate for your site. You'll submit your site through the Add URL link on the bottom of the subcategory page.

Make sure you create an effective title and description. Don't list keyword after keyword. Don't make a marketing pitch. Make it honest and professional.

Q. *What if the site isn't accepted into the index within a few weeks? What should you do?*

A. Make sure you've submitted the site in the proper category. Spend some time surfing the ODP and find the category that's just right for your site. Then, resubmit it again.

Wait a few weeks. If you still don't get in, write a note to the editor of that category.

When writing to the editor, be very nice! I've gotten some of the nastiest notes, yet they expect me to stop what I'm doing and accept their site into the index. It doesn't work that way!

Instead, be very nice and professional. Explain that you submitted the site on a certain date, then again on another date. Give the editor the following information in your e-mail:

> URL of the site
> Title
> Description

> When writing to the editor, be very nice! I've gotten some of the nastiest notes, yet they expect me to stop what I'm doing and accept their site into the index. It doesn't work that way!

Exact path to the subcategory, such as Arts: Music: Marching: Colorguard: College

Q. *If we have a solid reason to request that our site be listed in another category, can we write a special request to the editor?*

A. Certainly! Again, be very nice, and give the same information that I mentioned above.

Explain why it's important that your site be listed in another category. Most editors are very receptive to requests if they're made in a professional and friendly manner.

Q. *ODP editors are volunteers. How do you like being an editor?*

A. I enjoy it! It's fun being able to put a Web site "on the map" in the ODP.

Q. *How can you become an ODP editor?*

A. At the ODP, there's a link to information on how to become an editor. Editors get to choose their subcategories, so go through the ODP carefully and find areas where there are no editors. You'll have a much better chance getting in if there's not already an editor in that category. Then, you complete a form to apply to become an editor, and you have to list a few sample sites that you would add to the index if you were an editor.

That's it. You're notified if you've been accepted.

Once you're accepted and have some experience, you can request to become an editor in additional subcategories. But start out slowly first in a subcategory that is small and where there are no editors.

How to Suggest a Change to Your OPD Listing

If you are currently in the ODP database but would like to change your category, title, or description, first go to the category page in the ODP that lists your site. At the top right side of the page, where the Add URL link is, you'll also see the Update URL link. Click there and follow the directions. As with Yahoo! change requests, don't

> Explain why it's important that your site be listed in another category. Most editors are very receptive to requests if they're made in a professional and friendly manner.

waste the editor's time with unrealistic requests or in an effort to simply improve your site's rankings. Submit only appropriate requests and do so politely.

Getting Support

If all else fails, it is possible to e-mail directly to a category editor. Just click on the name of the editor at the bottom of your category page. You'll be able to see what other categories the editor may edit, and you'll find a link to an e-mail address. Use this option sparingly. You don't want to annoy an editor. Further, there may be several editors listed for your category, and you can't be sure which one reviewed your site.

From the Experts

At the time of this writing, the search industry had experienced a shift toward directories such as the ODP. With such emphasis and importance being attached to human-edited directories, what is the fate of the search engines?

Chris Sherman, About.com's Guide to Web Search (*websearch.about.com*), responded:

> I think the shift to directories is a natural response to the generally poor results offered by most search engines. In using the word "poor," I'm not necessarily blaming the engines. The problem is that when you have a vast index of pages and try to identify the most relevant documents based on one- or two-word queries, it's almost like doing mind-reading.
>
> Directories, because they are relatively small and are created by (ostensibly) selective editors, will naturally offer a more focused result set for a search. The problem with them is that they also miss large portions of the Web, so they're really not suitable for comprehensive searches.
>
> I think their popularity has two main drivers: First, they're easier to use for newcomers to the Net. Second, specifically in

> Don't waste the editor's time with unrealistic requests or in an effort to simply improve your site's rankings. Submit only appropriate requests and do so politely.

the case of the Open Directory, the data is free for anyone to use, so the major search engines had an economic incentive to incorporate them into their own services.

I don't see spiders fizzling out—there will always be a need for a comprehensive index to the Web. I do see fewer companies doing spidering—there will probably be a core group that specializes more on search (as opposed to the other services offered by portals) who will continue to improve their spiders. With the advent of XML and other META data, it will theoretically be possible for spidered indexes to become much better, especially if we can get to the point where there's enough semantic information available in documents that search engines can evolve into "reasoning" engines. This is the vision of Web creator Tim Berners-Lee, and I think if enough people support META data projects, it will likely come about.

AOL Search

search.aol.com

Although AOL Search did not make the top ten of the StatMarket.com rankings for 1999, it is a power to be reckoned with because of AOL's impressive subscriber base (20 million members for AOL and 2.2 million for CompuServe), its aggressive pursuit of powerful partners, and its history-making merger with Time Warner. Whether this merger will affect the way AOL Search operates is not known at the time of this writing. However, it is very possible that AOL Search will grow further away from dependency on its search partners and move toward unique search solutions. Therefore, be sure to spend time at AOL Search's Add URL pages to learn the most recent information before submitting.

AOL Search, like Netscape Search and MSN Search, benefits from the power of the portals. Netscape and IE5 browsers offer their proprietary search services as the default search service, giving them a significant added advantage, particularly to "newbies" who don't yet know how to change their defaults. AOL Search has that same advantage.

> With the advent of XML and other META data, it will theoretically be possible for spidered indexes to become much better, especially if we can get to the point where there's enough semantic information available in documents that search engines can evolve into "reasoning" engines.

AOL Search replaced its predecessor AOL NetFind and combines information from the Open Directory for its directory component, and Inktomi for its search engine component. It also lists popular Web sites even if they're not in the ODP. The Web Articles section is powered by Inktomi.

Tips for AOL Search

Since AOL Search combines results from the Open Directory Project and Inktomi, look at the submission guidelines for those two areas. Though you may submit to the Open Directory Project through the AOL Search forms, there is no known advantage for doing so. Instead, submit directly to the Open Directory Project.

Though you may submit to the Open Directory Project through the AOL Search forms, there is no known advantage for doing so. Instead, submit directly to the Open Directory Project.

For more information on this topic, visit our Web site at www.businesstown.com

Chapter 29

Yahoo!

Yahoo!

www. yahoo.com

The oldest major search service on the Web, Yahoo! is showing no signs of aging. Instead of slowing down, it has become the big bruiser of the search engines, with the power to make or break a Web site. Technically a directory rather than a search engine, it has grown to be one of the seven largest "portals" on the World Wide Web and, by all measures, is by far the most popular search service in the world. In its role as a portal site, it offers more than it did when it was *only* the powerhouse search engine: news and sports headlines, Wall Street updates, weather, its own brand of e-mail, and much more. Essentially, Yahoo! has grown from being a "starting point" to becoming a "one stop" resource on the Web, bookmarked by millions for daily visits.

This is why getting listed in the Yahoo! directory—and getting listed within your most important category and with your most effective title and description—should be the number-one goal of every Web marketer.

Failing at your Yahoo! submission is a marketing disaster. Don't take any chances; do it right the first time.

How Does Yahoo! Differ from a Search Engine?

Yahoo! is not a search engine—it is a directory. Therefore, the words you place within the META tags and content of your Web pages have no direct, automated influence on how your site is ranked within Yahoo! Instead, it is the information you complete within the Yahoo! online submission form that will help determine where and how you are ranked. The submission form will be the key determinant of whether or not your site gets listed in a Yahoo! category at all—when it is reviewed by the Yahoo! editor. To add insult to injury (or frustration to anxiety), even if you do get listed, a Yahoo! editor may determine that your requested category isn't the right one and so may place you into an altogether different category. Further, the title or description you request may be slightly or severely edited by the Yahoo! editor.

Here's another way in which submitting to a directory and an engine is different. When a search engine spider visits a Web site, it lists each page from the site independently from one another. Ranking of each page depends on the content and coding of each page and not on the Web site in general. That's why it's appropriate to submit every important page separately to the engines. However, with Yahoo!, you submit your *entire* Web site by submitting the home page alone, not individual pages. You do this by completing an online form with information about your site and the URL of your home page. An editor approves or rejects the submission, and your site is added to the directory if it's approved.

Another difference between Yahoo! and most search engines is that, whereas search engines have spiders constantly collecting new Web sites, Yahoo! does not seek out new listings for its categories. Therefore, your site will probably never be listed in Yahoo! category, unless you submit it. You may find your site picked up and listed as a "Web Page" match through Inktomi, but that doesn't give a site the same marketing effectiveness as that of being accepted into a Yahoo! category. For more information on Inktomi, see Chapter 25.

We started this chapter by telling you that META tags have no automatic effect on a Yahoo! submission. This is true—META tags, ALT tags, and other similar coding are not automatically used by Yahoo! to quantify or qualify your Web site. However, because an editor reviews each submitted site thoroughly, it makes sense to have the META tags consistent with the content of the site. Mixed messages might create some uncertainty for the editor, and this could affect your site's submission.

Make your submission preparation a first-class effort. Review your entire site carefully to make certain that it is in top-notch shape with no incomplete content, broken links, missing images, or notices of "under construction." Check out your competition in your desired Yahoo! category. Does your site look as professional as your competition? Are you offering any new or expanded content?—a big plus with Yahoo!'s editors.

> With Yahoo!, you submit your *entire* Web site by submitting the home page alone, not individual pages.

Don't try to pull a fast one on Yahoo!'s very capable human editors. Make sure that the content of your site reflects the description you include on the submission form. It will be checked! Approach Yahoo! with respect, and chances are Yahoo! will respect you.

Keeping in mind that only about 30 percent of the submissions to Yahoo! ever make it into the directory, you should feel some modicum of success if you get in at all, even if it's not into the most desirable category. But there are ways to increase the odds for Yahoo! success significantly, so read on.

How Yahoo! Works

In order to craft a Yahoo! submission that will work most effectively for marketing your site, first it is helpful to understand how Web surfers use Yahoo! There are two very different ways for a Web surfer to obtain information through Yahoo! One is by entering words into the search box at the top center of the Yahoo! home page to elicit one page or more of returns; the other is by drilling down through the categories that begin on the home page. For example, to find out about the elementary schools in an area you're considering moving to, you might start at the Yahoo! home page by clicking on the category listing "Education." This will take you to a page listing several dozen subcategories, of which you would choose and click on "K-12." This brings you to another listing of subcategories, of which you would choose "schools," then "elementary," "by region," "United States," and finally the state and city of interest. Although this drilling down approach takes a few seconds more than doing a keyword search, researchers can learn a lot along the way, and it is a preferred method of accessing Yahoo! information by some visitors.

When you perform a search at Yahoo!'s search box, you will generally receive results derived from two different databases:

1. From Yahoo!s own database
This is the database we have been discussing when talking about submitting to a Yahoo! category. It is the preferred method for establishing a Yahoo! presence.

> Keeping in mind that only about 30 percent of the submissions to Yahoo! ever make it into the directory, you should feel some modicum of success if you get in at all.

2. From the Inktomi search engine

You can tell at a glance if a site is in a Yahoo! category instead of being in the Inktomi database. The first thing you see in Yahoo! search results are the category listings that match your search criteria. Under those categories, you'll see Web Site Matches, which are sites that are in Yahoo!'s database. Below that, you will see Web Pages, which are results from the Inktomi index. When you view the results, one of the easiest ways to learn if you're looking at a Yahoo! listing or an Inktomi listing is to look at the menu bar at the top of the page. If Web Site Matches is highlighted on the menu bar, you're viewing results from the Yahoo! index. If Web Pages is highlighted, you're viewing Inktomi results.

This is how, even if your Web site has never been accepted into a Yahoo! category, it may appear within the returns of a Yahoo! search.

In order to get listed in the supplementary search results from the Inktomi engine, you'll need to submit your site successfully to HotBot, which we've discussed in Chapter 25.

Remember, though it is important to have a presence in Inktomi because of the various engines it feeds, it is not enough in Yahoo! The Inktomi-fueled matches are presented *after* any Yahoo! matches, and we all know it is better to be at the top of the returns!

Submission Guidelines and Tips from Yahoo!

In the following section, we're pasting (**in bold**) the most recent information available from the Yahoo! Web site regarding Yahoo!'s submission guidelines and tips. However, when you're ready to complete your online submission form, you should go to *add.yahoo.com/fast/add?152024* to see if any changes that may affect your submission have occurred after this book's publication date. Our comments about Yahoo!'s guidelines are printed in non-bold type.

When you perform a search at Yahoo!'s search box, you will generally receive results derived from two different databases:

1. From Yahoo!s own database
2. From the Inktomi search engine

Direct from Yahoo.com

The following form is for suggesting sites to the Yahoo! directory.

- **If your site is already listed in Yahoo! and you would like us to make changes, please use the change form (*add.yahoo.com/fast/change*).**

  If your site is already listed in a Yahoo! category, and you wish to change its URL, description, title, or category, you'll have to use the change form that Yahoo! provides: (*add.yahoo.com/fast/change*). There will be more about this procedure later in this chapter.

- **If you are suggesting a chat area, scheduled chat or live broadcast, including audio or video, please submit directly to Yahoo! Net Events**

  Please verify the following before you proceed:

- **You have read the brief explanation of how to suggest a site (*docs.yahoo.com/info/suggest*) to Yahoo!.**

- **You have searched the directory and confirmed that your site is not already listed in a Yahoo! category.**

  Check for your site by entering the complete URL into the search box. If your site shows up with Web Site Matches indicated on the menu bar, it is already in the directory. If it doesn't show up at all, you will want to submit to Yahoo!. However, your site may show up but not be listed under a category or with Web Pages indicated on the menu bar. In this case, it is in the complementary database fueled by Inktomi, and you will want to submit to Yahoo!

- **You have found an appropriate category for your site. (If you haven't already done so, please read our detailed explanation for help finding that category.)**

  It is critical that you choose an appropriate category for your site's submission. If you don't, there are several things that might happen, most of which are not desirable.

First, the editor may accept your submission, putting your site into the inappropriate category you have suggested. You'd probably have to learn to live with this since getting Yahoo! to reconsider after

> It is critical that you choose an appropriate category for your site's submission.

the fact is difficult. The editors have enough to do dealing with first-time submissions.

Second, the editor may balk at the category you have chosen and place your site into another category, one that is not to your liking. Third, you may get lucky and the editor will place you into the category you should have suggested in the first place. And fourth, the editor may reject your submission altogether.

One way to help you determine the most appropriate category for your site is to focus first on the best keywords for your site. Review our discussion about keywords in Chapter 4 before formulating your keyword strategy for Yahoo!. Then go to the Yahoo! search box on the home page and enter in the keywords, one at a time. What categories come up? The key to success here is to determine which of the keywords is the most important one for your site—which keyword will your potential customers use when trying to find a site like yours? Whatever category is pulled up by entering that keyword is probably the one that is best for you.

However, keep in mind that many searchers pick the first category they see in the results. So, if you can choose the first category, or at least one toward the top of the page, it's to your benefit.

If the category pulled up is not the right one for you, consider another category, or rethink the strength of the keyword with which you have been searching.

If you're still not sure about what category is appropriate for your site, spend some time on this very informative page:

www.yahoo.com/info/suggest/appropriate.html

And while we're talking about appropriate categories, let us remind you that there are appropriate Yahoo! directories to be considered, too. For example, non-English–language sites may not be accepted into the parent Yahoo! directory (*www.yahoo.com*) if there is an international Yahoo! directory for sites in that site's language, such as Yahoo! Italia (*www.yahoo.it*) and Yahoo! Chinese Properties (*chinese.yahoo.com*). And sites that are purely regional should be submitted to one of Yahoo!'s regional sites, linked off the bottom of the Yahoo! home page.

However, submitting to any of the regional directories will get your site into the main Yahoo! index.

> The key to success here is to determine which of the keywords is the most important one for your site—which keyword will your potential customers use when trying to find a site like yours?

> Sometimes there is more than one category that might make sense for your Web site.

- **You have clicked on the "Suggest a Site" at the bottom of the page from the category you think most appropriate.**

Suggest your site *from* the category you think most appropriate. The best way to determine this is to become familiar with all the categories relevant to your site. Start on the Yahoo! home page and drill down through the categories. Wherever you find your most successful competitors, make note. This is a category you will want to examine more carefully.

Sometimes there is more than one category that might make sense for your Web site. Read more about choosing your category later in this chapter.

When you determine the best category for your site, go to that page in Yahoo! and click on the "Suggest a Site" link at the very bottom of the page.

Proceed to Step One

If you answer "Yes" to all of the above, then please:

Suggest a Site: Step 1 of 4

Category:

You are suggesting that we add your site to the following category:

Recreation/Outdoors/Paddling

- If you think this is not the most appropriate category, then please find the one you want and click on the "Suggest a Site" link at the bottom of the page from there.
- Quick reminders: regionally specific sites belong in "Regional" categories; commercial sites belong in "Business and Economy" categories; personal homepages belong in the "Society and Culture:People:Personal Home Pages" category.
- You will have a chance (during this process) to suggest to us an additional category for your site listing.
- **Please note that the final placement of your site is determined by Yahoo!.**

Site Information:
Title:

- **Please keep the title brief.**
- **Use the official business name for the title of a commercial site.**
- **Please do not use ALL capital letters.**
- **Please do not include marketing slogans or superlatives (e.g., "The Best site on the Internet" or "We're the Number One Dealer…")**

URL:

http://

- **Not sure what this is? It's the address of your site that begins with "http://"**
- **Please supply the entire URL and double check to make sure it is correct.**

Description:

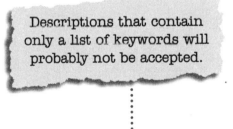

Descriptions that contain only a list of keywords will probably not be accepted.

- **Please write a brief, readable phrase or sentence—no longer than twenty five words.**

Descriptions that contain only a list of keywords will probably not be accepted; that is, if your site sells apples, do not submit a description that reads: "McIntosh apples, Granny Smith apples, red delicious apples, golden delicious apples, etc." Try, instead, "Offering gift baskets containing many varieties of apples, including McIntosh, Granny Smith, red delicious, and golden delicious."

If your site is a business site, briefly describe your products or services.

If your location (country, city and/or town) is important, make sure to include it within this description. For example: "Offering gift baskets containing many varieties of apples, including McIntosh, Granny Smith, red delicious, and golden delicious at locations throughout Vermont."

- **Avoid repeating the site title or category name in the description.**
- **Do not use ALL capital letters.**
- **Please Do Not Capitalize the First Letter of Every Word.**

For the title, you may capitalize the first letter of each word in the title; remember, if your site is a commercial site, the title must be the company name. For the description, you may capitalize the first letter in the sentence and elsewhere where appropriate.

- **HTML tags are not allowed.**
- **Please refrain from using marketing slogans such as, "We're Number One," or "The Best Site on the Internet!"**

Hype of any kind is not looked at kindly by Yahoo! editors. It is probably also best not to include brand names.

Yahoo! reserves the right to edit suggested descriptions.

> Hype of any kind is not looked at kindly by Yahoo! editors. It is probably also best not to include brand names.

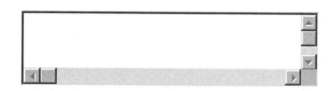

Proceed to Step Two

Suggest a Site: Step 2 of 4

Category Suggestions (Optional):

Is there an *additional* Yahoo! category where you think your site belongs? If yes, please let us know here:

Obviously, this is the place to put your second choice of category for your site. Briefly explain the reasoning behind your suggestion. If there is no good match for an additional category, leave this field blank.

Remember, businesses cannot be listed in noncommercial categories. If you have a business site, you should begin your drill-down category search from Yahoo!'s home page at the "Business and Economy" text link, the second category listed.

Further, if your site is purely a regional site, that is, if you have a retail flower shop with locations only in California, you should submit to a regional Yahoo!. See the listings of regional Yahoo!s at the bottom of the Yahoo! home page (Yahoo! Get Local). The submission of a regional site to the parent directory may be ignored.

Do you feel Yahoo! should create a *new category* to list your site and others like it? If yes, please let us know here:

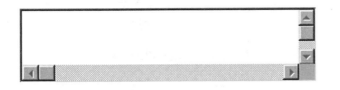

> If your site is purely a regional site, that is, if you have a retail flower shop with locations only in California, you should submit to a regional Yahoo!. See the listings of regional Yahoo!s at the bottom of the Yahoo! home page.

Again, only fill out this box if there is a yet uncreated category that you feel would be helpful, not only to your site, but to the people who use Yahoo! for their searches. Find an existing category that is relevant to your site, then refine the category by suggesting a new subcategory. Briefly explain the reason for your suggestion for an additional category.

Proceed to Step Three

With most companies today, employees come and go, so it might be best to use a generic webmaster@mydomain.com address for Web site submissions. This way, any webmaster employed by your company may correspond with Yahoo! about your site as needed.

Suggest a Site: Step 3 of 4

Contact Information:

In the event that we have questions about the placement of this site and to ensure that listings in Yahoo! cannot be changed by unauthorized persons, please provide the following:

Contact Person:

Contact Email:

Please note that this information will be kept strictly confidential.

Make a note of the e-mail address you supply since you will need to provide this in order to change your listing in the future. With most companies today, employees come and go, so it might be best to use a generic webmaster@mydomain.com address for Web site submissions. This way, any webmaster employed by your company may correspond with Yahoo! about your site as needed.

Geographical Location of the Site (if applicable):

City:

State/Province:

Country:

Postal Code:

Proceed to Step Four

Suggest a Site: Step 4 of 4

Time-Sensitive Information (if applicable):

Will this site only exist for a specific period of time? Please provide us with the date it will no longer be accessible. Format the date Month/Day/Year, for example 03/24/1999.

Will this site only exist for a specific period of time? Please provide us with the date it will no longer be accessible. Format the date Month/Day/Year, for example 03/24/1999.

End Date of Site:

Is the site about an event? Please provide the date (or dates) of the event. Again, format as Month/Day/Year, as in 03/24/1999.

Start Date of Event:

End Date of Event:

Time-sensitive sites can be quite successful in Yahoo! Don't hesitate to fill out these forms if your site is about an event that is going to begin and end on set dates. If the beginning date is close at hand, it is particularly important to let the Yahoo! editor know.

Final Comments:
Finally, if you have additional information that will help us place this site, please let us know. For example, if your site is not in English, an English description would be most helpful.

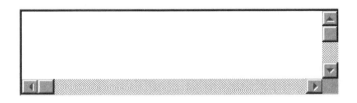

> Time-sensitive sites can be quite successful in Yahoo! Don't hesitate to fill out these forms if your site is about an event that is going to begin and end on set dates.

Yahoo! reserves the right to choose which URLs appear in the directory.

Here's where you get to tell Yahoo! what you think! If you've been trying for months to get listed, you can make a note of that fact here, as long as you do so in a nice, constructive way. If you have a great reason behind your second category or additional category request, you can reinforce it here by adding additional information. And, as with everything else in life, it probably doesn't hurt to say "Thank you."

Before you click on the Submit button, save the submission pages to your disk or printout. It is not unusual to have to resubmit to Yahoo!, and you'll save yourself time and needless errors by working from a saved copy. Pushing the Submit button even from a saved page will work if you're connected to the Web.

Review each step of the submission form one more time before you click Submit because once you're in Yahoo!, it is very difficult to change your listing.

> Review each step of the submission form one more time before you click Submit because once you're in Yahoo!, it is very difficult to change your listing.

More About the Title of Your Submission

When you're crafting the title and description of your Yahoo! submission, keep in mind the importance of understanding your best keyword strategy (Chapter 4). This is critical in Yahoo! because Yahoo! checks its index of Web sites and returns listings in this order:

> Yahoo! categories containing the keyword
> Sites with the keyword in their titles
> Sites with the keyword in their descriptions

Note: Try not to split your important keyword phrase in your title!

When people browse Yahoo! listings by category, sites are listed alphabetically. Therefore, having a title that begins with a letter at the beginning of the alphabet means the site will appear higher on the page, boosting the odds that someone will find the listing and click through to visit your site. When searchers go past the listing of categories and straight to the Yahoo! Site Matches, the Web sites are no longer listed in total alphabetical order. If the entire title is the keyword phrase, the site may be listed toward the top. If the keyword phrase isn't split in the title or description, the site may be listed more toward the top. Splitting the keyword phrase will generally cause you to lose ranking.

The biggest challenge for established companies may be that Yahoo!s policy is to accept submitted titles that match the name of the company or Web site. So, you can't choose a title simply for its effectiveness with Yahoo! search rankings. If your Web site or company name begins with a letter toward the end of the alphabet, you may try submitting a title very similar to the Web site's name but with a better alphabetic order, and hope for the best. Understand, though, that the editor may do what she does best—edit!

Another tactic that we have seen used with varying success is this: Create a new Web site independent of your main site that is lying lackluster at the end of the alphabet in its Yahoo! category. Name the new site with a beginning letter of the alphabet.

Warning: If the sites are not distinctive enough, Yahoo! may refuse the listing, or it may remove the existing listing and replace it with a listing for the "new" site.

Refrain from using ASCII characters such as ! and # in your title in an effort to get a higher ranking, or you'll risk a delay in getting your site indexed if it gets indexed at all, and Yahoo! editors will probably change it anyway. However, if you are already using ASCII characters throughout your site, and particularly if your company's legal name includes an ASCII character, it should be accepted.

Don't try the old Yellow Pages technique of beginning your submitted title with "AAA" before your company name. The Yahoo! editors won't allow this, and it could cause a delay or rejection of your site.

> If the sites are not distinctive enough, Yahoo! may refuse the listing, or it may remove the existing listing and replace it with a listing for the "new" site.

Cut the Hype!

Sites with honest titles without marketing hype will generally get priority over those with titles that need close review. Here are some title notes from the Yahoo! Web site:

> If it is early enough in your company's gestation to do so, give it a name that reflects what it does.

Please make sure that the title is no longer than five (5) words and not all capital letters (e.g. XYZ CORPORATION or THE BEST SITE ON THE INTERNET, etc.). For companies, the title MUST be the company name. Any request to change a business name to something other than its actual name will be ignored.

Here's a suggestion that may work for startups a lot better than established companies. If it is early enough in your company's gestation to do so, give it a name that reflects what it does. For example, if you sell green widgets, a name like Acme Green Widgets is much stronger than Acme Ventures, Inc.–not only for the search engines, but for letting the public know what you're all about in every marketing venue–from print ads, to signs, to the lettering on your trucks. Even an established company may want to consider changing its name for better effectiveness in Yahoo!, or creating a subsidiary with its own Web site and unique content.

More About the Description for Your Submission

Your description must include as many of your most important keywords as possible, but the description should be aptly crafted and not just a list of keywords. Remember, this is what surfers will find when your site is returned in a search, so you want the description to represent your site well and attractively. Make your description accurate and enticing without making it a blatant sales pitch.

The maximum number of words in your description is twenty five, or two hundred characters, including spaces. Try not to split your important keyword phrase in your description. Use your important keywords early and often. If you use hyphenated keywords, Yahoo! will probably count them as one word instead of two.

Yahoo's Business Express Submission Service

Yahoo! offers an express service for businesses that want a more rapid than usual review of their Web site submission. For a $199 fee, Yahoo! Business Express guarantees that your Web site will be reviewed for possible inclusion in Yahoo! within seven business days. Notice that it does not guarantee that your site will be indexed by Yahoo!, just that it will be reviewed within that timeline.

Do not kid yourself into thinking: "Aha! Here's how I finally get my fraudulent title into Yahoo!." The criteria for submissions and acceptance remain the same. Don't try to get duplicate listings in Yahoo! by submitting another Web site in a different category. The word out there is that Yahoo! is watching for this practice carefully.

An advantage to submitting through the Business Express Service is that you'll know within seven days if your site has made it into the index. If it doesn't, you'll receive an e-mail explaining why. Then, you can change your site accordingly in order to meet their criteria. With this service, unlike submitting through regular channels, you have recourse if your site doesn't make it into the index.

Business Express is not for everybody. If you are patient and can afford not to get listed quickly in Yahoo!, sit out the eight-week or longer wait—never knowing if your site will even be reviewed this time around or if you will have to resubmit and wait even longer out there in the cold and dark.

However, if your site meets the following qualifications, seriously consider using Business Express.

To qualify for Business Express, you must meet these conditions as outlined at Yahoo! 's Web site:

How to qualify
To qualify for Business Express you must meet and accept all of the following conditions. Please check the box next to each item to indicate you understand and accept each condition:

> Don't try to get duplicate listings in Yahoo! by submitting another Web site in a different category. The word out there is that Yahoo! is watching for this practice carefully.

❑ I have read and agree to be bound by the Business Express Terms of Service.

❑ I have verified that my site does not already appear in the Yahoo! Directory and I understand that this is not the place to request a change for an existing site. [Section 2.6]

❑ My site supports multiple browsers and capabilities. (For example, Java-only sites will not be listed). [Section 3.1]

❑ My site must be in the English language and my business is based in the United States. [Section 3.1]

❑ I understand that there is no guarantee my site will be added to Yahoo! [Section 2.5]

❑ I understand that Yahoo! reserves the right to edit and place my site as appropriate. [Section 4.1]

❑ I understand that if my site is added, it will be treated as any other site in Yahoo! and will receive no special consideration. [Section 4.1]

❑ My site must be up and running 24 hours a day, seven days a week. [Section 3.1]

❑ No parts of my site are under construction. All links on the site work. [Section 3.1]

❑ My site contains substantively unique content that is not already accessible from the Yahoo! Directory. (For example: a user that submits multiple portals to the very same content is not submitting substantively unique content.) [Section 3.1]

> Keep in mind that you must join Yahoo! and get a Yahoo! password before being allowed to use the Business Express.

Keep in mind that you must join Yahoo! and get a Yahoo! password before being allowed to use the Business Express. This means that they'll have a record of you and your submissions, which they can access at any time.

If Your Site Is Accepted

If your site is accepted into a category by Yahoo!, you will receive an e-mail message with only a few of the details you really want to know. It will read like this:

The URL you submitted has been added to Yahoo!. It will appear after our next update, which will probably occur within the next 2–4 days. You can find your listing at that time by looking through the "What's New" listing or by doing a keyword search. In order to keep Yahoo! accurate, please let us know of changes to your listing in the future.

If you're like most of us, you'll be on pins and needles wondering, "Did I get into the *category* I really want? Did they change my *title*? Oh, no, I hope they didn't put me into a *regional* directory!"

After you spend a few days nervously rejoicing, telling everyone you know about your Yahoo! success, and checking the "What's New" section every 15 minutes to see your listing, you'll finally find it under "What's New." A few days after that, your site will also appear in its permanent category or categories. You'll be at the top of the list during this time, and a "new" icon will be put next to your listing, which is a big traffic booster. Enjoy your moment of glory because soon your site will slip down to its permanent, alphabetical placement—however lofty or lowly that may be.

If Your Site Isn't Accepted

Try again!

If you have submitted your site and it doesn't get listed within two weeks using the regular submission process, it could simply be that an editor didn't have time to visit the site, and not that there's a problem with the site itself. Remember that if you're submitting to a very popular category, the number of submissions is astronomical. So, keep on trying!

Resubmit your site. If you don't get in, send an e-mail to their special e-mail address, which we'll discuss later in this chapter. Wait two weeks, and if you don't get in, call their phone number, which will also be discussed later. You won't be penalized for resubmitting your site, and sometimes you have to do it in order to get listed. You might want to consider submitting to an alternative category if your submission keeps failing, though it is hard to know unless you've

If you have submitted your site and it doesn't get listed within two weeks using the regular submission process, it could simply be that an editor didn't have time to visit the site, and not that there's a problem with the site itself.

received a formal rejection. Further, look carefully at your site and consider what improvements could be made to make the site better.

What if Your Site Gets Rejected?

Remember that only about 30 percent of all submissions ever make it into Yahoo!, so your site being rejected, is, regretfully, a possibility. However, according to our sources, the most common reason a site isn't listed is that Yahoo! did not have time to review it. Further, it is probable that some sites are reviewed and rejected though you're not officially informed of this decision. It has been suggested by more than one Web marketer that Yahoo! omits sending formal rejection messages in order to cut down on follow-up arguments and hassles. We don't know, but we concur that a timely response to a submission would be helpful to all submitters.

So, where does that leave you? You could be resubmitting your site over and over again, wasting your time and Yahoo!'s. Should you give up? We don't think so. We have seen instances, though, where a site was rejected once, but then accepted later, and Yahoo! is important enough to muster up the strength for another try.

To help determine whether your site was rejected or simply neglected because of the time crunch, you need to watch your server logs for at least two weeks immediately following a submission. You should be able to spot a Yahoo! surfer who has visited your site. Here's what to look for.

When you submit your site, Yahoo! sends out a spider to verify your page. This will appear in your server logs something like this:

add.yahoo.com - - [23/Feb/1999:12:34:23 -0800] "GET / HTTP/1.0" 200 5640

This means that the spider retrieved your page, not that a human reviewer has seen it.

However, a Yahoo! reviewer or editor generally will leave a different "trail" in your server logs a few days after the spider has visited.

> Remember that only about 30 percent of all submissions ever make it into Yahoo!, so your site being rejected, is, regretfully, a possibility.

This statement:
surf.yahoo.com/submissions/980119/568912-7960.html

shows you that this was a visit from a reviewer. If your site was accepted, you'll be notified soon. If you don't hear anything, it is likely that your submission was rejected.

Again, don't give up. Reread this chapter, continue to improve your site, and then resubmit it after you've given the revision your all. If after this your submission still fails, consider submitting to an alternative category. With the right keyword strategy, you may still be able to pop up in the rankings when searches are made for your most important keywords.

E-mail Support Address

Yahoo! offers an e-mail support address for those having problems getting listed or getting changes made. If you're submitting a new site, submit the site as outlined earlier. If your site isn't indexed within two weeks, resubmit it following the same procedure. If the site still isn't indexed within two weeks, send an e-mail to:
url-support@yahoo-inc.com

Include in your e-mail the exact URL that you submitted, but you do not need to include the categories you submitted to or the actual dates you submitted on. Make sure that you're totally honest about how many times you've submitted the site because the editor just might check on it.

If you're submitting changes to an existing site, the procedure is different. You need to submit the changes on Yahoo!'s change form:
add.yahoo.com/fast/change

Wait at least seven to ten business days for processing, and then send them an e-mail to the same e-mail address:
url-support@yahoo-inc.com

> Make sure that you're totally honest about how many times you've submitted the site because the editor just might check on it.

With change requests, include the URL, the exact date of the change request, and the desired categories.

Using the e-mail support address does not give you a better chance at being accepted, nor is it a way to get around the normal "add" or "change" submission process. It is a feature for those who have done all the right things but who still haven't gotten the action they requested. For example, don't use the address to tell Yahoo! that you've just done a submission and wanted to make sure they got it. And never use it for a first-time submission.

Note for Web marketing firms: Yahoo! requests that Web marketers who deal with multiple sites not use the support addresses for more than five URLs per week. Yahoo! will check into your past submissions and e-mail requests to them, so always play it on the up and up.

Here's a copy of the e-mail you'll receive if you submit your site to Yahoo!s e-mail address. For submission success, pay careful attention to these guidelines.

E-MAIL

You have reached the Yahoo! User Support Department. We handle queries regarding listings in the directory. If your request is related to one of our regional directories (e.g. Yahoo! UK & Ireland, Yahoo! Australia & NZ, Yahoo! France etc.), please direct your message to the appropriate directory's Webmaster or user support department.

The User Support Department assists users who are experiencing problems getting their site or change requests reviewed. Due to the volume of requests we receive, we are unable to personally respond to each message; therefore, we have included a copy of the guidelines that must be followed before the User Support Department will open an inquiry. If your request does not meet these guidelines, your query will be ignored.

New Submissions
- **Please make at least two attempts (several weeks apart) to submit your site via our online form.**

> Using the e-mail support address does not give you a better chance at being accepted, nor is it a way to get around the normal "add" or "change" submission process.

- Follow all of the guidelines listed on the submission form.
- Do not submit multiple requests in a short period of time for the same URL. We consider this spamming, and your requests will be dropped from consideration.
- For information on how to submit a request, please read our detailed instructions at *www.yahoo.com/info/suggest*. If you are having a problem finding the "Suggest a Site" link, please re-read step number 3 on that page. If you are creating and submitting sites for other people, please limit the number of URLs you send us to five (5) per week. If you send us a laundry list of URLs, we will review the first five (5) and ignore the rest.
- Yahoo! wants to be as inclusive as possible, but we cannot guarantee your site will be included in the index, even if you have followed the guidelines listed above.

Change Requests

In order to locate a change request, we will need the URL and the exact date you submitted the request form. We are unable to locate change requests without the exact date. If you do not know the exact date, please resubmit your request via our online form at *add.yahoo.com/fast/change*, and allow several weeks for review. Don't forget to make a note of the date you submit your request.

If you cannot remember the original e-mail address used to submit the site, please use our online form anyway. Please include any alternate addresses in the "additional instruction" fields.

Search Results/Site Position Requests

Please note that site positioning is determined by a complex algorithm based on relevance, and we cannot change the order in which sites appear. For more information on how search results are compiled, please see our How-To Guide located at *howto.yahoo.com*. If you have followed these guidelines, rest assured that your e-mail will be reviewed—there is no need to send multiple copies of the same request. Again, due to the large volume of e-mail we receive, we are not always able to inform you of our

> Do not submit multiple requests in a short period of time for the same URL.

decision(s). Please be aware that a real person reviews all requests; therefore, the review process is not an immediate one.

Thank you for taking the time to read this message.

Yahoo! User Support Team

Is There Anything Else You Can Do to Get into Yahoo!?

Yahoo! has a special telephone number for listing inquiries, and calling this number is probably your best bet if resubmissions fail to get you listed or if a change request doesn't go through.

Call (408) 731-3333 in the United States and Canada; or 001-408-731-3333 from outside the United States and Canada.

When you call, leave your name, URL, phone number, e-mail address, and the date you submitted your site or change request on their answering machine.

You can also try posting a note on one of their feedback forms: *www.yahoo.com/info/support/contacts*

Another option is to send a snail mail letter to Yahoo!. The current address is:

Yahoo! Inc.
3420 Central Expressway
Santa Clara, CA 95051

> Keep in mind that if you get listed through any channels other than the traditional submission way, your description will more likely be written by an editor, and the description may or may not be what you would have written for the site yourself.

Keep in mind that if you get listed through any channels other than the traditional submission way, your description will more likely be written by an editor, and the description may or may not be what you would have written for the site yourself.

How to Suggest a Change to Your Yahoo! Listing

Yahoo! has a separate page for those wishing to change their listings: *add.yahoo.com/fast/change*

The suggestion, or change, form can be used if you need to:

Change the URL of your listing
Change the title of your listing
Edit the description of your listing
Suggest additional or different categories for your listing
Change the email address associated with your listing

Yahoo! spells it out for us: "Yahoo! must have a compelling reason to make changes to your listing. We will not change information that is already accurate."

So, you'll likely have better luck getting the change request to go through if it's perceived as something more than a reworking of your description or title for the sake of improving your ranking. Instead, combine your request to update your description with a more acceptable and serious reason for the change if you can find one. For example, if you've created a new domain name for your site, request that your description is changed at the same time. This could help improve the odds that Yahoo! will act upon your request.

Keep in mind that it is extremely difficult to get a change request to go through. Once editors place a site in Yahoo!'s index, they don't like to change it!

Some Additional Do's and Don'ts

Do's

- Do expect to wait a while to hear from Yahoo! unless you have used the Yahoo! Business Express Service. Submissions to Yahoo! often take six to eight weeks before a response is received. Sometimes, a response is never received from an initial submission. If you have not heard after two weeks, resubmit and begin the waiting period again.
- Do put whatever resources are at your disposal to get your site looking as sharp as possible and working as well as possible before you submit to Yahoo!. If your first choice category is already pretty thick with listings, consider adding new and

> "Yahoo! must have a compelling reason to make changes to your listing. We will not change information that is already accurate." You'll likely have better luck getting the change request to go through if it's perceived as something more than a reworking of your description or title for the sake of improving your ranking.

unique content to your site before submitting to Yahoo! Take a look at the competitors in your category: Does your site shape up? Does it look professionally designed? How is the navigation? The benefits of this exercise are twofold: Your site will look better to the Yahoo! editor and more attractive to the prospective buyers you hope to draw to your site.

- Do include link pages because Yahoo! seems to like them.
- Do take advantage of regional directories if your site is region specific. Acceptance into one of Yahoo!'s regional directories will accomplish two things for you: It will get you into the directory used by the potential customers who live in your region; and it will also get you into the parent Yahoo! directory, albeit most strongly for regionally oriented searches. If you have a regionally specific Web site, submit it to the appropriate Yahoo! regional directory. Regional submissions have a better chance of getting in since those editors often don't have as many submissions to consider as parent directory editors, and they are aiming to build a site with true regional flavor and a broad array of choices within that region. If you submit to a regional directory, your site will also be listed in Yahoo!'s main directory. Further, submitting to a regional directory may speed up the indexing process.

If you have a Canadian Web site, visit these helpful URLs:

ca.yahoo.com/docs/info/help.html
ca.yahoo.com/docs/info/suggest.html

- Do include a copyright notice and date on your home page, conventionally found at the bottom of Web pages. This is good practice anyway, plus it may give you a slight edge with Yahoo!

> Put whatever resources are at your disposal to get your site looking as sharp as possible and working as well as possible before you submit to Yahoo!

Real-World Stories

One colleague has had great success getting pages listed in Yahoo within 72 hours by submitting to a local Yahoo (i.e., Los Angeles, San Francisco) Don't forget—local counts and will put you on the search results page as a Category Match.

Don'ts

- Don't use any automated submission tools when submitting to Yahoo! If you are using a submission service to submit your Web site, make sure the service you use will hand-submit to Yahoo! And make sure, in writing, that you are in agreement about the title, description, and category the submission service will use for your site.
- Don't submit multiple doorway pages to Yahoo!.
- Don't submit a site unless it's top notch and ready for business. If you have any broken links, missing images, or under construction signs, your site won't get in.

Some people have tried to increase their Yahoo! presence by purchasing an additional domain that incorporates the keyword phrase, and titling the company or page also using the keyword phrase. If you decide to do this, use your new domain address as your e-mail address, use a different phone number, and make sure your two domains don't look alike or have the same content. Make sure that none of your submission information matches what you've submitted to Yahoo! before because, believe us, they will check. The only time this practice should even be considered is if each domain stands on its own and is truly appropriate for different audiences and different categories.

For example, if your company sells software, but you also provide consulting services to others, purchasing a domain for each aspect of your company might be appropriate.

> Don't submit a site unless it's top notch and ready for business. If you have any broken links, missing images, or under construction signs, your site won't get in.

How Can You Get Your Site in Bold Text or with the @ Symbol at the End?

You can't.

These designations are determined by Yahoo! when listing your site. You have no control over it, nor can you request it. A bold listing means that there are sublistings for a particular company or site. Clicking on a bold listing will take you to a special Yahoo! page for that company or site that contains links to and related to the site.

Having said this, we can report the experience of a colleague who was able to get his site in bold text, to which he could then add additional links under that listing. This is what he did:

> I submitted the company and main Web page to Yahoo! and ensured that the description was right for the category. Once this was done, I went back under my company link and filled out the Yahoo! submission form to add subpages to it. Some had to be submitted a few times until you get an editor that can see what you're doing and assist you. Some editors will see it and think you're trying to cheat, when in reality, you're getting more specific results for the people searching for your specific info.

The @ symbol is essentially a navigation helper on Yahoo! It indicates that a particular category is cross-linked in various areas in Yahoo!.

The @ symbol is essentially a navigation helper on Yahoo! It indicates that a particular category is cross-linked in various areas in Yahoo!.

For more information on this topic, visit our Web site at www.businesstown.com

The Popularity
Engines:
Snap, Direct Hit,
and Google

A s the Web continues to grow at an incredible rate, search technology continues to evolve, trying to meet the challenge of indexing the 7.7 billion pages anticipated on the Web by 2002 (Business 2.0 Magazine, 8/99). A fairly recent trend in this technology is to provide search results that have been highly affected by the relative "popularity" of indexed sites. The reasoning is: If a particular Web site has many other sites offering links to it or is a highly trafficked site, it must be a useful, important Web site for search engine visitors.

This trend complicates things for positioners who cannot instantly create popularity. However, its most serious consequences are for new sites that cannot hope to compete for top rankings against established sites with a strong network of links. This approach to providing search results also limits the variety of available offerings to surfers, which is antithetical to the very nature of the "traditional" World Wide Web. Fortunately, some of the popularity engines still offer a subdatabase that operates with algorithms unaffected by popularity, so those wishing to see all results, and not just popular results, can still scroll down past the top listings to find pay dirt.

There are many variations to the technologies that measure popularity and to the ways that popularity is incorporated into the ranking algorithms. Following are some of the details about three of the fastest growing, popularity-focused search engines and directories.

> A fairly recent trend in this technology is to provide search results that have been highly affected by the relative "popularity" of indexed sites.

Snap

www.snap.com
Owned by CNET, Snap is a joint venture with NBC. It isn't a search engine but a directory of Web sites, similar to Yahoo!. Snap uses GlobalBrain technology (globalbrain.net) to refine its results and deliver the most popular sites into the top slots of any search returns. This specialized technology records click-throughs—monitoring which indexed sites Snap visitors are clicking through to and then continuously rearranging its database so that the most popular sites move into the top rankings.

When visitors drill down through categories, they will still see sites arranged in alphabetical order, but when they use the search box, the rankings are returned based on the algorithms, including the popularity measure.

Danny Sullivan of SearchEngineWatch.com explains the workings of GlobalBrain and Direct Hit technology as, essentially, a democratic approach to searching on the Web:

> Both systems watch to see which pages users actually select from among the search results. These pages are considered better than others, especially if a person spends much time viewing them. In this way, searchers invisibly vote for the pages they like.

Inktomi supplements Snap's own Web site listings and is called upon only if a match has not been found in, first, the parent directory, and next, in the Live Directory.

There's no way to submit to the Inktomi index that Snap uses. Instead, submit to HotBot.

Submission Guidelines and Tips from Snap

In late 1999, Snap introduced the Live Directory, the innovative first step in a two-tiered system. The Live Directory is a testing ground—anyone may submit a site to it and see it indexed within a few days. The submission is much quicker than gaining access to other directories, primarily because it is not reviewed by an editor at this point. Instead, it is a democratic "come one, come all" approach. However, once accepted, the submitted site must perform well in the Live Directory in order to move up to the larger directory located on Snap's home page.

Here's how it works, according to Paul Wood, Snap's Senior Product Manager for Search and Directory.

www.snap.com
Owned by CNET, Snap is a joint venture with NBC. It isn't a search engine but a directory of Web sites, similar to Yahoo!.

The Snap Directory has been hand-built by our editors . . . everything in the Snap Directory has been tested and edited. The Live Directory, however, has not.

However, he says that a site can move from the Live Directory to the parent directory if it earns enough popularity points, as measured by GlobalBrain technology. "Once a site reaches a certain level of popularity, that will notify one of Snap's editors and we will transfer that site from the Live Directory to the main directory."

Another innovation for this directory is that, once you register as a submitter with Snap, you can check on the popularity status of every site you've submitted every time you visit Snap.com.

> "Once a site reaches a certain level of popularity, that will notify one of Snap's editors and we will transfer that site from the Live Directory to the main directory."

Submitting Tips for Snap

Determining your category in Snap.com is similar to determining your best category in Yahoo!. From the home page, Snap.com, click on the top tab labeled "Directory." This brings you to the Live Directory. Then, perform a search for the most important keywords of your site. Study the categories returned, see where your chief competitors are, and then choose the category most appropriate to your site. It sometimes seems as though there is no "just right" category fit for a Web site. Find the one closest to the ideal and submit to it, keeping in mind that Snap creates new categories regularly and your listing may some day be moved into a more appropriate one when it is created. Read more in Chapter 29 about determining directory categories that are best for your site.

If you've already had success with your Yahoo! submission, earning desirable rankings for your most important keywords, consider using your Yahoo! description when submitting to Snap. For Snap, though, you'll need to edit the description down to ten to fifteen words. Craft an appealing and keyword-studded submission while avoiding marketing hype.

Submit your site to only one category. Unlike Yahoo!, you can't opt to submit to a primary category and then request an additional category. However, the Snap editors may choose to cross-link your site in a couple of categories.

If You Don't Get Listed

If you don't get listed in the directory within six weeks, submit your site again. Before resubmitting, though, make sure you've chosen the best category and that a more appropriate category hasn't been created in the meantime. If you're submitting your site for the second (or more) time, use the "Update old entry" option instead of the "Submit new entry" option. Don't abuse the option though because the editors will be able to tell how many times you've submitted.

Direct Hit

www.directhit.com
Recently acquired by Ask Jeeves, Direct Hit, claiming over one hundred million Web pages indexed, is another popularity engine increasing in importance. In addition to its self-standing search service at directhit.com, it provides supplementary results at other engines, such as HotBot and Lycos. As it says at its site, Direct Hit:

> "provides highly relevant results for any Internet search. Our Popularity Engine tracks the sites that people actually select from the search results list. By analyzing the activity of millions of previous Internet searchers, Direct Hit determines the most popular and relevant sites for your search request. . . ."

So, like in Snap, sites that get clicked on more than others in Direct Hit's search results get ranked higher in Direct Hit. Direct Hit works in the background, watching what visitors search for and recording the pages they visit from those searches. Web sites that are visited most frequently will move to the top, and Web sites that aren't visited often will move to the bottom.

HotBot's top results are being refined by Direct Hit now by default, rather than this being an option available to Web users. If

www.directhit.com
Recently acquired by AskJeeves, Direct Hit, claiming over one hundred million Web pages indexed, is another popularity engine increasing in importance. In addition to its self-standing search service at directhit.com, it provides supplementary results at other engines, such as HotBot and Lycos.

enough results haven't been gathered for that search term, the Direct Hit option won't be available. So, you can see where this service is better suited to more general keyword(s) of just one or two words, rather than a string like, "children's humorous book authors," or whatever.

Direct Hit uses the Open Directory Project for category listings, but here, too, it throws in the popularity curve, returning listings for categories based on their popularity algorithms.

For you do-it-yourselfers: Can you click your way to the top of a popularity engine like Direct Hit? Probably not because of the sheer amount of data that Direct Hit analyzes. It would be hard to imagine influencing that much data. Further, attempts to spam the engine will likely be spotted, perhaps by the use of cookies. More about cookies and submissions are mentioned in Chapter 17.

> Direct Hit uses the Open Directory Project for category listings, but here, too, it throws in the popularity curve, returning listings for categories based on their popularity algorithms.

Submitting Your Site to Direct Hit

www.directhit.com/util/addurl.html

To add your Web site to the Direct Hit index, please complete the form below.
URL:

> http://

E-mail Address:

Keywords:

(Enter descriptive words or phrases separated by commas).

(Author's note: Currently, the keyword box accepts up to sixty characters. Make them your best sixty!)

Please note the following:

- Any site that spams the Direct Hit URL submission service will be immediately removed from the Direct Hit search engine.
- After submitting your URL, it may take up to a few weeks before your site is included in the Direct Hit index.
- The Direct Hit rankings are based on actual search activity of millions of Internet users. New sites submitted or found when our spider crawls the Web are listed in the search engine and given an opportunity to be found by searchers. Sites that users visit and spend time at for particular search topics are then ranked higher than other sites.
- For complete details about the Direct Hit spider, read this (*www.directhit.com/util/spider.html*) If you have questions, please send e-mail to dhfeedback@directhit.com.

Google

www.google.com

Google has a silly name and a great PR team. It has been gathering press interest faster than you can say "Google!" Founded in 1998 by Larry Page and Sergey Brin, Stanford University Computer Science graduate students, Google is similar to Direct Hit. However, with between seventy and one hundred million Web pages in its index, this engine offers a different twist; each page in the index has a rank, based on the number of other pages linking to it and the importance of those pages. For example, a link from very important Yahoo! would be more helpful to a site than several links from "unimportant" sites, like your local car dealer or florist. So, it's the overall link count and who among the big players think you're worthwhile that matters with Google, not the number of people who click on the site in their search returns.

Google still relies on a fundamental search technology in order to analyze submitted pages for relevancy—what words are used on a page, where and how they're used, and so on. But then to determine

> Sites that users visit and spend time at for particular search topics are then ranked higher than other sites.

how to return that page within a set of listings, Google uses a technology invented by its founders called VC PageRank. If you are fortunate enough to have some big, highly trafficked Web sites offering a link to your site, don't assume that Google has indexed that page. Instead, take it upon yourself to submit it. Otherwise, you may not be properly leveraging your popularity.

Unfortunately, at this writing, Google is quite slow in indexing new submissions, keeping submitters waiting up to several months. However, as Google's influence grows, so should your efforts to getting ranked well there. Already, this new engine is the default engine for Netscape, if matches with Open Directory are not found. Reportedly, its recent addition to the Netcenter portal page has got traffic zooming even higher.

Google recently set up the Google Directory, where it takes results from its own database of sites and combines them with results from the ODP. Now when you search Google, you're presented with Google results as in the past. However, you'll also see a statement at the top of the page that lists a "Category." Clicking on that link will take you into the Google Directory, which is composed of ODP listings that have been ranked according to Google's link analysis system.

Submission Guidelines

www.google.com/addurl.htm/

As it says at the Web site, "Add a URL here and we will likely add your Web page to our index the next time we crawl. Note that it may be quite a while before we get around to your page." Google crawls the Web itself and tries to update most of its index each month.

Because Google makes extensive use of the text within hyperlinks, it can find matching pages even when the pages themselves haven't been indexed. So, your pages may still show up within Google's results because of indexed sites that offer links to yours. Because of this feature, link analysis, a Google executive estimates that their searches cover up to 254 million pages on the Web.

> If you are fortunate enough to have some big, highly trafficked Web sites offering a link to your site, don't assume that Google has indexed that page. Instead, take it upon yourself to submit it.

Read more about how Google returns information on this page of its site: *www.google.com/help.html#interpretscout*

Google and RealNames

Google has joined the RealNames fan club. This is how RealNames is used, from their site *www.google.com/help.html#interpretscout*

> When the Internet Keyword matches Google's first result, the Internet Keyword and RN mark will appear at the end of the title. When the Internet Keyword differs from Google's first result, it will appear above Google's results.

Straight from the Horse's Mouth

Q & A with Cindy McCaffrey, director of Corporate Communications for Google.

Q. *We understand that each page in your index has a ranking, based on the number of other pages linking to it and the "importance" of those pages. For example, a link to a site from CNET would give a higher value to that site than a link to it from a car dealership site in Timbukto. Is this correct, and can you give us any additional information about VC PageRank and your relevancy algorithms that will be helpful to our readers?*

A. Correct. PageRank Technology performs an objective measurement of the importance of Web pages and is calculated by solving an equation of millions of variables and more than two billion terms. Google does not count links; instead PageRank uses the link structure of the Web as an organizational tool. In essence, Google interprets a link from Page A to Page B as a "vote" by Page A for Page B. Google assesses a page's importance by the votes it receives. Google also analyzes the page that casts the vote. Votes cast by pages that are themselves "important" weigh more heavily and help to make other pages "important." Important, high-quality pages receive a higher PageRank

> Because Google makes extensive use of the text within hyperlinks, it can find matching pages even when the pages themselves haven't been indexed.

and are ordered higher in the results. Google's technology uses the collective intelligence of the Web to determine a page's importance. Google does not use editors or its own employees to judge a page's importance.

Q. *How often does Googlebot crawl?*
A. We try to crawl about once a month.

Q. *How large is your index?*
A. We currently have a total of 254 million URLs in our repository, out of which 138 million are fully indexed.

Q. *How many visitors used Google during 1999 to perform their searches? On average, how many use Google daily now?*
A. The information that we currently publicly refer to is number of searches performed on our site. At the end of 1998, we had about 10,000 searches per day; at the close of 1999, we had about 9 million searches per day. And that number is growing rapidly.

Q. *How long does it take for a site to get indexed, from submission to posting within the index?*
A. We try to update our index every month or more frequently. However, we consider a page's PageRank when inserting it for the first time, so lower PageRank pages may take longer to get into the index. PageRank in this situation does not represent our judgment of quality. New pages may have a low PageRank until high-PageRank people in the related area discover the page and link to it.

Q. *Will Google allow cloaked pages within its index?*
A. Because of PageRank, spamming like this is a much less significant issue for Google than for other search engine. If the cloaking is done for illegitimate reasons, high-quality sites are unlikely to link to the cloaked sites, meaning Google will not rate them highly no matter what they do. On the other hand, if the cloaking is legitimate, it is likely high-quality pages will get scored highly by Google regardless of the Web techniques they use.

> At the end of 1998, we had about 10,000 searches per day; at the close of 1999, we had about 9 million searches per day. And that number is growing rapidly.

Chapter 31

The Paid-for Engines: GoTo, FindWhat, and RealNames

GoTo

goto.com

Internet purists or traditionalists (if something as new as the Internet can be said to have traditions!) aren't going to like GoTo. It flies smack in the face of the sharing and free access spirit that grew the WWW to what it is today. But searchers might like this alternative to the rest of the search world.

Founded in 1997 by Bill Gross, GoTo is one of the few major search engines that sells listings, allowing Web sites to buy high rankings. GoTo keeps its user interface simple, unlike the more cluttered portal sites, and it delivers results quickly. It claims that its search results are more relevant than those of the free engines and here's why:

> Advertisers bid in an open auction for placement in the results for search terms that are relevant to their sites. And they pay only for consumers who click on their listings. So they have an incentive to bid for top placement only on search terms where they are going to meet consumers who are looking for what they have to offer.

Advertisers bid against each other to be ranked well for popular search terms, and the advertiser willing to fork out the most money will be at the top. Simple as that. Search results begin with the advertiser who is paying the most, followed by the others, then the supplementary nonpaid listings from Inktomi.

The engine supplements its results from the Inktomi search engine. So, nonpaid results come from Inktomi. Submit to HotBot in order to be in the nonpaid results for GoTo. Nonpaid results appear right after the paid results.

After advertising with GoTo, many people find that their traffic increases significantly from META search engines like DogPile, which incorporates GoTo results.

In order to become an advertiser with GoTo and to be included in their paid listings, visit:

www.goto.com/d/about/advertisers

goto.com
Internet purists or traditionalists (if something as new as the Internet can be said to have traditions!) aren't going to like GoTo. It flies smack in the face of the sharing and free access spirit that grew the WWW to what it is today.

Submission Tips for GoTo

Before bidding on a keyword, keep these important tips in mind.

1. Choose keyword terms for your site and link them to pages within your site. You can send people to your home page, or you can send them to any page within your Web site. You can change the designated URL at any time.
2. In order to choose a search term, GoTo offers a suggestion service (*www.goto.com/d/about/advertisers/othertools.jhtml*) that allows you to enter a few words to see how popular they are. Refine your keyword terms to ones that will bring you the most qualified leads, not the most traffic.
3. Buy the plural word and you'll also get the singular; if you bid on "boats," you should also appear for "boat."
4. After entering the search term in their form, you have to set a bid amount. This is how much you will pay for each person who clicks through on your listing to your site.

    Start with one cent, which is as low as you can bid. If your keyword isn't highly competitive, this can sometimes provide you with a ranking in the first page of results. Some keywords, though, are fetching prices over $5 to $6 per click-through to the site.
5. Bids can be changed at any time, so if you aren't getting the traffic, you can up your bid amount.
6. Enter a title for your listing. Words in the title have nothing to do with your ranking. But make it attractive and appealing. Your title can be forty characters long.
7. Enter a description, up to 190 characters long. Again, words in the description have nothing to do with your ranking, but a compelling description will increase click-throughs.

    You need to indicate an opening budget amount. The minimum is $25, but you can go higher. You get charged for each person who clicks on your listing, and the clicks cost you whatever you bid. The charges come out of your budget. When your budget is exhausted, your listing will no longer appear in the paid results. When your budget is spent, you'll

> After entering the search term in their form, you have to set a bid amount. This is how much you will pay for each person who clicks through on your listing to your site.

receive an e-mail from GoTo, and you can add additional funds to your budget if you choose.

Potential Problems with GoTo Listings

Recently, a colleague was concerned about discrepancies between his server reports and GoTo's reports concerning traffic. He wondered if the higher click-through rate reported by GoTo for which he was being charged could have been caused by a nasty tactic used by one of his competitors. Could, he asked, the unethical but clever competitor be repeatedly eliciting search returns at GoTo that included his paid listing, and then repeatedly clicking through to his Web site in order to significantly raise his costs? Here's what a GoTo client service representative replied in an e-mail message:

E-MAIL

We understand why you are concerned about the source of those clicks. We take your concern seriously and would like to offer a few reasons why you might be seeing those clicks on your account. We have several processes that identify unusual clicking activity. We do eliminate those clicks from our calculations to ensure that you are not charged for them. We offer some suggestions but hopefully this e-mail will answer the sources of those clicks.

In our ongoing effort to increase the amount of targeted traffic to our clients' Web sites, GoTo.com partners with META-search companies to provide search results on their Web sites.

Some of the current partnerships that are already driving traffic to your site include DogPile, Mamma, Apple, Cyber411, Profusion, Savysearch, Guide, Infospace, The Globe, and XCrawler. It's important to note, however, that while searches from these sites return GoTo.com's results, your server logs will reflect the META-searcher's URL, not ours.

If you would like to track the amount of traffic you receive from GoTo.com, we recommend that you change the URL you have listed with us to a tracking URL. Following are a few simple instructions on what to do so that you can track the traffic you receive from us:

> Could, he asked, the unethical but clever competitor be repeatedly eliciting search returns at GoTo that included his paid listing, and then repeatedly clicking through to his Web site in order to significantly raise his costs?

To change a URL such as www.leopards-r-us.com/
to a tracking URL add:

?source=goto so your URL will look this:

www.leopards-r-us.com/?source=goto

If the URL already has a question mark in it, you will have to add "&source=goto" to the end.
Examples:

From: www.leopards-r-us.com/home/index.html
To: www.leopards-r-us.com/home/index.html?source=goto

From: www.leopards-r-us.com/search.cgi?q=feline
To: www.leopards-r-us.com/search.cgi?q=feline&source=goto

If the URL has a # sign, the "?source=goto" will need to be inserted before the # sign.

From: www.leopards-r-us.com/#leo
To: www.leopards-r-us.com/?source=goto#leo

We recommend that you test the new tracking URL to verify that the modified URL works as well as the original. You should also avoid putting the modified URL on your site, and do not distribute it, as these actions would frustrate your ability to use it to observe GoTo clicks.

By completing this process, you should be able to look for "source=goto" in your access logs. If your Web server behaves normally, it should appear once for every click-through on one of your GoTo search results.

Keep in mind that most search engines won't index a site with a ? in the URL, so if you want the page listed in the other engines, be sure to submit the URL without the ? in it. For more information about using symbols in URLs, see Chapter 20.

If you would like to track the amount of traffic you receive from GoTo.com, change the URL you have listed to a tracking URL.

FindWhat

www.findwhat.com

A newcomer on the block, FindWhat has taken a very aggressive approach to getting its name on the map in the search engine industry.

FindWhat was launched in September of 1999 by Craig Pisaris-Henderson and Tony Garcia and is a pay-for-placement search engine with supplemental listings supplied by Inktomi.

To learn more about how you can promote your site at FindWhat, visit:

findwhat.com/static/ab_promote.html

Straight from the Horse's Mouth

Craig Pisaris-Henderson, president of FindWhat, says,

> FindWhat.com is a pay-for-position search engine based on an open automated bidding system whereas advertisers can bid for top placement for any keyword or key phrase in real time. The bidding process allows advertisers to dictate their placement with the results displayed after a search giving them the opportunity to get in front of their target market everytime. When a consumer finds what they are looking for and clicks through to an advertisers site, that advertiser pays the bid amount for that targeted person.

> As of Dec. 31, 1999, more than 5,000 Web sites were participating in the FindWhat.com search engine which was launched in September 1999. Additionally, Web site publishers or their advertising agencies were bidding on more than 750,000 search keywords or key phrases. The numbers of participants accumulated in just a few short months shows the willingness of the online market to adopt the "pay-for-performance" model.

www.findwhat.com
A newcomer on the block, FindWhat has taken a very aggressive approach to getting its name on the map in the search engine industry it is a pay-for-placement search engine with supplemental listings supplied by Inktomi.

RealNames

customer.realnames.com/GetYourRealNames/GetYourRealNames.asp
Many domain names are just not memorable. Corporate America is spending billions on television and radio spots and on print ads to publicize their Web sites, but a problem occurs when prospective customers finally get to their computers to check out what they saw advertised. Unless they remember the URL exactly, which means remembering how to spell it correctly, they can't get where they want to go. The result: a frustrated *wannabe* customer and wasted ad dollars.

Professional positioners have significantly helped to solve this problem by making sure home pages are optimized for commonly misspelled company and product names, but even then, this works only when the prospective customer goes to the search engines, and it's not foolproof.

RealNames created a clever new way of helping Web sites get found. It is an alternative addressing system for the Web that makes use of "real names" instead of URLs. With this system, visitors can type in the name they remember, such as the company or product name, and RealNames will deliver them to the correct Web site or offer choices related to the URL. It takes away the need to remember an exact URL, figuring out whether the "www." comes first or not, and whether it's a ".com," ".net," or ".org."

RealNames is following the modus operandi for successful search ventures—acquiring important partners quickly. RealNames was really put on the map by its early partnership with AltaVista, where RealNames links were displayed within many search results, thus taking the viewer to subscribing Web sites or to the RealNames search engine itself. RealNames has moved on to add other impressive relationships, including a promising one with Inktomi, which may eventually deliver many of Inktomi's impressive partners: HotBot, Yahoo!, AOL, and more. The Go Network (InfoSeek) will also be integrating RealNames though it is uncertain at this time how that will be effected.

Other areas that use RealName technology are LookSmart, NeoPlanet browser, and Fireball (Germany's largest search engine).

> Visitors can type in the name they remember, such as the company or product name, and RealNames will deliver them to the correct Web site or offer choices related to the URL.

RealNames has now been incorporated into Microsoft's Internet Explorer 5.0 browser. Of course, each new partner acquired means a greater value for the subscribing sites' $100 purchase.

How RealNames Works

Each of RealNames navigation partners incorporates the RealNames information differently. The META search engine, DogPile, just returns the RealNames information as it does any other engine data within its long list of returns. However, one nice feature of DogPile is that you can customize it to have your favorite engines' data returned first, second, or third, for example. So, if someone wants to use RealNames regularly but would also like input from favorite non-paid engines, DogPile could be a real find.

LookSmart is returning listings from RealNames similarly to the way AltaVista does; there is a link at the bottom of the first page of site matches that invites a visitor looking for "Schwinn" to click-through to that site's home page. It looks like this:

> *Schwinn(RN)*
> *Go there directly with this Internet Keyword.*

One important benefit of RealNames is that even if your positioning isn't great, you can still, in a sense, make it on to the first page of returns for your most important keywords in the AltaVista engine!

When someone searches AltaVista for a keyword that is used in the RealNames title or description, the service resolves the request by pulling selected sites containing the keyword in their titles or descriptions. So, not only will you get traffic from the "real name" itself, but you'll get traffic from indirect "resolutions" (matches made by the RealNames engine). However, as of the writing of this book, AltaVista is the only RealNames partner who is using indirect matches. So, with AltaVista alone, a search for a keyword found in a RealName title or description will produce a listing of possible matches.

One important benefit of RealNames is that even if your positioning isn't great, you can still, in a sense, make it on to the first page of returns for your most important keywords in the AltaVista engine!

With RealNames' other partners, you have to type in the entire RealName in the search query window in order for it to be a match in the results.

Search results from RealNames come from three sources and are generally listed in this order: paid listings, editor selections, and picks found by a Web crawler. However, site popularity does come into play, so popular sites can appear higher if enough people click on them.

Obtaining a RealNames

Each RealNames term costs $100 a year, and there is no limit to the number of terms you can purchase. When a searcher searches for a related term, depending on the exact name and number of names registered, RealNames offers up a link to your site as a possible match.

You cannot register generic names, but can link your company name to generic names for broader exposure. For example, the Schwinn Company couldn't register a RealNames for "bicycles," but it could for "Schwinn bicycles."

Editorial Picks

In order to make the system more useful, editors at RealNames have created RealNames for thousands of products, companies, and services. Out of the three million names in its index, one million are editorially produced, and two million are domain names, whereas only ten thousand are paid RealNames.

RealNames also has information from about a half-million Web sites that it has spidered. This information provides matches when no paid or editorial picks exist. You cannot suggest a site to be spidered by RealNames.

> Search results from RealNames come from three sources and are generally listed in this order: paid listings, editor selections, and picks found by a Web crawler.

Tips for Registering a RealName

1. Since you can't register generic names, add your keyword(s) to the end or beginning of your title, such as Schwinn Bicycles. Keep in mind that this strategy works only with AltaVista as of the writing of this book. However, considering the potential traffic to your site through a major player like AltaVista, it's well worth the $100.

2. Create a short description to go with your name or names and incorporate other important search terms. Make your description enticing but not misleading.

3. You can send people to a different URL rather than your main page if you choose.

4. Go to the signup form at this Web site: *customer.real-names.com/GetYourRealNames/GetYourRealNames.asp*

5. Enter the first name you want, the URL, and a description. Although RealNames doesn't list a title or description length limit, if yours is too long, they'll ask you to cut it down.

   As a guideline, keep your title under 80 characters including spaces, and keep your description under 140 characters.

   When you're finished, choose "proceed" to continue to the credit card section to complete the transaction.

6. After completing the form, you'll be notified of the permanent approval of your account.

7. If your name has been rejected, you can choose another name or you'll lose the registration fee, which is nonrefundable for rejections.

For support, send an e-mail to support@realnames.com.

A colleague said:

> After going through this exercise and looking into your recommendation of RealNames, I have purchased two RealNames for my site. I researched the company; looked at who was making investments ... in fact a representative from Central Corp (now RealNames) even called me; explained what they were all about; what they were trying to do and helped me craft two RealNames (now called Internet Keywords).

> Create a short description to go with your name or names and incorporate other important search terms. Make your description enticing but not misleading.

After spending a couple hours looking around, I was impressed. It appears to be a good time to do this now not only because of the recent investments but because of this reason. When they started out as a company, they sent out a Web crawler and came up with many names in a number of categories. Those names are listed without the RN logo next to them. Now that it is a pay per name at $100 per year per name, your RN will go to the top of the list.

For example, if you do a search on Indiana, you will get 13 million hits on AltaVista. If you click on RealNames, there are about 40 listings but none are registered. When mine gets out this week, I will be at the head of the list. I could not ask for better coverage on a term that has 13 million hits!

From another colleague:

About three months ago, I decided to give RealNames a try. They had a two-month trial special going on. My site is hopping now! I'm getting between 100 to 200 hits per day! Half of those are due to ranking; the other half to RealNames. I'm very pleased! I'm even starting to get a couple of Web design clients from my site now ... yipppee!

Straight from the Horse's Mouth

Q & A with Keith Teare, CEO of RealNames.

Q. *What is the process a Web marketer or Web owner should use to determine how to choose an Internet Keyword?*

A. If you're a major brand marketer with an already existing brand, it makes every sense for your keywords to be the same as your product names and brand. So, it would be very sensible, for example, for Sony for its camcorder brand to have as its Internet Keyword "Sony Handy Cam." That's a far better keyword that simply the keyword "camcorder" which doesn't leverage the strong Sony brand at all. The main purpose of an Internet

> If you're a major brand marketer with an already existing brand, it makes every sense for your keywords to be the same as your product names and brand.

> The main purpose of an Internet Keyword for a brand marketer is not to get found in an AltaVista.

Keyword for a brand marketer is not to get found in an AltaVista. It is, in your TV, radio and print ads, to have the consumer recognize it so they can act on it. It's for enhancing the media ad.

If you're a new Web company, if you're launching an online company, I think there's a little twist there. You then have to determine what your identity is. Is it Amazon or is it amazon.com, for example. Depending on your answer to that question, your Internet Keyword could be the same as your domain address.

The first thing is who are you, want do you want to be? That question really arises for offline entities much more than for online. Depending on that, you'll take one or the other keyword. If you take the dot com as a keyword, then in addition to the ability that DNS already gives you with the dot com, you additionally get the ability for the consumer to type your dot com into all of the search engines that have RealNames and come right to the top of the search. If you test it out, that doesn't always happen with the dot coms in search engines if they're not additionally keywords—they generally won't come up unless you type them in. They're typically not even found at all in some search engines.

The third type is the online marketer who doesn't really have a strong brand and doesn't have the budget for print and TV ads, for example. Therefore, he's mainly looking to get the Web site found by online users. For these people, the most important Internet Keyword platform is the search engines. For these marketers, it is appropriate to do two things. One is, of course, to take the Internet Keyword that is their identity. But in addition to that, buy additional keywords to include outside their identity the generic categories they participate in. For example, let's say there's a Web site "Joe's garage." And let's say Joe's Garage does Nissan repairs. As well as taking the keyword "Joe's garage," they should also take the keyword "Nissan repairs." And all the other categories they participate in would be appropriate keywords. In many of our implementations, for example, AltaVista, if the user were just to type "Nissan repairs,"

"Joe's garage Nissan repairs" would be one of the results the user would get to see and could choose from. So, for a small business, that's a pretty good strategy.

Q. *Is there an infinite number of companies that can subscribe to any particular generic keyword?*

A. The first, most pointed answer, which is true most of the time, is there's no need to rush. If you have an identity which you securely own, we wouldn't give your keyword to someone else. For example, we'd never give your dot com keyword to someone else because you're the unique owner and nobody else is. We'd never give your brand name to someone else if you are the strong, recognized owner of the brand—Pepsi to Coca Cola, Ford to General Motors, or anything like that.

If you don't have a strong identity and let's say you're "Joe's Garage" and there's 5,000 Joe's Garages in the USA, then there is the issue of timing. When there's an ambiguous ownership, we have a policy called, "First appropriate, first served." Not "First come, first served." You must be appropriate.

Q. *If the first Joe's Garage got that, and another appropriate Joe's Garage came along. . . .*

A. We'd ask them to be "Joe's Garage San Jose," or something like that. Some identity that distinguishes that from the first one.

Q. *So, if someone types in generic "Joe's Garage," both listings would come up if they were both appropriate, but who would come up on the top of the list—whoever signed up first?*

A. Right now the order is very similar to the Direct Hit search engine. We order by popularity, which is measured by the number of clicks each one gets. It's kind of a user-driven popularity measure of testing. I would say that we do not always control our list. I've described an experience to you that is typically the AltaVista requirement, but in some of our implementations, the partner has chosen to take only what we call "exact match" results. For example, MSN.com only takes exact match results, and the GO Network only takes exact match results. So, in those

> If you don't have a strong identity then there is the issue of timing. When there's an ambiguous ownership, we have a policy called, "First appropriate, first served." Not "First come, first served." You must be appropriate.

Monitor your traffic closely to see the results from these buys. In particular, you'll want to determine the quality of these hits by tracking them through, whenever possible, to determine if they become sales.

cases, it really is your job as the owner of the keyword to market that keyword to your customer base so they type it in exactly and then you'll come up top."

Are Paid-for Keyword Strategies Worth the Cost?

Of course, you'll want to monitor your traffic closely to see the results from these buys. In particular, you'll want to determine the quality of these hits by tracking them through, whenever possible, to determine if they become sales. There are several different ways to do this, beginning with the simple start of providing different versions of your URL: for example, for DirectHit, you may mirror your home page and name it www.mydomain/dh/mykeyword.html; and for RealNames, you may name that same page www.mydomain/rn/mykeyword.html.

Further, your reception and sales staff must become diligent about asking inquiries how they heard about your company or product, and this information becomes part of the tracking process.

As companies continue to struggle to quantify and qualify their marketing efforts throughout the Web–trying to measure the effectiveness of banner ads, sponsorships, and so on–more and better software products will evolve that will help you determine the best routes for your marketing plan.

The demographics of both the paid-for and free search engines each have some unique characteristics that will help determine whether your rankings there deliver solid sales. Once you determine which engines are best for your bottom line, you'll need to act accordingly, even if it means paying for results.

For more information on this topic, visit our Web site at **www.businesstown.com**

Other Engines: Northern Light, whatUseek, Jayde, and Fast

Chapter 32

Northern Light

www.northernlight.com/search.html
Northern Light is a popular search engine among researchers because of its large index and its ability to cluster documents by topic. The engine has over 200 million Web pages in its index, which makes it one of the largest engines on the Web.

Gov.Search, a search engine that focuses on information from U.S. government sources, was opened in May 1999. The service is jointly produced by Northern Light and the U.S. Commerce Department's National Technical Information Service. Searching is not free, but the service probably has the largest collection of government Web sites available on the Net.

Northern Light now also provides a Special Collection index, which is a research version of its service. This index has information from over 5,400 publications, much of which is not available on the Web. Searching is free, but the documents can be purchased for between $1 and $4.

> *www.northernlight.com/search.html* has over 200 million Web pages in its index, which makes it one of the largest engines on the Web.

How Can You Get Your Site Indexed with Northern Light?

Visit this Web site and complete the form:
www.northernlight.com/docs/regurl_help.html

1. Submit only one page from your Web site. Gulliver, their spider, can find your other pages by following links from this one page.
2. Northern Light cannot delete URLs at the request of the user. Their crawler is scheduled to make periodic passes through their index of Web sites and will automatically update or delete any old or obsolete links at that time.
3. If you have any questions about the service, please send an e-mail to:
   crawler@nlsearch.com

Submission Tips for Northern Light

Keep these important submission tips for Northern Light in mind.

1. It takes two to four weeks for both submitted and nonsubmitted pages to be indexed.
2. Northern Light supports frames and image maps.
3. Tips from a Northern Light representative:

    Regarding doorway pages, our spider will examine every page by following links from the index page, index each page, etc. If doorway pages are not included in those links, the spider won't find them. Submit the main site URL; then submit each individual doorway page.

Additional Tips for Northern Light

These added tips will help you when submitting to Northern Light:

1. Northern Light now considers site popularity for relevancy.
2. The use of META tags doesn't give your site a boost in this engine.
3. Northern Light doesn't index the text in ALT or comment tags.
4. The engine uses word stemming, which means it will search for variations of words based on their stems.
5. Try using your keyword phrase "outside" the <title> tag but within the <head> </head> section, like this:
   <html>
   <head>
   keyword phrase
   <title>keyword phrase</title>
   </head>
6. Use your keyword phrase in your link text, like:
   <A HREF="www.yourweb site.com">keyword phrase</A>
7. Use your keyword phrase in your body text.
8. Northern Light doesn't index hidden form data.

> Northern Light now considers site popularity for relevancy.

9. Northern Light doesn't index within a URL link, like:
<A HREF="www.yourweb site.com/keyword-phrase.html>

Your Title Tag and Northern Light

Title tags can be eighty characters long with this engine. As with all engines, be sure to begin the tag with your important keyword phrase.

Your Description Tag and Northern Light

Northern Light takes your description from the first 150 to 200 words found on the page itself. So, make them shine!

What Does Northern Light Consider to Be Spamming?

The engine doesn't consider the use of META refresh tags or tiny text to be spamming.

whatUseek

www.whatuseek.com
To submit a site to whatUseek, visit this URL:
www.whatUseek.com/noshock/addurl-tableset.shtml

Tips from whatUseek Itself

These tips will keep you on the right track for whatUseek.

Your page will be visited and indexed by whatUseek's spider, Winona Spider, generally between 1 and 24 hours.

Northern Light takes your description from the first 150 to 200 words found on the page itself. So, make them shine!

Webmasters can sign up to receive a Webmaster Newsletter that contains information such as:

When the index will be updated

What type of reindex will be performed

Submission tips in general

Visit this Web site to sign up to receive the newsletter: *www.whatUseek.com/webmaster*

Submission Tips for WhatUseek

Keep these additional tips in mind.

1. Use your keyword phrase near the top of the page as well as near the bottom of the body of the page itself.
2. Use the plural form of your keyword phrase in addition to the singular form when possible.
3. whatUseek is case sensitive, so use uppercase, lowercase, and capitalized versions of your keyword phrase.
4. Top ranking sites with whatUseek have an average of over 400 words in the body of the page and a keyword weight of 1 percent.

Jayde.com

www.jayde.com

The following information was taken from Jayde.com's newsletter:

How to Raise Your Site's Ranking on Jayde

Jayde.com is a cross between a search engine and a directory, which has resulted in some confusion as to how Web sites are ranked. Here are some important guidelines to keep in mind when you submit or resubmit your site:

- Jayde.com does NOT index sites by spidering the Web. The content of your Web site pages and the use of META tags within them is irrelevant to our indexing process.

> Jayde.com is a cross between a search engine and a directory, which has resulted in some confusion as to how Web sites are ranked.

alltheweb.com
Ultimately wants to power other search engines, rather than compete against existing portal sites, similarly to the way that Inktomi powers HotBot. Its first major engine to partner with in this regard is Lycos, where it provides results in Lycos's advanced search feature.

- What is relevant to your site ranking is your Site name and description. Every word in your site name and description is indexed, except for words that are 3 letters or less.
- Since site descriptions are limited to twenty five to thirty words and words like "and," "a," and "the" are not indexed, careful thought should be given to the wording you provide.
- To score a high ranking for a particular keyword or keyword phrase, your site name and/or description must contain the keyword or keyword phrase. Repetition of the word or phrase will enhance your site's ranking.
- If 2 or more sites contain an equal number of keyword matches, then ranking is determined by submission date with more recently submitted sites given a higher ranking.

FAST (All the Web)

alltheweb.com

Fast Search & Transfer, a Norway-based company, has launched a new site called alltheweb.com. The engine's goal is to have the largest index of Web pages. Ultimately, it wants to index the entire Web, at an estimated 500 to 600 Web pages.

Fast currently powers Lycos's MP3 specialty engine and their FTP search feature. It ultimately wants to power other search engines, rather than compete against existing portal sites, similarly to the way that Inktomi powers HotBot. Its first major engine to partner with in this regard is Lycos, where it provides results in Lycos's advanced search feature.

To submit to Fast, visit this URL:
www.alltheweb.com/addurl.html

Submissions to Fast make it into the index in 4 to 6 weeks.

For more information on this topic, visit our Web site at www.businesstown.com

Appendix I: Glossary

Appendices

Glossary

Algorithm: Ranking criteria that are used by each individual engine in determining ranking. An engine's ranking algorithm changes quite frequently, and an algorithm for one engine is different from an algorithm in another engine.

Case sensitive: When an engine is "case sensitive," it will search for the keyword exactly as you have entered it. For example, if you enter "NEW ORLEANS" in the search query window, a case-sensitive engine would only search for the keyword phrase in all caps. Some engines are case sensitive for certain searches, but not for other searches (like AltaVista). So, your best bet is to search for your keyword phrase in all variations (all caps, all lowercase, and capitalized) to see if the search results differ.

Cloaking: Also called food script or stealthing, cloaking allows you to show the engines different pages than what you show human visitors. Cloaking is sometimes used if your Web page uses technology that will make it difficult, if not impossible, for your pages to get top rankings. With cloaking, you create separate pages for each of the engines, taking into account what each engine likes to see on a Web page in order to give your page the most relevancy. The script then detects whether you have a visitor or a search engine spider visiting your site. If it's HotBot's spider, for example, the script will serve up (or show) your HotBot page. If the script determines that a human visitor is at your site, it shows up the beautifully designed and presented page that will impress your visitors but would present ranking problems with the engines due to the technology used.

Comment tag: A comment tag is used to describe something within your HTML code that is not viewed by people visiting your site. Most of the engines don't consider the content of comment tags when determining relevancy.

Directories: Directories rely on submissions from Web site owners to build their indexes. They don't use spiders to index Web sites. Examples are Yahoo! and the Open Directory Project.

Doorway page: A page that has been created for the sole purpose of ranking higher in the search engines for a particular keyword or set of keywords, the name of your company, or even for a specific engine. These pages act as additional "doorways" into your site, thus increasing traffic through those doorways. Doorway pages should be content-rich information pages that explain in detail the concept involved, rather than pages slapped up there with little thought as to the content.

Dynamic HTML: Pages that are generated via CGI script or database delivery. Pages using dynamic HTML will have ranking problems because most of the time, symbols are used in the URLs, which cause the engines to stop indexing when they spot those symbols. Further, because the pages are database delivered "on the fly" (instantly depending on what the user has requested), there's nothing for the engines to index.

Frames: Divide Web pages into multiple, scrollable regions. An example of a Web site with frames can be found at Search Engine Watch: *searchenginewatch.internet.com/webmasters/ examples/frames/example1.html*

Invisible text: Stuffing keywords in a font color that is the same (or a similar) color as the background of the page.

Keyword "weight": Refers to the number of keywords appearing on your Web page in relation to the total number of words appearing on that page. Keyword weight is also referred to as "keyword density."

META refresh tag: A tag that automatically takes visitors to a different page within the Web site. Engines don't like META refresh tags, as a general rule. If you use one, make sure that you set it at thirty seconds or higher. For an example of a META refresh, go to: *www2.netdoor.com/~smslady* To view the source code of any page that uses a META refresh tag, even a very fast META refresh, type "view-source:" before the URL in the browser window, like this: *view-source:www2.netdoor.com/~smslady*

META tag stuffing: Stuffing your META tags with your keywords, over and over again.

META tags: HTML tags that are placed in the <head> section of your Web page and offer content to the search engines. Important META tags are the META keyword and the META description tags.

Open Directory Project (ODP): A directory of Web sites that is operated by thousands of volunteers. This directory provides directory results to Lycos, HotBot, Netscape, AOL Search, and more.

Punctuation sensitive: Indicates if an engine recognizes symbols in the URL, such as the ampersand (&), percent sign (%), equals sign (=), dollar sign ($) or question mark (?).

Relevancy: How well a document provides the information a user is looking for, as measured by each search engine's algorithm. The higher the relevancy, the higher the ranking in the search engine results.

Root-domain wise: If an engine is root-domain wise, you do not need to include the index.html when submitting your home page.

Search engine positioning: The art or science of positioning your Web pages well in the search engines. In other words, search engine positioning strategies will put you on the right track to getting top search engine rankings for your site. Also known as Web positioning or search engine optimization.

Search engines: Search engines are one of the primary ways that Internet users find Web sites. Search engines use spiders to crawl the Web, which is how they build the index of Web sites that you use when searching. After you submit your Web site to these engines, they send their spiders to your site to index it. Examples of search engines are AltaVista, GO/InfoSeek, Excite, HotBot, Lycos, WebCrawler, and Northern Light.

Site popularity: The "popularity" of your Web site as evidenced by the quantity and quality of related sites that considered your site important enough to link to. Also called link popularity, the popularity of your site is tied to the number of relevant sites that offer links to your site and may also consider the importance of those linking sites. Site popularity can also refer to the amount of click-through traffic to a site from a particular engine or directory.

Spider: Also called a robot, a "spider" is a program that scans the Web looking for URLs. It starts at a particular Web page and indexes all links from it, then moves to another page.

Stop words: Words that some engines leave out when they index a page, or words they may not search for during a query. Examples are: "and," "the," "too," etc.

Tiny text: Repeating your keywords over and over again in a very small font size, usually at the bottom of your page. Many engines consider this to be spamming.

Word stemming: Some engines use "stemming" or "word stems," which means that searches for root words will also include variations of that word. For example, a search for "prevent" would also produce "prevention," "preventative," etc.

WYSIWYG HTML editors: This stands for "What You See Is What You Get." Using these editors is like typing in a word processor. You don't view the tags or codes. These editors generally add unimportant META tags to your pages (such as the generator tag) and place those tags above your important keyword-containing METAs. They also often place your <title> tag beneath other META tags at the bottom of the <head> section. Move your title tag to the top of the <head> section!

Appendix II:
Search Engines
Chart

Search Engines Chart

Engines-at-a-Glance Chart

	ALTAVISTA	EXCITE	HOTBOT
Size in Web pages	250 million	214 million	110 million
Crawls Web every	4–6 weeks	2–3 weeks	Twice a month
Indexes sites in	1–3 days to 1 month	1–3 weeks	2 wks–2 mos.
Submit important pages?	Usually 1 pg per site	Usually 1 pg per site	Yes
Daily submission limit	1–5 pages	25 pages	50 pages
Word count minimum?	No	No	No
META tags for relevancy	Yes	No	Yes
Use META description?	Yes	Yes	Yes
Description length	150 chars.	395 chars.	249 chars.
Title length	78 chars.	70 chars.	115 chars.
Keywords count toward relevancy in the:			
Title tag	Yes	Yes	Yes
URL	Yes	Yes	Yes
Link area	Yes	Yes	Yes
Headline tag	Yes	Yes	Yes
Domain name	Yes	Yes	Yes
Top of doc	Yes	Yes	Yes
Comment tags	No	No	Yes
ALT tags	Yes	No	No
Hidden form tags	Spam	Spam	Spam
Gives more weight to:			
Home pages	Yes	Yes	Yes
Uncommon keywords	Unknown	Yes	Yes
Keyword weight preferred	5 percent	3–8 percent	2 percent
Link popularity important	Yes	Yes	Yes/Site
Case-sensitive searches	Yes	No	Partial
Word stemming used	No	No	No
Frames support	Yes	No	No
Image maps support	Yes	No	No

SEARCH ENGINES CHART

GO	LYCOS	NORTHERN LIGHT	WEBCRAWLER	YAHOO!
90 million	50 million	211 million	2 million	1 million
Two months	6 weeks	Monthly	2–3 weeks	Doesn't crawl
1–6 wks	3–6 weeks	2–4 weeks	1–3 weeks	2–8 weeks
Only 1 pg per site	Yes	Yes	Yes	Only 1 pg per site
1 per day	50 per day	No limit	25 pages	Only 1 pg per site
75 words at least	100 words at least	No	No	No
Yes	No	No	No	No
Yes	Sometimes	No	Yes	Submission form
170–240 chars.	135–200 chars.	150–200 chars.	395 chars.	25 words (200)
70–75 chars.	60 chars.	80 chars.	59–60 chars.	5 words (40)
Yes	Yes	Yes	Yes	Submission form
Yes	No	Unknown	Yes	No
Yes	Yes	Unknown	Yes	No
Yes	Yes	Unknown	Yes	No
Yes	Unknown	Yes	Yes	No
Yes	Yes	Unknown	Yes	No
No	No	No	No	No
Yes	Yes	No	No	No
Spam	Spam	Spam	Spam	No
Unknown	Yes	Unknown	Yes	No
Yes	Unknown	Unknown	Yes	No
5–6 percent	1–2 percent	Unknown	3–5 percent	N/A
Yes	Yes/Site	Yes	Yes	No
All caps	No	Yes, title	No	No
Yes	Yes	Yes	No	No
No	Yes	Yes	No	N/A
Yes	No	Yes	No	N/A

	ALTAVISTA	EXCITE	HOTBOT
Will index:			
Active server pages (.asp)	Ok	Ok	Ok
Cold fusion (.cfm)	Ok	Ok	Ok
Server side incls (.shtml)	Ok	Ok	Ok
? symbol	No	No	Yes
Perl (.pl)	Ok	Ok	No
Has stop words	Yes	Yes	Yes
Offers RealName searches	Yes	No	Yes
Has a connected directory	LookSmart	Yes	Yes
Spam:			
Tiny text	Spam	No	Spam
Invisible text	Spam	No	Spam
META refresh tags	Spam	No	No
Identical pages	Spam	Unknown	Spam
Keyword stuffing	Spam	Spam	Spam
Extra hints	Short titles and long pages	Use KWs in style tags	Short pages
Extra hints	Use hidden links	Root pgs indexed faster	Incl. all links on main page
Extra hints	Likes spider to find	Submit every two weeks	KWs in links
Extra hints	Try no KW tag	Use hidden links	Submit to directory

SEARCH ENGINES CHART

GO	LYCOS	NORTHERN LIGHT	WEBCRAWLER	YAHOO!
Ok	Ok	Ok	Ok	N/A
Ok	Ok	Unknown	Ok	N/A
Ok	Ok	Unknown	Ok	N/A
No	Yes	Unknown	No	N/A
No	Ok	Unknown	Ok	N/A
Yes	Yes	No	Yes	Yes
No	No	No	No	Yes
Yes	Yes	No	No	Is a directory
No	Spam	No	Spam	N/A
Spam	Spam	Spam	No	N/A
Spam	Spam	No	No	N/A
Spam	Spam	Unknown	Unknown	N/A
Spam	Spam	Spam	Spam	N/A
Comma- separated phrases	Run site thru HTML validator	Takes descr from page	Problem w/ dyna pages	Choose appropriate categories
Evenly spaced KWs	Try multiple title tags	Supports META robots tag	Use hidden links	No marketing hype
Try no KW tag	Use tiered documents	Indexes all text on pg	Submit every two weeks	Top-notch Web site
Use hidden links	Not root domain wise		Use KW in style tags	Keep trying!

Appendix III:
In a Nutshell

In a Nutshell

Which Engines Require You to Submit Each Page?

Yahoo!	Submit just one page
AltaVista	Generally submit the main page and add hidden links to the rest
Excite	Generally submit the main page and add hidden links to the rest
GO/InfoSeek	Submit the main page and add hidden links to the rest
HotBot	Not necessary—spider finds
Lycos	Optional
WebCrawler	Submit the main page and add hidden links to the rest
Snap	Submit just one page
Northern Light	Submit all important pages

How Long Does It Take Each Engine to Index Submitted Pages?

Yahoo!	2 to 8 weeks
AltaVista	Maximum of 1 to 3 days, but it can take as long as a month
Excite	1 to 3 weeks
GO/InfoSeek	1week to months
HotBot	2 weeks to 2 months
Lycos	2 to 6 weeks
WebCrawler	1 to 3 weeks
Snap	2 to 8 weeks (Snap Live Directory is almost immediate, though)
Northern Light	2 to 4 weeks

How Long Does It Take Each Engine to Index Nonsubmitted Pages?

Yahoo!	N/A
AltaVista	1 day to 1 month
Excite	3 weeks
GO/InfoSeek	1 to 2 months

HotBot	2 weeks
Lycos	2 to 3 weeks
WebCrawler	1 to 6 weeks, if at all
Northern Light	2 to 4 weeks

How Many Pages Beyond the Submitted Page Does the Search Engine Gather Information?

("No limit" means that the engine will try to gather everything they can find at a Web site. It doesn't mean they succeed, but they do try. "Sample" means that they gather a sampling of Web pages from a Web site. Some gather a larger sampling than others.)

Yahoo!	N/A
AltaVista	No limit
Excite	Sample
GO/InfoSeek	Sample, but the spider is crawling deeper since they only accept index pages through their submission process
HotBot	No limit
Lycos	Sample
WebCrawler	Sample
Snap	N/A
Northern Light	No limit

Can the Search Engine Follow Frame Links?

(If it can't, the engine is probably missing much of your site, so be sure to study the information provided on how to overcome problems with search engines.)

Yahoo!	N/A
AltaVista	Yes
Excite	No
GO/InfoSeek	No
HotBot	No
Lycos	Yes
WebCrawler	No
Snap	N/A
Northern Light	Yes

Which Engines Recognize META tags?

Yahoo!	No
AltaVista	Yes (but seems to rank sites high that don't use the keyword META tag)
Excite	Supports the META description tag
GO/InfoSeek	Yes
HotBot	Yes
Lycos	No
WebCrawler	Supports the META description tag
Snap	No
Northern Light	No

Which Engines Are Case Sensitive?

(These are the engines that notice if keywords have been capitalized or not. If an engine is case sensitive, you'll need to include both capitalized and lowercase versions of your keywords.)

Yahoo!	No
AltaVista	Yes
Excite	No
GO/InfoSeek	No (except for all caps)
HotBot	Mixed
Lycos	No
WebCrawler	No
Snap	No
Northern Light	Mixed/title

Which Engines Use Data Entered on a Submission Form to Determine Your Site's Ranking, and Which Use a Spider?

Yahoo!	Submission form
AltaVista	Spider
Excite	Spider
GO/InfoSeek	Spider
HotBot	Spider
Lycos	Spider
WebCrawler	Spider
Snap	Submission form
Northern Light	Spider

IN A NUTSHELL

For Which Engines Do Stop Words Affect How a Page Is Ranked?

Yahoo!	N/A
AltaVista	Yes
Excite	Yes
GO/InfoSeek	Yes
HotBot	Yes
Lycos	Yes
WebCrawler	Yes
Snap	N/A
Northern Light	No

Which Engines Consider Link Popularity?

Yahoo!	No
AltaVista	Yes
Excite	Yes
GO/InfoSeek	Yes
HotBot	Yes–click through popularity
Lycos	Yes–click through popularity
WebCrawler	Yes
Snap	No–click through popularity
Northern Light	Yes

Which Engines Use an Alphabetical Ranking to Determine a Relevancy Score?

Yahoo!	Yes, within Yahoo! categories
AltaVista	No
Excite	No
GO/InfoSeek	No
HotBot	No
Lycos	No
WebCrawler	No
Snap	Yes, within Snap categories
Northern Light	Unknown

Which Engines Consider Keyword Weight?*

Yahoo!	Yes, but only on words you enter on their submission form
AltaVista	Yes (5% keyword weight)
Excite	Yes (3–8% keyword weight)
GO/InfoSeek	Yes (5–6% keyword weight)
HotBot	Yes (2% keyword weight)
Lycos	Yes (first 270 characters or so) (1–2% keyword weight)
WebCrawler	Yes (3–5% keyword weight)
Snap	No, frequency and prominence only
Northern Light	Unknown

* Keyword weight of visible text

Which Engines Consider the Title Tag for Relevancy?

Yahoo!	Yes, but only on the title you enter on their submission form
AltaVista	Yes
Excite	Yes
GO/InfoSeek	Yes
HotBot	Yes
Lycos	Yes
WebCrawler	Yes
Snap	Yes, but only on the title you enter on their submission form
Northern Light	Yes

Which Engines Consider the Prominence of Keywords in the Title Tag?

Yahoo!	Yes, but only for the title you enter on their submission form
AltaVista	Yes
Excite	Yes
GO/InfoSeek	Yes
HotBot	Yes
Lycos	Yes
WebCrawler	Yes

Snap   Yes, but only for the title you enter
                  on their submission form
Northern Light   Yes

Which Engines Consider the Comment Tags for Relevancy?

Yahoo!   No
AltaVista   No
Excite   No
GO/InfoSeek   No
HotBot   Yes
Lycos   No
WebCrawler   No
Snap   No
Northern Light   No

Which Engines Consider the ALT Tag for Relevancy?

Yahoo!   N/A
AltaVista   Yes
Excite   No
GO/InfoSeek   Yes
HotBot   No
Lycos   Yes
WebCrawler   No
Snap   N/A
Northern Light   No

Which Factors Are Considered Spamming by These Engines?

(The factors are META refresh tags, the use of invisible text, and the
use of tiny text)

Yahoo!   N/A
AltaVista   META refresh, invisible text, tiny text
Excite   All are okay
GO/InfoSeek   META refresh, invisible text (tiny text is okay)
HotBot   Invisible text, tiny text (META refresh is okay)
Lycos   Invisible text, tiny text, META refresh
WebCrawler   Tiny text (META refresh and invisible text are OK)
Snap   N/A
Northern Light   Invisible text (META refresh and tiny text are OK)

Maximum Length of Titles?

Yahoo!	40 characters (unless company name is longer)
AltaVista	78 characters
Excite	70 characters
GO/InfoSeek	70–75 characters
HotBot	115 characters
Lycos	60 characters
WebCrawler	60 characters
Snap	40 characters (unless company name is longer)
Northern Light	80 characters

Maximum Length of Keyword META tags?

Yahoo!	N/A
AltaVista	Unknown
Excite	N/A
GO/InfoSeek	1000 characters
HotBot	Unknown
Lycos	N/A
WebCrawler	N/A
Snap	N/A
Northern Light	N/A

Maximum Length of Description?

(Engines form their descriptions from the first text they find on a page or from the META description tag, if they support it. This shows the description length in all cases.)

Yahoo!	200 characters; no more than 25 words total
AltaVista	*150 characters
Excite	*395 characters
GO/InfoSeek	*170–240 characters
HotBot	*249 characters
Lycos	135–200 characters
WebCrawler	*395 characters
Snap	15 words
Northern Light	150–200 characters

*Those engines that support the META description tag.

Total Number of Web Sites Indexed?

Yahoo!	Approximately 1 million Web Sites
AltaVista	250 million Web pages indexed
Excite	214 million Web pages indexed
Fast	300 million Web pages indexed
GO/InfoSeek	90 million Web pages indexed
Google	138 million Web pages indexed
HotBot	110 million Web pages indexed
Lycos	50 million Web pages indexed
Northern Light	211 million Web pages indexed

*As of February 3, 2000, according to Search Engine Watch:
searchenginewatch.com/reports/sizes.html

Total of Unique Visitors Who Visited the Site in February 2000 (indicating its popularity)

Yahoo!	**120,000,000 (465 million page views per day)
AltaVista	*11,969,000
Ask Jeeves	*7,631,000
Excite	*15,552,000
GO/InfoSeek	*19,487,000
GoTo	*7,208,000
HotBot	*9,341,000 (December '99)
LookSmart	*8,812,000
Lycos	*27,121,000
WebCrawler	*Unknown
Snap	*10,923,000
Northern Light	*Unknown

*According to MediaMetrix.com,February, 2000:
mediametrix.com
**According to a Yahoo! Press Release dated January 11, 2000:
docs.yahoo.com/docs/pr/4q99pr.html

> Yahoo! boasts 465 million page views per day.

Appendix IV:
Helpful Links

Appendices

Helpful URLs

Note: Live links to all these URLs may be found at the authors' Web site: *www.searchengineadvice.com*

Check Submission Status

AltaVista	Search for *host:yourdomainname.com*
Excite	Search for: *www.yourdomainname.com*
GO/InfoSeek	*www.go.com/* *AddUrl?pg=CheckURLStatus.html*
HotBot	*hotbot.lycos.com/help/checkurl.asp*
Lycos	*www.lycos.com/addasite.html*
Yahoo!	Search for your URL

> Become an ODP editor at *dmoz.org/about.html*

Dynamic Pages

A Users Guide to URL Rewriting with the Apache Webserver:
www.engelschall.com/pw/apache/rewriteguide

Spider Trap:
www.spider-trap.com/trap.html

CloakCheck:
se.make-it-online.com/

IP Delivery:
www.searchengineadvice.com

Editor (How to Become)

Go Guides: *beta.guides.go.com/*
Open Directory Project: *dmoz.org/about.html*

Examples

@NetDetective 2000:
www.netdetective2000.com/netdetective2000.html

Clear gif example:
www.robinsnest.com/clr.gif

Dana Rader Golf School:
www.welcomecenters.com/find/br/golf_dana_rader_ex.htm

Helpful Links

Drew University/Roxbury High School:
www.cyberguild2000.com/arv34.htm

Hallway page example:
www.whootnews.com/atlantic-city-links.html

Hotel reservations Las Vegas:
www.placesforfun.com/hotel_reservations.htm

Hypnosis board:
www.welcomecenters.com/find/hb/hypnosis_board_is.htm

Image map example at Concierge.com:
www.concierge.com/cgi-bin/maps.cgi?link–intro

JavaScript example at SearchEngineWatch:
searchenginewatch.com/search.html

Joshua Syna, Clinical Hypnotherapist:
www.besttexasbusiness.com/syna/smoke.html

META refresh example:
www2.netdoor.com/~smslady

Orange county bail bonds:
www.bindersbailbonds.com/orange-county-bail/as/index.htm

Site map example:
pages.ebay.com/sitemap.html

Tables example at TechEncyclopedia:
www.techWeb.com/encyclopedia/

Tiny bullet graphic example:
www.robinsnest.com/circle1.gif

Virtual flower showroom:
www.advinfo.com/tropcon/virtual-flower.html

Wholesale Mortgage Inc.:
www.wholesalemortgageinc.com/

Wisconsin Home Builders:
www.wickhomes.com/wisconsin.htm

Free Information and Newsletters

InternetDay (free newsletter):
internetday.com

Internet Marketing Center (free newsletter and information):
www.marketingtips.com

MarketPosition (free newsletter):
www.webposition.com/newsletter.htm

Notes on helping search engines index your Web site:
www.w3.org/TR/REC-html40/appendix/notes.html#h-B.4

Search Engine Watch (free newsletter and information):
www.searchenginewatch.com

Web Search at about.com (free information):
websearch.about.com/internet/websearch

> Web search at about.com is an excellent source of free information about the search engines: *websearch.about.com/ internet/websearch*

Helpful URLs

javElink:
www.javelink.com

List of Sites That Use the Open Directory Project:
dmoz.org/Computers/Internet/WWW/Searching_the_Web/ Directories/Open_Directory_Project/Sites_Using_ODP_Data

Search engines and frames at Search Engine Watch:
searchenginewatch.com/webmasters/frames.html

What is a bridge page or entry page:
searchenginewatch.internet.com/webmasters/bridge.html

Keywords

GoTo's Search Suggestion List:
www.goto.com/d/about/advertisers/othertools.jhtml

Plumb Design Visual Thesaurus:
www.plumbdesign.com/thesaurus

Roget's Internet Thesaurus:
www.thesaurus.com

What people search for:
searchenginewatch.internet.com/facts/searches.html

WordNet:
www.cogsci.princeton.edu/~wn

WordSpot:
www.searchengineadvice.com

Word Tracker.com
www.wordtracker.com

Keyword Weight

KeywordCount.com:
keywordcount.com/keys/search

Keyword Density Analyzer:
www.searchengineadvice.com

Link Popularity

LinkPopularity.com:
www.linkpopularity.com

META Tags

How to use HTML META tags:
www.searchenginewatch.com/meta.htm

Search engine design tips:
searchenginewatch.com/webmasters/tips.html

Trademarks in META tags OK, with good reason:
searchenginewatch.internet.com/sereport/98/05-metatags.html

What can <META> do for you:
www.hotwired.com/webmonkey/html/96/51/index2a.html

Paid Subscription Newsletters

Search Engine Watch:
www.searchengineadvice.com

Planet Ocean:
www.searchengineadvice.com

Referrer Logs

Funnel Web:
ctcr.investors.net/funnelWeb/Webreport.html

eXTReMe tracking:
www.extreme-dm.com/tracking/?home

FlashStats:
maximized.com/products/flashstats

"There's gold in them there log files!" by Charlie Morris:
www.wdvl.com/Internet/Management

WebTrends:
www.Webtrends.com

Robots and Spiders

Robots Exclusion:
info.Webcrawler.com/mak/projects/robots/exclusion.html

Robots.txt syntax checker:
www.tardis.ed.ac.uk/~sxw/robots/check

Spider spotting chart—robot agent and host names:
searchenginewatch.internet.com/webmasters/spiderchart.html

Subscribe to Planet Ocean's newsletters for the latest information about the search engines: *www.searchengineadvice.com*

Search Engine Addresses and Phone Numbers

AltaVista Company
Phone: 650-617-3496

Excite@Home
450 Broadway Street
Redwood City, CA 94063
Phone: 650-556-5000

Fast Search & Transfer, Inc.
1700 West Park Drive
Westborough, MA 01581
Phone: 508-616-2400

GO Network
1399 Moffett Park Drive
Sunnyvale, CA 94089-1134
Phone: 800-781-4636

HotBot
660 Third Street
Fourth Floor
San Francisco, CA
Phone: 415-276-8400

Lycos, Inc.
400-2 Totten Pond Road
Waltham, MA 02451
Phone: 781-370-2700

Northern Light Technology Inc
222 Third Street, Suite 1320
Cambridge, MA 02142
Phone: 617-621-5100

Yahoo! Inc.
3420 Central Expressway
Santa Clara, CA 95051
Phone: 408-731-3333

Search Engine E-mail Addresses and Feedback Forms

AltaVista	*doc.altavista.com/help/contact/contact_us.shtml*
Excite	*www.excite.com/feedback*
Fast	*www.alltheWeb.com/cgi-bin/feedback.php3*
GO/InfoSeek	Comments@go.com
	comments.go.com/comments.html
HotBot	Feedback@hotbot.com
	hotbot.lycos.com/help/supportform.asp
Lycos	Webmaster@lycos.com
Northern Light	cs@northernlight.com
Search.com	Support@search.com
Web Crawler	*www.webcrawler.com/feedback*
Yahoo!	url-support@yahoo-inc.com
	www.yahoo.com/info/support/contacts

Search Engine on Your Site

SearchButton.com:
www.searchbutton.com

Search Engines and Directories

AltaVista	www.altavista.com
Anzwers.com	*www.anzwers.com*
AOL Search	*search.aol.com*
Ask Jeeves	*www.askjeeves.com*
Canada.com	*www.canada.com*
Direct Hit	*www.directhit.com*
Electron Search	*electronsearch.com*
Excite	*www.excite.com*
Fast	*alltheweb.com*
FindWhat	*findwhat.com*
GO/InfoSeek	*infoseek.go.com*
Google	*google.com*
GoTo	*www.goto.com*
HotBot	*www.hotbot.com*

Inktomi	*www.inktomi.com/products/search*
Jayde	*www.jayde.com*
LookSmart	*www.looksmart.com*
Lycos	*www.lycos.com*
Magellan	*magellan.excite.com*
MSN Search	*search.msn.com*
NetGuide Live	*www.netguide.com*
Northern Light	*www.northernlight.com*
ODP	*dmoz.org*
Search.com	*www.search.com*
Snap	*www.snap.com*
WebCrawler	*www.webcrawler.com*
WhatUseek	*www.whatuseek.com*
Yahoo!	*www.yahoo.com*
Yep	*yep.com*

Search Engine Positioning Classes

Academy of Web Specialists:
www.academywebspecialists.com

Search Engine Positioning Companies

@Web Site Publicity.com:
websitepublicity.com

Software Programs

Cookie Crusher:
www.thelimitsoft.com/cookie.html

IP Delivery:
www.searchengineadvice.com

Keyword Density Analyzer:
www.searchengineadvice.com

Help visitors find what they're looking for at your site by installing an onsite search engine by *SearchButton.com*

Search Engine Optimizer:
www.searchengineadvice.com

Site Promoter:
www.searchengineadvice.com

WebPosition Gold:
www.searchengineadvice.com

TopDog Software:
www.searchengineadvice.com

Take a class in Search Engine Positioning Strategies at the Academy of Web Specialists
www.academywebspecialists.com

Spammers: Where to Report Them

AltaVista	*www.altavista.com/av/content/ help_block.html*
Excite	*www.excite.com/feedback*
GO/InfoSeek	E-mail to: comments@GO.com
HotBot	E-mail to: feedback@hotbot.com
Lycos	E-mail to: Webmaster@lycos.com
Northern Lt	*www.northernlight.com/docs/gen_help_prob.html*
WebCrawler	*www.webcrawler.com/feedback*
Yahoo!	E-mail to: url-support@yahoo-inc.com

Statistics

Accessibility and distribution of information on the Web:
www.wwwmetrics.com

GVU's Tenth Annual WWW User Survey:
www.cc.gatech.edu/gvu/user_surveys/survey-1998-10/graphs/use/q52.htm)

GVU's WWW User Survey:
www.gvu.gatech.edu/user_surveys

MediaMetrix.com:
mediametrix.com

Search engine sizes at SearchEngineWatch.com:
searchenginewatch.com/reports/sizes.html

StatMarket.com:
statmarket.com/SM?c=WeekStat

Submission Guidelines

AltaVista	*www.AltaVista.com/cgi-bin/query?pg=addurl*
AOL Search	*search.aol.com/add.adp*
Ask Jeeves	*www.ask.com/docs/about/policy.html*
Direct Hit	*www.directhit.com/util/spider.html*
Excite	*www.excite.com/info/getting_listed*
Fast	*www.ussc.alltheweb.com/add_url.php3*
FindWhat	*findwhat.com/static/ab_promote.html*
GO/InfoSeek	*go.com/AddUrl?pg=SubmitUrl.html*
Google	*www.google.com/addurl.html*
GoTo	*www.goto.com/d/about/advertisers/*
HotBot	*hotbot.lycos.com/help/addurl.asp*
Jayde	*www.jayde.com/submit.html*
LookSmart	*www.looksmart.com/r?page=/h/info/submitfaq3.html*
Lycos	*www.lycos.com/addasite.html*
Magellan	*magellan.excite.com/info/add_url*
MSN Search	*search.msn.com/help_addurl.asp#proc18*
NetGuide Live	*www.netguide.com/aboutus/aboutreviews.html*
Northern Light	*www.northernlight.com/docs/regurl_help.html*
ODP	*www.dmoz.org/add.html*
Snap	*www.snap.com/LMOID/resource/0,566,-516,00.html*
Web Crawler	*www.webcrawler.com/info/add_url*
WhatUseek	*www.whatUseek.com/noshock/addurl-tableset.shtml*
Yahoo!	*docs.yahoo.com/info/suggest*
Yahoo! How To Guide	*howto.yahoo.com*
Yep	*yep.com/YEP/Register*

Submission URLs for Search Engines and Directories

AltaVista	*www.altavista.com/cgi-bin/query?pg=addurl*
Anzwers.com	*www.anzwers.com/cgi-bin/print_addurl.pl?*
AOL Search	Submit to ODP: *dmoz.org*
Ask Jeeves	E-mail to: url@askjeeves.com
Canada.com	*www.canada.com/search/web/addurl.asp*
Direct Hit	*www.directhit.com/util/addurl.html*
Excite	*www.excite.com/info/add_url*
Fast	*alltheWeb.com/addurl.html*
FindWhat	*findwhat.com/static/ab_promote.html*
GO/InfoSeek	*go.com/AddUrl?pg=SubmitUrl.html*
GO—if submitting more than 50 a day or adult sites	E-mail to: www-request@infoseek.com
Google	*www.google.com/addurl.html*
GoTo	*www.goto.com*
HotBot	*hotbot.lycos.com/addurl.asp*
Jayde	*www.jayde.com/submit.html*
Jayde Online Market Links (listing of numerous submission URLs)	*www.jayde.com/webprm.html*
LookSmart	*www.looksmart.com/h/info/submitfaq.html*
LookSmart Changes	*www.looksmart.com/h/info/confirm.html*
Lycos	*www.lycos.com/addasite.html*
Magellan	*magellan.excite.com/info/add_url*
MSN Search	Submit to HotBot: *hotbot.lycos.com/addurl.asp*
NetGuide Live	*www.netguide.com/aboutus/aboutreviews.html*
Northern Light	*www.northernlight.com/docs/regurl_help.html*
ODP	*www.dmoz.org/add.html*
Search.com	E-mail to: submit@search.com
Snap	*home.snap.com/LMOID/resource/ 0,566,-1077,00.html?st.sn.ld.0.1077*
WebCrawler	*www.Webcrawler.com/info/add_url/*

WhatUseek	*www.whatUseek.com/noshock/ addurl-tableset.shtml*
Yahoo!	*www.yahoo.com*
Yahoo! Changes	*add.yahoo.com/fast/change*
Yahoo! Chinese Properties	*chinese.yahoo.com*
Yahoo! Italia	*www.yahoo.it*
Yep	*yep.com/YEP/Register*

Tutorials

HTML Goodies:
www.htmlgoodies.com/tutors

Online Web Training:
www.onlinewebtraining.com

ZDNet Developer:
www.zdnet.com/devhead/filters/homepage

Need help positioning your site? Visit *websitepublicity.com*

STREETWISE® BOOKS

New for Fall 2003!

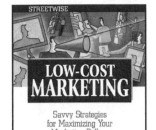

Low-Cost Marketing
$19.95 (CAN $31.95)
ISBN 1-58062-858-3

Business Valuation
$19.95 (CAN $31.95)
ISBN 1-58062-952-0

Also Available in the *Streetwise*® Series:

24 Hour MBA
$19.95 (CAN $29.95)
ISBN 1-58062-256-9

Achieving Wealth Through Franchising
$19.95 (CAN $29.95)
ISBN 1-58062-503-7

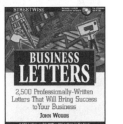

Business Letters with CD-ROM
$24.95 (CAN $37.95)
ISBN 1-58062-133-3

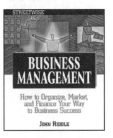

Business Management
$19.95 (CAN $29.95)
ISBN 1-58062-540-1

Complete Business Plan
$19.95 (CAN $29.95)
ISBN 1-55850-845-7

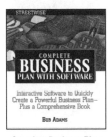

Complete Business Plan with Software
$29.95 (CAN $47.95)
ISBN 1-58062-798-6

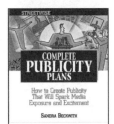

Complete Publicity Plans
$19.95 (CAN $29.95)
ISBN 1-58062-771-4

Customer-Focused Selling
$19.95 (CAN $29.95)
ISBN 1-55850-725-6

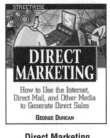

Direct Marketing
$19.95 (CAN $29.95)
ISBN 1-58062-439-1

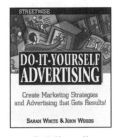

Do-It-Yourself Advertising
$19.95 (CAN $29.95)
ISBN 1-55850-727-2

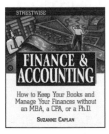

Finance & Accounting
$17.95 (CAN $27.95)
ISBN 1-58062-196-1

Financing the Small Business
$19.95 (CAN $29.95)
ISBN 1-58062-765-X

Get Your Business Online
$19.95 (CAN $28.95)
ISBN 1-58062-368-9

Hiring Top Performers
$17.95 (CAN $27.95)
ISBN 1-55850-684-5

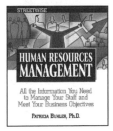

Human Resources Management
$19.95 (CAN $29.95)
ISBN 1-58062-699-8

Independent Consulting
$19.95 (CAN $29.95)
ISBN 1-55850-728-0

Internet Business Plan
$19.95 (CAN $29.95)
ISBN 1-58062-502-9

Landlording & Property Management
$19.95 (CAN $29.95)
ISBN 1-58062-766-8

Low-Cost Web Site Promotion
$19.95 (CAN $29.95)
ISBN 1-58062-501-0

Managing a Nonprofit
$19.95 (CAN $29.95)
ISBN 1-58062-698-X

Managing People
$19.95 (CAN $29.95)
ISBN 1-55850-726-4

Marketing Plan
$19.95 (CAN $29.95)
ISBN 1-58062-268-2

Maximize Web Site Traffic
$19.95 (CAN $28.95)
ISBN 1-58062-369-7

Motivating & Rewarding Employees
$19.95 (CAN $29.95)
ISBN 1-58062-130-9

Project Management
$19.95 (CAN $29.95)
ISBN 1-58062-770-6

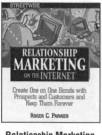

Relationship Marketing on the Internet
$17.95 (CAN $27.95)
ISBN 1-58062-255-0

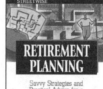

Restaurant Management
$19.95 (CAN $29.95)
ISBN 1-58062-781-1

Retirement Planning
$19.95 (CAN $29.95)
ISBN 1-58062-772-2

Sales Letters with CD-ROM
$24.95 (CAN $37.95)
ISBN 1-58062-440-5

Selling Your Business
$19.95 (CAN $29.95)
ISBN 1-58062-602-5

Small Business Start-Up
$17.95 (CAN $27.95)
ISBN 1-55850-581-4

Small Business Success Kit with CD-ROM
$24.95 (CAN $35.95)
ISBN 1-58062-367-0

Time Management
$17.95 (CAN $27.95)
ISBN 1-58062-131-7

Start Your Own Business Workbook
$9.95 (CAN $15.95)
ISBN 1-58062-506-1

Take Your Business Online Workbook
$9.95 (CAN $15.95)
ISBN 1-58062-507-X

Available wherever books are sold.
For more information, or to order, call 800-872-5627 or visit www.adamsmedia.com
Adams Media, an F+W Publications Company, 57 Littlefield Street, Avon, MA 02322